Poetry and the Sense of Panic

COSTERUS NEW SERIES 124

Series Editors:
C.C. Barfoot, Theo D'haen
and Erik Kooper

Poetry and the Sense of Panic

Critical Essays on Elizabeth Bishop and John Ashbery

edited by
Lionel Kelly

 Rodopi Amsterdam-Atlanta, GA 2000

ISBN 90-420-0720-6

Printed in The Netherlands

CONTENTS

INTRODUCTION

LIONEL KELLY

Surely there is an element of mortal
panic and fear underlying all works of art?[1]

A kindly gnome
of fear perched on my dashboard once, but we had all been instructed
to ignore the conditions of the chase.[2]

Poetry and the sense of panic is a topic which recurs in several of the
contributions to this collection of essays on Bishop and Ashbery, particularly
though not exclusively in the essays on Bishop. The passage from Bishop's
stunning memoir of Marianne Moore I have used as one of my epigraphs comes
at a moment where Bishop rebukes feminist critics of Moore for describing
her as a "poet who controlled panic by presenting it as whimsy". Bishop has
no animus against whimsy for itself, and acknowledges its presence in Moore,
along with "humour". Panic, however, she appropriates as one of the residual
and necessary conditions of art, whether its sources are personal, social, political
or global, and the function of the work of art is to mediate that sense of panic
through the formal devices which structure the work. The poetry of Bishop
and Ashbery flourishes as much through what it conceals as what it reveals,
and concealment may be read as one resource for controlling that impetus
towards self-exposure which attends the writing of poetry, as in the example
of Moore's acrostic on the name of one of her oldest and closest friends, semi-
concealed, as Bishop tells us, "by being written upside down".[3] As this anecdote
suggests, the constraints of formal verse forms are one means which allow
revelation and concealment to work in unison, as in Bishop's "Sestina" and
her villanelle "One Art". In Ashbery's poetry there are countless instances of a
haunting, melancholic voice which expresses the sense of loss in a tone of
muted anguish as in this from the title poem of *And The Stars Were Shining*:

---

1. Elizabeth Bishop, *The Collected Prose*, ed. Robert Giroux, New York, 1984, 144.

2. John Ashbery, *Wakefulness*, Manchester, 1998, 3.

3. Elizabeth Bishop, *The Collected Prose*, 142.

I let so many people go by me
I sort of long for one of them, any
one, to turn back toward me,
forget these tears. As children we played at being grownups.
Now there's trouble brewing on the horizon.

As is characteristic of Ashbery, loss is quickly modified by "sort of" in the second line, and the resort to cliche with "trouble brewing": despite these modifications the expression of loss is achieved and survives through the following verse:

So – if you want to come with me,
or just pull at my sleeve, let them make that discovery.
Summer won't end in your lap,
nor are the stars more casual than usual.
Peace, quiet, a dictionary – it was so important,
yet at the end nobody had any time for any of it.
It was as if all of it had never happened,
my shoelaces were untied, and – am I forgetting anything?[4]

We feel compelled to ask who is the "I" and "me" of these lines, a question Ashbery's work seldom allows us to resolve. For he is a master of concealment as in the way he repeatedly denies the attribution of pronouns to names. Indeed, John Shoptaw's *On the Outside Looking Out* (1994) is a study of Ashbery predicated on what he takes to be Ashbery's "encrypted" meanings. Responding to an interviewer's question about his work, Ashbery commented, "I don't think my poetry is inaccessible. People say it's very private, but I think it's about the privacy of everyone", and we may take this as a sufficient way of reading the pronominal voice in "And the Stars were Shining". To express the experience of loss, pain, damage, psychic mutilation, to write these conditions is to take risks: to guise them is to control panic. There are other dimensions of the poetry of both these poets, and Ashbery's comedy is rightly celebrated as a counter-weight to the plangent melancholic mood I have signalled here. But Bishop's notion of the "element of mortal panic and fear underlying all works of art" is clearly appropriate to Joanne Feit Diehl's reading of the psychic presence of threat in Bishop's work, and to Peter Robinson's examination of poetry as self-therapy in "Crusoe in England": and the subtitle of Geoff Ward's account of Ashbery in the 1990s "Voice, Syntax, and Panic", is an occasion where panic certainly has a wider valency than the senses I have touched on.

We may trace the pressure of panic in the poetry of Ashbery and Bishop through the anxiety of origination which goes with the practice of poetry, and

---

4. John Ashbery, *And The Stars Were Shining*, Manchester, 1989, 100.

in their covert representation of the biographical. In relation to the traditions and public office of poetry Ashbery characteristically resorts either to the comedic, or to what Geoff Ward calls his "darkly Romantic" faith in the "talking cure", and whilst Ward finds particular evidence of the striving for this cure in Ashbery's prolific output in this last decade, Ashbery's faith in the word is clearly of long duration. For Ashbery's comedy we might turn to "And *Ut Pictura Poesis* Is Her Name", where the demands of originality confront the long tradition of the "picture-poem" with the constraint that "You can't say it that way any more."[5] In recorded readings of "And *Ut Pictura Poesis* Is Her Name" Ashbery certainly plays it for laughs, yet its subject of "how it may now be said" is central to his concerns. If the practice of a predecessor poet is foregrounded in this poem, more often in Ashbery the predecessor is occluded, as in "Can You Hear, Bird", where Walt Whitman is not named but seems implied in the apparent summons to Whitman's hermit thrush, in the acknowledgement that "The road started to get rough with me", and the closing assertion that "After all who blubbered the truth / It wasn't I",[6] where the form of the first person pronoun certainly suggests Whitman, as "blubbered" suggests his self-proclaimed "barbaric yawp". As to the biographical, Ashbery has suggested, apropos of "Fragment" from *The Double Dream of Spring* that it is a love poem "like maybe all of my poems", yet "Fragment" equally lends itself to philosophical analysis as an expression of Romantic irony, so that the narrative of love is subsumed within another mode, as is also true, if in different terms, of *Three Poems*. If in Bishop's case her surrealist practice in *North & South* marks a deliberate turning away from her American and modernist predecessors, it was also a way of keeping panic at bay as she struggled to define herself as a poet. And over the arc of Bishop's career, the biographical pressures of familial, psychological, sexual and religious issues become more insistent in the poems, as in her prose writings, despite her reputation for reticence.

These essays were first given as papers at an international conference at the University of Reading in the summer of 1996. They take a variety of critical routes, philosophical, psychoanalytic, religious, gender based, and through poetics. If some of them collude in an interest in the tensions which generate the work of these poets that must be seen in the context of the high esteem in which Bishop and Ashbery are held. Studies of Bishop have proliferated in the years since her death in 1979, and she is now understood as one of the major American poets of the second half of this century. Ashbery, who reviewed Bishop's *Collected Poems* in 1969, was not the only reviewer to hope there would be more poems to come. Earlier in his career Ashbery found the poems

---

5. John Ashbery, *Houseboat Days*, Harmondsworth and New York, 1977, 45.

6. John Ashbery, *Can You Hear, Bird*, Manchester, 1996, 24.

of *North & South* (1946) a liberating example in their difference from the dominant idioms of mid-twentieth-century American poetry, a compelling example of what was possible. His own creative journey into the possible is difficult to keep pace with, for even as I write these notes another collection of his work appears, *Wakefulness*, his fifth book of poems published in this decade. If the "gnome of fear" hovers over Ashbery's work we note that he thinks it "kindly", a generous attendant on the poetic psyche, the spirit who holds our "mortal panic" at bay.

Mark Ford's account of the impact of French poetry on Bishop and Ashbery is signalled through their common embrace of escapism, not as limitation or failure but as a strategic means of defying the literary and social conventions they found so constricting, as in Bishop's time in France in the mid-1930s and Ashbery's longer residence there from 1955 to 1965. Ford reads the French inflections of Bishop's first book *North & South* (1946), which Ashbery "read, reread, studied and absorbed". Ford writes of Bishop's admiration for the mercurial shifts of tone in Laforgue and his ability to represent the mind's vacillations, reminds us that Baudelaire was one of Bishop's favourite poets, and reads the influence of French Surrealism in the ""dreamily opaque" quality of the poems of *North & South*. Whilst Ashbery has denied the importance of French poetry to his development, Ford finds allusions to and borrowings from French writers surfacing persistently throughout Ashbery's oeuvre, and attends particularly to the impact of Pierre Reverdy on Ashbery's *The Tennis Court Oath*, and the appeal of Raymond Roussel's fusion of the utilitarian and the fantastic.

Joanne Feit Diehl deploys Melanie Klein's psychoanalytic theory of aggression and reparation to the pervasive inscription of the presence of threat and the means to contain it in Bishop's work. In Klein's theory the girl–child's aggression is equivalent to the boy's Oedipal conflict, and centres on the sadistic desire to rob the mother's body of its contents. In response to the anxiety created by this phantasy of maternal mutilation, the girl later seeks to make reparation which may take the form of creative work. As the child matures, the psychic assault on the mother is experienced as an attack upon the self, and reparation becomes a self-recuperative gesture in which the work of art is the vehicle of restitution. In Bishop's case this infantile anxiety situation was intensified by the absence of both parents. Feit Diehl uses this network of psychic circumstances to adduce the "profoundly revelatory" origins of the nascent creative self in Bishop.

Helen M. Dennis uses the "Brazil" sequence of *Questions of Travel* (1965) to investigate the discontinuities between the poet as speaking subject and the foreign worlds she travels to in order to trace the ways in which travel is deployed as a metonym for the post-romantic self's relation to the world. Dennis calls on the concept of the "negative sublime" as an aesthetic category of difference rather than identity to suggest how the poem "Questions of Travel" registers difference rather than similarity in its gaze on the foreign and the other, unlike some of the other "Brazil" poems where she finds traces of "a colonial mentality, an embedded sense of civilized superiority" accompanying Bishop's fascination with the other.

Thomas Travisano's consideration of Bishop as a postmodernist reminds us that all the grand totalizing terms of literary history are patient of many meanings as Arthur O. Lovejoy long ago demonstrated in his discrimination of the varieties of Romanticism. Travisano finds a version of postmodernism to be an appropriate description of Bishop's aesthetic, a covert aesthetic she shared with John Berryman, Randall Jarrell, and Robert Lowell. The terms of this aesthetic may only be constructed through an analysis of their intuitions about poetry and its practice in their poems, letters, and essays, for it was never articulated as a formal manifesto – a mode they all refused, as they commonly refused to locate themselves either side of the formal versus open verse debate. However, there is evidence of their early attempts to clarify an emerging aesthetic agenda significantly different from their modernist elders such as Eliot and Pound, and their immediate mentors such as Allen Tate, John Crowe Ransom and Marianne Moore. This aesthetic is principally concerned with "dramatizing the individual's problems of knowledge, identity, traumatic loss, and repressed or otherwise feelings of displacement, confusion, anger, and grief", in brief a poetics of loss. This is distinct from Frederick Jameson's characterisation of the "impersonality" of postmodern aesthetics, is a realm occupied by the "embattled self", and it is in these terms that Travisano investigates Bishop's poetry and her creative negotiations with Berryman, Jarrell and Lowell.

Peter Robinson argues that poetry and the life of writing, and the solitude and devotion it requires, are inextricably interwoven with the suffering and damage which impels the act of writing, and he takes Bishop's late poem "Crusoe in England" as an exemplary version of this predicament. He sees the poem as challenging our inherited belief in the healing powers of poetry. The difficult achievement lies not in resolution of the damage or illness which compels composition, but in the poem's articulation of the conditions of its making. In Bishop's own words, "Writing poetry is a *way of life*, not a matter of testifying but of experiencing". Robinson traces the autobiographical pressures of self-therapy in the poem's preoccupation with solitude whilst it negotiates the equally imperative pressures of communication with a world of readers. In this reading the issue is how the poem escapes the confines of its own self-delighting imagination in the way it "focuses on the dilemma of the solitary imagination's relation to society, and also the self". "Crusoe in England" is one more endeavour to find moments in which "objects and events become outward criteria for the isolated and unspeakable inner life". Thus, if the poem is readable as a retold version of the Crusoe story, it comes into focus, in Robinson's view, as a Wittgensteinian double-aspect text in which we read it as a poem about Crusoe but understand it, metaphorically "as a commentary on Bishop's own creative life". In this context Robinson finds Coleridgean rather than Wordsworthian affinities in the poem and argues that like Coleridge's "Dejection: An Ode", "its power and its failure are inextricably mixed".

If we take Bishop's poem "The Unbeliever" as offering a view of her own religious convictions, we might fairly assume she had lost that faith she was nurtured in as a child. Cheryl Walker offers contrary evidence in her account of the implications of metaphysical Surrealism in Bishop's poetry where the persistent impetus to reach beyond the pain and dreariness of the quotidian is always toward "another level of reality we might as well describe as the province of religion". Walker reminds us of the frequency with which Bishop pursues the theological topics of pride, human obtuseness, the Fall, and abandonment by God, topics central to the work of two of her favourite poets, George Herbert and Gerard Manley Hopkins, and reminds us also of Bishop's long familiarity with the writings of the Christian fathers and mystics. She calls on Michael A. Sell's *Mystical Languages of Unsaying* with its celebration of "apophasis", or unsaying, as providing a schema by which we may follow the four primary directions of Bishop's work – the just act, the acts of perception, the act of interpreting, and the act of love, and concludes this account of the religious dimensions of Bishop's work with an analysis of "Santarém" which she proposes as a visionary poem akin to the visionary writings of Henry Vaughan and George Herbert.

Benjamin Colbert reads Ashbery's "Fragment" from *The Double Dream of Spring* (1966) as embodying Frederick Schlegel's concept of romantic irony, inflected through Kantian and post-Kantian idealism, in which the notion of the fragment is seen as endemic to the classical and romantic endeavour to represent the unrepresentable "transcendental idea of totality". Thus whilst the ten-line stanza form of Ashbery's "Fragment" and its satisfying movement from departure to closure presents a "whole fragment", it defies the totality it appears to present, even as it negotiates a postmodern Romanticism which recognizes "how complicity with the past and freedom from it" are the simultaneous gestures that form the fulcrum of his art.

Dennis Brown argues for Ashbery's long poem "A Wave" (1983) as a fluid representation of postmodern experience in terms of an inherent "time philosophy" and sees Ashbery sharing with James Joyce, Virginia Woolf, and other modernists the development of a "fluxive temporality", evidenced by the shifting, dissolving materials of the poem's gaze. Brown situates "A Wave" within an extended twentieth century aesthetic genealogy and calls on Wyndham Lewis's *Time and Western Man* for an analytical grounding which connects mainstream literary modernism and postmodernism, against the dominant view of postmodernism's "turn" away from modernity and aesthetic modernism.

Ashbery's question, "Is there anything central?" from "The One Thing that can Save America" in *Self-Portrait in a Convex Mirror* (1975), is taken by Edward Larrissy as a teleological questioning of spiritual potential in its wider application in Ashbery, despite the extreme difficulties of locating the sense of a transcendental centre in the pervasive ironies and paradoxes of Ashbery's poetry. In the ensuing discussion of Ashbery's search to "isolate the postmodern religious sensibility", especially in the first section of *Three Poems*, Larrissy finally points to a degree of consonance between the phenomenology of Maurice Merleau-Ponty and Ashbery's attempt to depict what Larrissy calls "the first movement beyond the void", a movement in Ashbery frequently given Christian connotations.

Krystyna Mazur writes that in Ashbery "meanings reside in the difference repetition makes", and uses "Self-Portrait in a Convex Mirror" and the title poem from *Hotel Lautréamont* (1992) to reveal Ashbery's use of two distinct models of poetic repetition. If in "Self-Portrait", repetition is an ingrained feature of the poem's thematics as exhibited in its recurrent use of motif, pattern and figuration, in "Hotel Lautréamont" exact repetition of whole lines is dictated by the poem's pantoum form. She argues that in both poems repetition is a principle of change, defamiliarizing the familiar and "revitalizing calcified structures", so that despite the formal and thematic differences between them they offer powerful evidence of the appeal of repetition to Ashbery and that even as repetition asserts the failure of mimetic representation, it extends the meaning of what is repeated, endlessly generating new meanings.

John Pilling finds a nexus of English literary sources for Ashbery's *Three Poems* (1972). He notes Ashbery's swerve away from the tradition of the prose poem in French, despite his decade in Paris, and accepts the provenance of Gertrude Stein's *Stanzas in Meditation* as a model offering "possibilities" to those interested in what Ashbery calls a "way of happening". He centres the preoccupations of the "hybrid mix" of *Three Poems* in one thematic "story", that of a love affair whose happening and site is variously traced (and buried) in the poem's three sections. Pilling reads the verbal echoes which mark Ashbery's gestures to his American and Anglo-American antecedents such as Hawthorne, Whitman, Frost, and Eliot, but locates the primary stimulus and sense of spiritual sustenance in the absent presence to *Three Poems* of John Clare's autobiographical writings, Thomas Traherne's *Century of Meditations*, and W.H. Auden's *The Sea and the Mirror*. He adduces verbal evidence that *Three Poems* is framed by two classic poems in the English literary tradition, when it signals Keats's "Ode to a Nightingale" in its opening, and quotes from the first book of Wordsworth's *Prelude* towards its close. In this context Pilling suggests *Three Poems* as a propitious "prelude" to "Self-Portrait in a Convex Mirror", addressed like the *Prelude* to a "Friend".

For Peter Nicholls the Language poets' enthusiasm for Ashbery's *The Tennis Court Oath* (1962) and their less favourable view of his subsequent work provides occasion for a reading of Ashbery and the alternative poetics of the Language poets in relation to two opposed views of the current health of poetry in North America. Is it, as Joseph Epstein argues, driven to a "dark corner" of social irrelevance, or is there substance in Ron Silliman's counter claim that "we are living in a poetic renaissance unparalleled in our history"? Whilst Ashbery's dissolution of the self as the agency of the lyric voice and his anti-referential vocabulary in *The Tennis Court Oath* seems to enact an agenda comparable to that of the Language poets, Nicholls locates affinities between Ashbery's practice in this collection and the so-called "literary Cubism" of Pierre Reverdy, which operates by a "secret logic", what Ashbery called a constant movement between "meaningfulness" and "randomness". Nicholls suggests that whilst Ashbery's language in *The Tennis Court Oath* may be read as a parallel of the Language poets' privileging of rhetoricity over referentiality, he finds their pursuit of the "rich commonness" of language too often results in intractably opaque poems which undermines the democracy of their intentions. Ashbery's work is seen as not resolving the question of the health of contemporary North American poetry, but as a body of work which can be read as countenancing both conditions, the "dark corner" and "a renaissance".

Geoff Ward sets Ashbery's poetry of the 1990s in a long perspective from the political ambitions of North American poets of the Sixties to that of Ashbery's contemporaries in the present where that political ambition is characteristically ironised. However, Ward argues for irony not as a self-defensive posture but as a division or duplicity of tonal approaches, a practice of thinking in contradictions and alternatives, including the political, and he reads ironic duplicity as one of the markers of the idioms of poetry in the nineties. What connects Ashbery to this development is that sense of darkness which attends his work which Ward relates to a "darkly Romantic" faith in the "talking cure" for the poet and his world. Thus Ward defines Ashbery's collections in this decade as dominated by a shift from the poetry of the image to a poetry of syntax, evidenced in the recycling, repetitions, and remorseless "prolificity" of his work. Syntax is seen both as a stylistic equivalent of individuality and the verbal register of the journey, as in Rilke, where arrival is neither sought nor achieved. Furthermore, syntax may be associated with the tradition of male authorship, of "the fight against silence which evidently is death", and in Ashbery's case, the fight not to disclose the sexual psyche.

MONT D'ESPOIR OR MOUNT DESPAIR:
EARLY BISHOP, EARLY ASHBERY, AND THE FRENCH

MARK FORD

One

"(I'd time enough to play with names)", observes Bishop's Crusoe of his years on his "still / un-rediscovered, un'renamable" island. Back in England – "another island, / that doesn't seem like one, but who decides?" – the gap between names and things, *d'espoir* and despair, uses and meanings, island and mainland, dwindles to nothing:

> I'm old
> I'm bored, too, drinking my real tea,
> surrounded by uninteresting lumber.
> The knife there on the shelf –
> it reeked of meaning, like a crucifix.
> I lived. How many years did I
> beg it, implore it, not to break?
> I knew each nick and scratch by heart,
> the bluish blade, the broken tip,
> the lines of wood-grain on the handle ...
> Now it won't look at me at all.
> The living soul has dribbled away.
> My eyes rest on it and pass on.[1]

The "island-dweller" of John Ashbery's "The Skaters" suffers a similar awakening from his boy's own fantasy of life as a castaway. Like Crusoe he climbs to the island's highest point "to scan the distances", watches waterspouts that are "beautiful, but terrifying" – an echo, surely, of Bishop's "awful but cheerful" (CP, 61) – and forgets much of what he thought he knew. Fortunately he has a weathered child's alphabet on which some of the island's flora and fauna are pictured – "the albatross, for instance – that's a name I never would have remembered".[2] While Bishop's Crusoe blanks at the word "solitude" in Wordsworth's "I Wandered Lonely As a Cloud" –

---

1   Elizabeth Bishop, *Complete Poems*, London, 1983, 166. Subsequent references will be cited in the text as CP.

2.   John Ashbery, *Rivers and Mountains*, New York, 1977, 55–56. Subsequent references will be cited in the text as RAM.

"They flash upon that inward eye,
which is the bliss … " The bliss of what?
One of the first things that I did
when I got back was look it up   (CP, 164)

– Ashbery's marooned exile can only remember through the aid of his primer
the most famous Romantic property of all, Coleridge's "sweet bird",[3]
Baudelaire's "prince des nuées".[4] A storm erupts, and in the middle of a
drenching rain the fantasy is reluctantly abandoned:

Kerchoo … Goodbye, Storm-fiend. Good-bye vultures.

In reality of course the middle-class apartment I live in is nothing
    like a desert island.
Cozy and warm it is, with a good library and record collection.
                                                        (RAM, 56)

Dreams of escape occur throughout Ashbery's and Bishop's work. "I write
mainly for escapist purposes," Ashbery commented in an interview of 1977;
"I am aware of the perjorative associations of the word 'escapist', but I insist
that we need all the escapism we can get and even that isn't going to be
enough."[5] The attempt fails most plangently at the end of "Self-Portrait in a
Convex Mirror", as the poet realizes the limitations of his – and Parmigianino's
– art:

This could have been our paradise: exotic
Refuge within an exhausted world, but that wasn't
In the cards, because it couldn't have been
The point.[6]

Bishop's quests for an "exotic / Refuge within an exhausted world" tend to be
embodied in less aesthetic terms, but dramatize essentially the same
understanding. In "The End of March" she describes a walk taken with two
friends along the beach at Duxbury:

---

3. Samuel Taylor Coleridge, *Poems*, ed. John Beer, London, 1974, 175.

4. Charles Baudelaire, *Les Fleurs du Mal*, London, 1982, 192.

5. Sue Gangel, "An Interview with John Ashbery", in *San Francisco Review of Books*,
no. 3, November 1977, reprinted in *American Poetry Observed: Poets on Their Work*,
ed. David Bellamy, Urbana and Chicago, 1984, 13–14.

6. John Ashbery, *Self-Portrait in a Convex Mirror*, New York, 1975, 82. Subsequent
references will be cited in the text as SP.

> Everything was withdrawn as far as possible,
> indrawn: the tide far out, the ocean shrunken,
> seabirds in ones or twos. (CP, 179)

The poet hopes to reach her "proto-dream-house", a tiny primitive shack perched out on the dunes:

> I'd like to retire there and do *nothing*,
> or nothing much, forever, in two bare rooms:
> look through binoculars, read boring books,
> old, long, long books, and write down useless notes ...[7]

This "waking dream", like Ashbery's, inevitably collapses, proves "perfect! But – impossible". The quixotic lion sun, the suddenly multi-coloured stones, reconnect the poet to the processes of nature, just as Ashbery is left to sift the April sunlight for clues, to readjust to the "cold, syrupy flow" of time's "pageant" (SP, 83).

Ashbery's and Bishop's methods of relating to this "pageant" converge at many points. Both take it for granted that there is no ultimate metaphysical centre from which life's patterns become clear, "No Way of Knowing", as an Ashbery title puts it, only the "waking up / In the middle of a dream with one's mouth full / Of unknown words" (SP, 55). Bishop's Crusoe soliloquizes in a similar vein:

> Was there
> a moment when I actually chose this?
> I don't remember, but there could have been. (CP, 163)

Accordingly their figurations can never transcend the moment of their articulation, never aim to attain "the form, the pattern" of Eliot's Chinese jar that "moves perpetually in its stillness".[8] Ashbery's and Bishop's properties illuminate only for the duration of their usefulness: "our knowledge" Bishop insists at the end of "At the Fishhouses", is "historical, flowing and flown" (CP, 66). Returned to England Crusoe's flute and knife and shoes are so much "uninteresting lumber", while by the conclusion of "Self-Portrait in a Convex Mirror" Parmigianino's outsized hand has been wholly drained of purpose

---

7. The unnamed protagonist of the early story "In Prison" (1938) similarly longs for a hermit-like existence in jail with only "one very dull book to read, the duller the better" (Elizabeth Bishop, *The Collected Prose*, London, 1984. For a discussion of this theme in Bishop's work, see David Lehman's essay "In Prison: A Paradox Regained", in *Elizabeth Bishop and Her Art* eds Lloyd Schwartz and Sylvia P. Estess, Ann Arbor, 1983, 61–74.

8. T.S. Eliot, *The Complete Poems and Plays*, London, 1969, 175.

and memory – it "holds no chalk? And each part of the whole falls off / And cannot know it knew" (SP, 83). From the outset of their careers Bishop and Ashbery present experience as continually inflected, even determined by, the formulations of genre; they offer us not the world but a map, or rather the world as an endless series of maps. "How," Ashbery wonders in his discussion of the opening poem of *North & South* in his 1977 essay "Second Presentation of Elizabeth Bishop", "could the map-makers" colours be more delicate than the historians? … Precisely because they are what is given to us to see, on a given day in a given book taken down from the bookshelf for some practical motive.[9]

The poem "The Map" is itself a palimpsest of different kinds of maps:[10] Bishop's speculations overlay seemingly neutral topography with erotic, domestic, and metamorphic possibilities, lovely bays one might stroke, women feeling for the smoothness of yard-goods, Norway as a scampering hare. Bishop's absorption in the map mirrors her ideal of aesthetic experience best outlined in a letter of 1964 to Anne Stevenson: "What one seems to want in art, in experiencing it, is the same thing that is necessary for its creation, a self-forgetful, perfectly useless concentration".[11] The distance between cartography's severe codes of denotation and the poet's yearning for contact and self-expression vividly illustrates the space in which Bishop's – and Ashbery's – self-flexive poetrys both operate. "Only out of such 'perfectly useless concentration'," he suggests in his essay, "can emerge the one thing that is useful for us: our coming to know ourselves as the necessarily inaccurate transcibers of the life that is always on the point of coming into being" (EB, 10).

Ashbery's inaccuracies ("In New York we have winter in August"[12]) are obvious, excessive, and legion, predicated on the theory that "the man who made the same mistake twice is exonerated" (SP, 11), that two wrongs make, if not a right, at least an increased awareness of what any given discourse excludes or represses to sustain its illusions of coherence. This double vision is most literally embodied in the twin-columned "Litany", in which, as he once "half-jokingly" proposed, part of his "object was to direct the reader's

9. John Ashbery, "Second Presentation of Elizabeth Bishop" in *World Literature Today*, vol. 51, no. 1, Winter 1977, 9. Subsequent reference will be cited in the text as EB.

10. For an excellent discussion of the poem's relation to the history of map-making, see Mutlu Konuk Blasing, *Politics and Form in Postmodern Poetry*, Cambridge, 1995, 72–78.

11. *Elizabeth Bishop and Her Art*, eds Lloyd Schwartz and Sybil P. Estess, Ann Arbor, 1983, 288. Subsequent references will be cited in the text as EHA.

12. John Ashbery, *Houseboat Days*, New York, 1977, 49. For further discussion of the importance of the "inaccurate" to Ashbery's poetics, see Stephen Fredman, *Poet's Prose: The Crisis in American Verse*, Cambridge, 1983.

attention to the white space between the columns".[13] Bishop's "famous eye", on the other hand, would seem to leave her poetry less or even no margin for error. She fretted endlessly over minor literary transgressions – for instance her compounding of the February and March issues of the *National Geographic* in "In the Waiting Room"[14] – and was appalled by Lowell's cavalier attitude to his originals in *Imitations* (1962). "Please forgive my sounding like French 2A", she apologizes in a letter to him, before launching into an extensive catalogue of what "*look* like mistakes".[15]

Nevertheless, Bishop's poetry also consistently charts her longing to evade the premises and strictures of her seeing. In a 1948 article on Marianne Moore Bishop suggests that "one should constantly bear in mind the secondary and frequently sombre meaning of the title of her first book: *Observations*" (EHA, 278). In both Moore and Bishop one often feels the active gaze may be at any moment construed as its opposite, the poet become like poor Polonius at supper – "Not where he eats, but where a is eaten".[16] This occurs most dramatically at the end of "Quai d'Orléans", a poem written in the aftermath of a car accident in which Bishop and Margaret Miller, to whom the poem is dedicated, were involved. Miller was badly hurt, and part of her right arm had later to be amputated. In the poem the memory of what is seen is presented as endlessly imposing on its protagonists:

> "If what we see could forget us half as easily,"
>   I want to tell you,
> "as it does itself – but for life we'll not be rid
>   of the leaves' fossils."   (CP, 28)

In a mid-thirties journal, entitled "Recorded Observations", Bishop worries about poetry's ability both to transform and control what it observes: "It's a question of using the poet's proper materials ... to express something not of them – something, I suppose, *spiritual*. But it proceeds from the material, the material eaten out with acid, pulled down from underneath, made to perform and always kept in order, in its place".[17]

---

13. Peter Stitt, "The Art of Poetry XXXIII", in *Paris Review*, vol. 25, no. 90, Winter 1983, reprinted in *Poets at Work*, ed. George Plimpton, New York, 1989, 405.

14. In a 1977 interview with George Starbuck she worries: "Something's wrong about that poem and I thought perhaps that no one would ever know. But of course they find out everything. My memory had confused two 1918 issues of the *Geographic* ... I should have had a footnote". (EHA, 318).

15. Elizabeth Bishop, *One Art: The Selected Letters*, ed. Robert Giroux, London, 1994, 395. Subsequent references will be cited in the text as OA.

16. *Hamlet*, Act IV, Scene 3, line 19.

17. Quoted in Bonnie Costello, *Elizabeth Bishop: Questions of Mastery*, Cambridge MA, 1991, 3–4.

The anxiety voiced in that repetition "in order, in its place" permeates Bishop's work. Her poetry is continually attempting to escape the principle of order and place on which it knows it depends, just as the fantasies of "The Map" depend upon topography's refusal to display "favourites". The forces of instability and disorientation – the urge "to see the sun the other way around" (CP, 93) – express themselves in many ways in Bishop, through travel, word-play, whimsy, dream-scapes. In a number of poems in her first book, *North & South* (1946), they seem associated with Frenchness, which, like the Man-Moth's third rail, can be seen as intimating an enticing but potentially fatal realm that almost simultaneously promises and denies escape from the polarities of the book's title.

Two

The Man-Moth is himself a highly Laforguian creation, a moon-haunted clown derived from the Pierrots of *L'Imitation de Notre Dame La Lune* (1886). To the Modernists Eliot and Pound, Laforgue was a sort of late-flowering metaphysical whom Eliot adjudged "nearer to the 'school of Donne' than any modern English poet",[18] while Pound felt his work perfectly illustrated his ideal of "logopoeia" – "the dance of the intellect among words".[19] Bishop, though, responds to less sovereign aspects of Laforgue's poetics, "the quickness, the surprise, the new sub-acid flavor" (EHA, 283). In "Rhapsody on a Windy Night" Eliot develops his Laforgue-inspired lunar cityscape into a vision of disgusted, helpless alienation. The speaker's nocturnal rambles serve to harden him for the battles ahead, almost to exorcize his individuality. The Man-Moth's antics and compulsions escape any such narrative. His frustrations are eternal and comic; after each failure he "falls back scared but quite unhurt".

As she makes clear in her 1956 review of William Jay Smith's translation of Laforgue's poems, it was Laforgue's mercurial shifts of tone, his ability to represent the mind's vacillations, that attracted her. While Pound and Eliot figured Laforgue as a master rhetorician – "a deliverer of nations ... a father of light"[20] as Pound grandiloquently described him in 1918 – Bishop valued his undermining of rhetorics and the closeness of his poetry to the speaking voice. She stresses the sceptical wryness of his *ars poetica*, and approvingly quotes his remark that "I find it stupid to speak in a booming voice and adopt a platform manner".[21] The Man-Moth is equally unwilling to assume a public role:

---

18. T.S. Eliot, *Selected Prose*, ed. Frank Kermode, London, 1975, 66.

19. Exra Pound, *Literary Essays*, London, 1960, 25.

20. Quoted in *Poems of Jules Laforgue*, trans. Peter Dale, London, 1986, 20.

21. "The Manipulation of Mirrors", in *The New Republic*, Nov. 19, 1956, 23–24.

Then from the lids
one tear, his only possession, like the bee's sting slips.
Slyly he palms it, and if you're not paying attention
he'll swallow it. However, if you watch, he'll hand it over,
cool as from underground springs, and pure enough to drink.   (CP, 15)

The lines might be read as an implicit critique of the "platform manner" that
had come to dominate the poetry of both of Laforgue's modernist champions.
Certainly his most complete opposite in Bishop's oeuvre would be the "tragic
... talkative ... honored ... old, brave ... cruel ... busy ... tedious ... wretched
man / that lives in the house of Bedlam" (CP, 133–35).

If Pound and Eliot were drawn to nineteenth-century French poetry as a
means of disciplining the "slushiness and swishiness of the post-Swinburnian
British line",[22] in Pound's words, Bishop and Ashbery looked to France as a
means of escaping the New Critical orthodoxies instituted by Modernism. In
his 1962 article "Reverdy en Amérique" (written in French), Ashbery laments
the dessicated nature of most contemporary American poetry which he depicts
as feebly languishing in Eliot's shadow:

> Les poètes qui lui ont succédé ont affaibli ou dénaturé le contenu
> intellectuel de la poésie d'Eliot, mais ils en ont retenu certains aspects
> superficiels: le langage sec et digne, ou le ton de J. Alfred Prufrock –
> celui d'un bourgeois sensible dépassé par les événements ... Pour les
> Français, i'expression ‹‹poésie de l'imagination›› peut sembler
> redondante. En Amérique, au contraire, c'est un concept entièrement
> neuf. La poésie de l'imagination, bien entendu. Voilà si longtemps que
> cette *autre* sorte de poésie nous ennuie en nous désole![23]

Reverdy appeals to Ashbery for much the same reasons Laforgue appealed to
Bishop, for his fluidity, his freedom from any over-determining system of
purpose, his ability to surprise:

> J'ai toujours regretté que les rythmes sombres d'Eliot et de Yeats, par
> exemple, soient au service d'une signification précise, et que leurs élans
> poétiques – différents, en cela, du faucon de Yeats – soient comme un
> cerf-volant dont le fil est fermement tenu par le poète rivé à sa terre. Ce
> qui nous enchante chez Reverdy, c'est la pureté de sa poésie, faite de
> changements, fluctuations, archétypes d'événements, situations idéales,

---

22. Ezra Pound, *Selected Letters*, London, 1950, 181. See his praise of Théophile Gautier:
"We may take it that Gautier achieved hardness in *Emaux et Camées*" ("The Hard and Soft in
French Poetry", *Literary Essays*, 285).

23. John Ashbery, "Reverdy en Amérique", in *Mercure de France* (Special Issue: Pierre
Reverdy), Paris, no. 344, Jan / April 1962, 110–11.

mouvements de formes transparentes, aussi nautrels et variés que les vagues de la mer. C'est l'étoffe même de la poésie, sa matière première pure de toute arrière-pensée métaphysique.[24]

Seven years later, in his 1969 review of Bishop's *The Complete Poems*, Ashbery deliberately separates her from the dry world of the poetry establishment to which she nominally belongs – "and the establishment ought to give thanks; she is proof that it can't be all bad" – by highlighting the "French" aspects of her work: "Her concerns at first glance seem special. The life of dreams, always regarded with suspicion as too 'French' in American poetry; the little mysteries of falling asleep and the oddness of waking up in the morning ... ". He compares her prose poems "Rainy Season; Sub-Tropics" to Jules Renard's *Histoires Naurelles* – though in fact the prose poems of Francis Ponge collected in *Le Parti Pris des Choses* (1942) are a more likely source[25] – and "The Burglar of Babylon" to Jean-luc Godard's *Pierrot le Fou* (EHA, 201–05).

"The Man-Moth" was published in the spring of 1936, by which time Bishop had lived half a year in France. She set sail at the beginning of August 1935, and passed the rest of the summer in Brittany working mainly on translations of Rimbaud, now, alas, lost. She spent the winter in Paris, a period she recalled twenty-five years later in her letter to Lowell concerning his translations of Rimbaud and Baudelaire: "I lived in Paris one whole winter long ago, and most of another one [that of 1937] – and that 'endless wall of fog' [from Baudelaire's "Le Cygne"[26]] haunts me still" (OA, 396). There is certainly something foggy, or at least dreamily opaque, about the poems in *North & South* which most obviously signal their "Frenchness" – "Paris, 7 A.M.", "Quai d'Orléans", and "Sleeping on the Ceiling". These were all composed before Bishop moved to Key West in 1938, and reflect her wide reading in French poetry, particularly that of the Surrealists who dominated French intellectual

---

24. *ibid.*, 111–12

25. John Mullen convincingly compares Ponge's "Escargots" (dated March 21, 1936) with Bishop's "Giant Snail", composed the following year, in "Elizabeth Bishop's Surrealist Inheritance", in *American Literature*, vol. 54, no. 1, 1982, 72.

26. Elsewhere in the letter she pronounces "Le Cygne" one of her "favourite Baudelaire poems" (OA, 395), and Baudelaire in general seems to have been among Bishop's best loved poets. When Ashley Brown visited Bishop in 1966 to interview her for *Shenandoah* he noticed above her worktable photographs of Baudelaire, Marianne Moore, and Robert Lowell (EHA, 289). In a letter to Anne Stevenson of January 8–20, 1964, she describes George Herbert and Baudelaire as "two of my favourite poets (not best poets)": quoted in David Kalstone, *Becoming a Poet: Elizabeth Bishop with Marianne Moore and Robert Lowell*, London, 1989, xi.

life in the thirties.[27] In later years Bishop looked nostalgically back to this period as to a golden pre-lapsarian age: "At the time I was writing the poems I like best", she wrote to Anne Stevenson in 1964, "I was very ignorant politically and I sometimes wish I could recover the dreamy state of consciousness I lived in then – it was better for my work, and I do the world no more good now by knowing a great deal more".[28] Other poems from the thirties such as "The Weed", "The Unbeliever", "The Monument", "A Miracle for Breakfast", "From the Country to the City", "Sleeping Standing Up", "Love Lies Sleeping", equally reveal Bishop's ability to appropriate surrealist techniques for her own ends. "This exteriorizing of the interior, and the aliveness all through", wrote Marianne Moore to Bishop in September of 1936 on receiving "The Weed" and "Paris, 7 A M.", "it seems to me are the essential sincerity that unsatisfactory surrealism struggles toward".[29]

But these dreamy poems are far from innocent in their implications. The yearning for a surrealist miracle is continually played off against more quotidian concerns, the need for breakfast. The speaker's rapturous vision in stanzas five and six of Bishop's sestina may be seen as more of a parody than an endorsement of Surrealism's organicist ideal. The envoy effectively returns the miracle to the speculative world of aesthetics, far from the Depression era souplines of the poem's political context:[30]

> We licked up the crumb and swallowed the coffee.
> A window across the river caught the sun
> as if the miracle were working, on the wrong balcony. (CP, 19)

The wholly liberated dreamer of "Love Lies Sleeping" also ends up on "the wrong balcony": unable to "dine" on others' hearts, he pays for revelation with his life:

---

27. In a 1966 interview Bishop told Ashley Brown that she "had read a lot of surrealist poetry and prose" (EHA, 297). For further discussion of her relation to Surrealism, see Richard Mullen, "Elizabeth Bishop's Surrealist Inheritance", *American Literature*, vol. 54, no. 1, 663–80. See also her translations of Max Jacob, *CP*, 265–68. Her library contained volumes by Apollinaire, Baudelaire, Char, Corbière (described in a letter of October 1, 1948, as "really a marvellous poet" (OA, 173), Jacob, Proust, Reverdy, and Rimbaud (Costello, 26).

28 Quoted in Victoria Harrison, *Elizabeth Bishop's Poetics of Intimacy*, Cambridge, 1993, 31.

29. Kalstone, 45.

30. In her 1966 interview Bishop described "A Miracle for Breakfast" as her "Depression poem. It was written shortly after the time of souplines and men selling apples, around 1936 or so. It was my 'social conscious' poem, a poem about hunger" (EHA, 297).

the image of

the city grows down into his open eyes
inverted and distorted. No. I mean
distorted and revealed,
if he sees it at all.[31]   (CP, 17)

For such as Breton and Aragon urban existence offered a potentially endless series of chance discoveries capable of gratifying the surrealist urge for the marvellous. "Love Lies Sleeping", in contrast, balances the dreamy, unlikely aspects of its immense city, imaged as "slowly grown / in skies of water-glass" like a "little 'chemical' garden in a jar", with its casually destructive powers that invert Nature's paradigm of fertility:

Then, in the West, "Boom!" and a cloud of smoke.
"Boom!" and the exploding ball
of blossom blooms again.   (CP, 16)

The poem's city is a place of "alarms", "stony walls and halls and iron beds", "Danger", and "Death". In the short poem "From the Country to the City" Bishop constructs an elaborate conceit in which the city is figured as the head tyrannically imposing its seductive anxieties on the country's "long black length of body": "'Subside', it begs and begs" (CP, 13). Bishop was happy, like the Surrealists, to use "dream-material"[32] as a source for poems, yet in "Sleeping Standing Up" charts the failure of dreams – pictured as blundering "armored cars" – to yield up the redemptive truths they promise. "How stupidly we steered", it ends, "until the night was past / and never found out where the cottage was" (CP, 30).

From a different angle, however, that perhaps of the sleeper "whose head has fallen over the edge of his bed", or of the wistful protagonist of "Sleeping on the Ceiling", such poems might also be read as embodying a yearning to confound the rationalist assumptions implied by their strict and elaborate forms. They are as much an attack of the New Critical ideals of controlled wit and formal discipline as they are of the surrealists' belief in "la liberté totale". "It is so peaceful on the ceiling. / It is the Place de la Concorde" (CP, 29), feelingly sighs the speaker of "Sleeping on the Ceiling". Like Wallace Stevens, Bishop

---

31. Bishop commented in a letter to Anne Stevenson of March 20, 1963: "I think the man at the end of the poem is dead" (Costello, 20).

32. Letter to Anne Stevenson, march 20, 1963: "I use dream-material whenever I am lucky enough to have any" (Costello, 26).

longs "to make the visible a little hard / To see,"[33] and thus escape being "too exactly [her]self". One technique for this borrowed from Stevens is the use of French titles as a means of complicating the reader's responses to the poem that follows; the titles of "Chemin de Fer", "Cirque d'Hiver", and "Trouvée", all impose a dandyish insouciance on the bleak narratives these poems develop. In "Paris, 7 A.M." on the other hand, the specifying of time and place serves to counteract the poem's blurring of the distinctions between imagination and reality.

"Paris, 7 A.M.", like "Love Lies Sleeping", explores the uncertain hinterland between dreams and waking, and the odd perspectives this in-between state permits on the life of the city. The poem collapses time and space ("Time is an Etoile"), but through a method exactly opposite that of the Surrealists' liberation of the unconscious. Bishop's speaker is trapped in a constrictingly over-determined series of patterns – "circles surrounding stars, overlapping circles" – that reduces her apprehension of the weather itself to "a dead wing with damp feathers". As in "Quai d'Orléans", the poet is paralyzed by the meanings relentlessly imposed by her "famous eye":

> It is like introspection
> to stare inside, or retrospection,
> a star inside a rectangle, a recollection. (CP, 26)

The insistent rhymes mimic the poet's compulsive generation of shapes, the addiction to order that diminishes all otherness to a geometrical version of the self and its history. The city itself comes to seem an embodiment of this impulse; "childish snow-forts, built in flashier winters", are imagined hardening into houses as claustrophobic and imprisoning as the architecture of Paris:

> their walls, their shape, could not dissolve and die,
> only be overlapping in a strong chain, turned to stone,
> and grayed and yellowed now like these. (CP, 26)

The poem finds no way of undoing the metonymic substitutions which translate the desire to create into its confining opposite – the star of the imagination into the schematic Etoile of the city, the sky into a dead pigeon. The opportunity to evade the limitations of time and space, seemingly promised by the apartment's divergent clocks, whose "ignorant faces" punningly figure the city's foreignness, in fact leads to the "endless intersecting circles" of a dizzying solipsism. Miraculously improbable as a permanent snow – or sand-fort, yet exhausting in its incessant formal repetitions, the poem's Paris oscillates

33. Wallace Stevens, *The Collected Poems*, New York, 1954, 310–11. For a discussion of Bishop's relation to Stevens, see Kalstone, 50–54.

between disorientating mirage and all-too-solid mausoleum, between dissolving south and freezing north, apparently stranded, despite the title's assurances, beyond the reach and records of time and place:

> When did the star dissolve, or was it captured
> by the sequence of squares and squares, and circles, circles?
> Can the clocks say; is it there below,
> about to tumble in snow?   (CP, 27).

Three

John Ashbery "read, reread, studied and absorbed" (EHA, 203) *North & South* when it was published in 1946, and had the experience of "being drawn into a world that seemed as inevitable as 'the' world and as charged with the possibilities of pleasure as the contiguous, overlapping world of poetry" (EB, 10).[34] Like Bishop, Ashbery began writing at a time when rigid New Critical principles held sway. For Ashbery's fellow New York school poets Kenneth Koch and Frank O'Hara, certain French poets seemed to signal – and in their poems to represent – a possible means of escaping or defying the literary and social conventions they found so constricting. "I dress in oil cloth and read music / by Guillaume Apollinaire's clay candelabra,"[35] O'Hara declares with a self-conscious flourish in the early "Memorial Day 1950". The names of French poets appear regularly in O'Hara's poetry, nearly always as a talismanic source of comfort or imaginative freedom:

> My heart is in my
> pocket, it is Poems by Pierre Reverdy   (FOH, 258)

> Aimé Césaire
> for if there is fortuity it's in the love we bear each other's
>   differences   (FOH, 305)

> René Char, Pierre Reverdy, Samuel Beckett it is possible isn't it
> I love Reverdy for saying yes, though I don't believe it   (FOH, 329)

In "Fresh Air" (1955) Kenneth Koch asks "who is still of our time?" and responds to his own question: "Mallarmé, Valéry, Apollinaire, Eluard, Reverdy, French poets are still of our time".[36]

---

34. Cf. Octavio Paz's general definition of twentieth-century French poetry: "It is a poetry where the world becomes writing and language becomes the double of the world" (quoted in *The Random House Book of Twentieth Century French Poetry* ed. Paul Auster, New York, 1982, xxxi.

35. Frank O'Hara, *The Collected Poems*, New York, 1979, 18. Subsequent references will be cited in the text as FOH.

36. Kenneth Koch, *Selected Poems*, New York, 1985, 38.

Ashbery, by contrast, has frequently denied the importance of French poetry to his development. Asked in a 1973 interview about the effects on his work of his expatriate years in France he insisted:

> I don't think that my poetry has been much influenced by French poetry, including French surrealist poetry, as people have often said – probably because I have lived in France. I think my poetry was surrealist, in a way, from the beginning. But I don't think there is any direct influence from French surrealist poetry, which, as a rule, I am not very interested in. There are a few exceptions, such as Raymond Roussel, who is not really a surrealist, and Pierre Reverdy. He was a surrealist of a kind, but not of the hard-core group of Breton, Eluard, and so on.[37]

In a 1977 interview he suggests:

> The fact is, as far as European poetry is concerned, German and Slavic poetry has been much more of an influence in my work. Only Rimbaud has managed to get beyond the *lucidity* of the French language, which doesn't allow you to do much "in the shadows". It becomes very clear and classical and illuminating, even the poetry of the surrealists.[38]

Nevertheless, allusions to and borrowings from French writers periodically surface throughout Ashbery's oeuvre, from the Roussel-inspired fantasy of "The Instruction Manual" to the parody of Baudelaire's "L'Invitation au Voyage" in Part II of "The Skaters", from the Maurice Sceve-influenced *dizains* of "Fragment" to the open house of the "Hotel Lautréamont", from the Surrealist-style collaborations with Kenneth Koch published in the second issue of *Locus Solus* (Summer 1961) to the version of Baudelaire's "Paysage" collected in *A Wave* (1984). In addition Ashbery has translated numerous French writers – Roussel, Reverdy, Max Jacob (also translated by Bishop), Marcelin Pleynet, Denis Roche, Arthur Cravan, Pierre Martory, André Breton, Paul Eluard, René Char – written articles on such as Michel Butor, Antonin Artaud, de Chirico's *Hebdomeros*, Roussel, and Reverdy, and written poems himself in French, which he then translated back into English. Of this last experiment he commented: "I wanted to see if my poetry would come out differently if I wrote it at one removed ... I don't think it did come out very differently.'[39]

The desire to live "at one removed" from his homeland was certainly one of the primary motivations behind Ashbery's decision to take up residence in

---

37. Louis A. Osti, "The Craft of John Ashbery", in *Confrontations*, New York, no. 9, Fall 1974, 86.

38. Gangel, 12.

39. Osti, 88.

Paris for most of the years from 1955–65. McCarthyism and the Korean War made the mid-fifties in America "a very humiliating and cynical period, a low point ... Everyone wanted to get out of the country and the political environment",[40] he recalled in an interview thirty years later. Ashbery looked to France, rather as Bishop had twenty years previously, as a way of discovering the fresh perspectives a foreign country inevitably forces on one's cultural and linguistic assumptions. Particularly in the radically polarized world of *The Tennis Court Oath* Ashbery presents himself responding to experience in the unsettling, self-divided, restless manner of the final stanza of Bishop's "Sleeping on the Ceiling":

> We must go under the wallpaper
> to meet the insect-gladiator,
> to battle with a net and trident,
> and leave the fountain and the square.
> But oh, that we could sleep up there ...   (CP, 29)

That any attempt to satisfy the need to escape is as likely to result in disorientation as peaceful sleeping upside down is one of the lessons repeatedly taught by Bishop's and Ashbery's poetrys. Imaginary and real journeys alike end up posing Bishop's fundamental questions of travel:

> Continent, city, country, society;
> the choice is never wide and never free.
> And here, or there ... No. Should we have stayed at home
> wherever that may be?   (CP, 94).

Ashbery's voyages are never as literal as those of Bishop's South American poems. An early unpublished piece "Embarkation for Cythera", based on Baudelaire's "Voyage à Cythère", turns on a couple of puns that unite travelling and music:

> Now the bow dragged over mournful strings
> Expands and breathes the tints of Cythera
> Into the fever's beat.[41]

In a similar fashion map and landscape prove inseparable in "Rivers and Mountains" ("you found / It all on paper but the land / Was made of paper process / To look like ferns, mud" (RAM, 10), and the high Symbolist sea-

---

40 John Murphy, "John Ashbery: An Interview" in *Poetry Review*, London, vol. 75, no. 2, August 1985, 22.

41. Quoted in John Shoptaw, *On the Outside Looking Out: John Ashbery's Poetry*, Cambridge MA, 1994, 40.

journeying of Part II of "The Skaters" flagrantly reveals its source in a pored-over atlas – "And we finger down the dog-eared coasts" (RAM, 44). As in Bishop's "The Map", cartography assumes an unpredictable life of its own. The early poem "The Instruction Manual" parades even more explicitly the extent to which Ashbery's travels are "at one removed".

"The Instruction Manual", composed in September of 1955, clearly reflects the influence of Raymond Roussel, as Ashbery has acknowledged.[42] Ashbery was introduced to Roussel by Kenneth Koch, who returned from his trip to France in 1951 with a copy of Roussel's *La Vue* (1904). This volume consists of three enormously long poems in which Roussel describes in exhaustive, indeed impossible, detail three miniature representations. The 4,000 lines of "La Vue" depict a beach scene set in the lens of a pen-holder, "La Source" presents the spa pictured on the label of a bottle of mineral water, while "Le Concert" is based on the sketch of a hotel adorning the heading of a letter written on the hotel's writing paper. Like "The Instruction Manual", each begins with a short portrayal of the solitary poet's immediate circumstances and ends by returning to this stark reality. The view in the lens clouds over, and Roussel is left only the

> souvenir vivace et latent d'un été
> Déjà mort, déjà loin de moi, vite emporté.[43]

In "Le Concert" he turns from the letter's heading to the letter itself:

> Puis, tous bas, je relis pour la centième fois,
> Essayant d'évoquer, à chaque mot, la voix   (LV, 110)

Ashbery seems to have been intrigued not only by the obsessive meticulousness of Roussel's imagination – for instance he observes of the eyebrows of a rower way out at sea that:

> son sourcil guache n'est pas pareil
> Au droit; il est plus noir, plus important, plus dense
> Et plus embroussaillé dans sa grande abondance   (LV, 11)

---

42. Gangel, 18. For a more detailed discussion of the relation btween Ashbery and Roussel see my "John Ashbery and Raymond Roussel", in *Verse*, vol. 3, no. 3 November 1986, 13–23.

43. Raymond Roussel, *La Vue*, Paris, 1963, 73. Subsequent references will be cited in the text as LV. Roussel's works, originally published at the author's expense by Alphonse Lemerre, were reprinted 1963–72 by Jean-Jacques Pauvert. Two volumes of a new edition incorporating manuscripts discovered in 1969 and lodged in the Bibliothèque Nationale as part of the *fonds Roussel* were published in 1994, also by Pauvert.

– but by the odd fusion the poems establish between the utilitarian and the fantastic: "the poet," he writes in his essay entitled "Re-establishing Raymond Roussel", "like a prisoner fascinated by the appearance of the wall of his cell, remains transfixed by the spectacle before his eyes, which is not even a real scene but a vulgar reproduction".[44] Roussel's "self-forgetful, perfectly useless concentration" on the tiny mass-produced images mirrors Bishop's absorption in the "commercial colors" of the map, which are, as Ashbery points out in his second Bishop essay, "the product, after all, of the expediencies and limitations of a mechanical process" (EB, 10). In "The Instruction Manual" too, the world of fantasy is presented as dependent upon the "press", the peremptory laws of commercial publishing:[45]

> City of rose-colored flowers!
> City I wanted most to see, and most did not see, in Mexico!
> But I fancy I see, under the press of having to write the
>   instruction manual,
> Your public square, city, with its elaborate little bandstand![46]

Ashbery's pun deftly encapsulates the antithetical realms of instruction manual and pastiche travelogue, and also implies that each is governed by an equally rigid code that makes them suitable for mass circulation. As in Bishop and Roussel, it is the uniting of seemingly incompatible genres that prompts speculation on which Ashbery has called the "confessional"[47] aspect of the poem. Its conclusion, however, grimly insists that the publisher's pressing deadlines and the cornball rose-coloured city are part of the same interminable loop:

> And as a last breeze freshens the top of the weathered old tower,
>   I turn my gaze
> Back to the instruction manual which has made me dream of
>   Guadalajara. (ST, 18)

---

44. John Ashbery, "Re-establishing Raymond Roussel", in *Portfolio & Art News Annual*, New York, no. 6, Autumn, 1962, reprinted in *How I Wrote Certain of My Books*, ed. Trevor Winkfield, Boston, 1995, under the title "Introduction" xvii. A footnote explains the essay was composed in 1960, vii.

45. Ashbery wrote the poem in the office of the publishers McGraw-Hill, where he was working at this time editing college text-books (Gangel, 18).

46. John Ashbery, *Some Trees*, New Haven, 1956, reprinted New York, 1978. Subsequent references will be cited in the text as ST.

47. Gangel, 18.

The poem's double-take leaves one marooned, rather as Bishop's "Paris, 7 A.M." does, neither reconciled to the schedule of instruction manuals, nor believing in the possibility of escaping them.

This dilemma is charted throughout Ashbery's oeuvre, but is most explosively dramatized in the poems written mainly in France and collected in his second volume, *The Tennis Court Oath* (1962).[48] Here *d'espoir* and despair collide at frightening velocity, at once polarized and inseparable: "This honey is delicious" observes a character in "They Dream Only of America", "*Though it burns the throat*" (TCO, 11). Ashbery's language, suddenly unleashed from symbolic and narrative constraints, evolves its own secret methods of connection and disjunction that aggressively refuse to be plotted according to pre-existing schema or value systems. The effect might be compared to that Ashbery experienced reading Reverdy: "C'est comme si on voyait pour la première fois un paysage naturel, n'ayant vu jusque là que des paysages peints".[49] The poems insistently juxtapose the forces of obsession and dispersal, desire and flux, as "To Redouté" graphically illustrates:

> My first is a haunting face
> In the hanging-down hair.
> My second is water:
> I am a sieve   (TCO, 21)

Ashbery's essay on Reverdy also helps make clear the extent to which the radical techniques of *The Tennis Court Oath* may be construed as a reaction against the stifling, overweening claims of Modernism:

> A l'inverse des écrivains importants de langue anglaise de ce siècle (Eliot, Pound, Yeats, Joyce), Reverdy parvient à restituer aux choses leur vrai nom, à abolir l'éternel poids mort de symbolisme et d'allégorie qui excède chez les auteurs que j'ai cités. Dans *The Waste Land* d'Eliot, le monde réel apparaît avec les reves qui lui sont propres, mais il est toujours artificiellement lié à une signification allégorique – l'uisine à gaz et le «dull canal», par exemple. Tanis que chez Reverdy un canal ou une usine sont des phénomènes vivants, ils font partie du monde qui nous entoure, dont le souffle cru se fait sentir partout dans sa poésie.[50]

The land – and mind-scapes of *The Tennis Court Oath* similarly resist being formulated in terms other than their own, like Reverdy seem "pure de toute

---

48. John Ashbery, *The Tennis Court Oath*, Middletown, 1962. Subsequent references will be cited in the text as TCO.

49. "Reverdy en Amérique", 111.

50. *ibid.*

arrière-pensée métaphysique" though Ashbery is not above the occasional sly jab at his precursors, as in "The Suspended Life": "In the hay states of Pennsylvania and Arkansas / I lay down and slept" (TCO, 37).

The vertiginous, disruptive, all-over poetics of *The Tennis Court Oath* can be traced back to any number of sources – Gertrude Stein's *Stanzas in Meditation*, the drip-paintings of Jackson Pollock, the musical experiments of Webern, Berio, or John Cage – but the dominant influence is surely again the work of Raymond Roussel, and in particular his late extremely rebarbative poem in four cantos, *Nouvelles Impressions d'Afrique* (1932), considered by Ashbery to be Roussel's "masterpiece". *Nouvelles Impressions* was originally intended to be a follow-up to *La Vue*. Roussel planned to describe "une miniscule lorgnette-pendoloque, dont chaque tube, large de deux millimètres et fait pour se coller contre l'oeil, renfermait une photographie sur verre, l'un celle des bazars du Caire, l'autre celle d'un quai de Louqsuor".[51] After five years work, however, Roussel abandoned this idea, and began the poem all over again. Though still set in Egypt, it develops a methodology wholly its own, for Roussel fractures its progress every few lines with a parenthetical thought, introduced by a bracket, which is itself interrupted by a new parenthesis, and so on and so on. The poem's Chinese box effect constitutes a further evolution of the Roussel "*procédé*" which generated the elements of the narratives that make up his novels and plays.[52] In "Re-establishing Raymond Roussel" Ashbery argues the "result is a tumultuous impression of reality which keeps swiping at one like the sails of a windmill … In *Nouvelles Impressions* the unconscious seems to have broken through the myths in which Roussel had carefully encased it: it is no longer the imaginary world, but the real one, and it is exploding around us like a fireworks factory, in one last dazzling orgy of light and sound". As in his discussion of the poetry of Bishop, which seems to present a world "as inevitable as 'the' world", or his praise for the "paysage naturel" embodied by the work of Reverdy, or his admiration for the "counterfeit of reality more real than reality"[53] offered by Stein's *Stanzas in Meditation*, Ashbery celebrates Roussel's power to create a poetry whose strangeness seems analogous in the fullest possible way to the strangeness of experience. Roussel's writings consistently defeat all expectations of purpose and meaning:

> What he leaves us with is a body of work that is like the perfectly preserved temple of a cult which has disappeared without a trace, or a complicated set of tools whose use cannot be discovered. But even though

---

51. Raymond Roussel, *Comment j'ai écrit certains de mes Livres*, Paris, 1935, 34.

52. For Roussel's own explanation of his "procédé", see *Comment j'ai écrit*, 11–25.

53. John Ashbery, "The Impossible", in *Poetry* (Chicago), vol. 90, no. 4, July 1957, 254.

we may never be able to "use" his work in the way he hoped, we can still admire its inhuman beauty, and be stirred by a language that seems always on the point of revealing its secret, of pointing the way back to the "republic of dreams" whose insignia blazed on his forehead.[54]

The fragmentations of *The Tennis Court Oath* seem motivated by just such ideals. "There was no longer any need for the world to be divided," he declares in "Measles", the implication being that the principle of endless division may itself become a totalizing force. Ashbery's collaged cut-ups such as "Europe" or "Idaho" or "America" seek in "the hazards of language" the sorts of juxtapositions he finds so convincing in *Nouvelles Impressions*, of which he observes: "The logic of the strange positions (a rephrasing of a line from his own *"Le Livre est sur la table"* [ST, 74]) of its elements is what makes the poem so beautiful. It has what Marianne Moore calls "mysteries of construction".[55]

To many, including Ashbery himself,[56] the "mysteries of construction" shaping *The Tennis Court Oath* have remained that bit too mysterious. Its most vociferous supporters, the Language poets, dislike much of the rest of Ashbery's poetry, while for critics eager to place Ashbery in the central traditions of American poetry such as Harold Bloom and Helen Vendler, the book is "a fearful disaster", "a mixture of wilful flashiness and sentimentality".[57] No other Ashbery volume has excited such conflicting responses, such *d'espoir* and despair, for this particular Crusoe has no time to play with names, only to live them:

> Everything is being blown away;
> A little horse trots up with a letter in its mouth, which
>   is read with eagerness
>   As we gallop into the flame.   (TCO, 58)

---

54. "Re-establishing Raymond Roussel", xxii. The phrase "republic of dreams" is borrowed from Louis Aragon, who declared Roussel "The President of the Republic of Dreams". The terms employed by Ashbery here return in the final paragraph of his second essay on Elizabeth Bishop: "Behind the multiple disguises, sometimes funny, sometimes terrifyingly unlike anything human, that the world assumes in Elizabeth Bishop's poetry, this moment of almost-transfiguration is always being tracked to its lair, giving the work a disturbing reality unlike anything else in contemporary poetry" (EB, 11).

55. "Re-establishing Raymond Roussel", xx–xxi.

56. For instance in Osti, on "Europe": "It was more of a therapy for me than anything that was meant to go into print. I am not displeased that it was published, but I look at it very much as part of a transitional phase", 94.

57. John Ashbery: *Critical Views*, ed. Harold Bloom, New York, 1985, 51, and 180.

AGGRESSION AND REPARATION:
BISHOP AND THE MATTER-OF-FACT

JOANNE FEIT DIEHL

Although initially it may seem perverse to emphasize the dynamics of aggression and reparation in a poet as nuanced and controlled as Elizabeth Bishop, throughout her work Bishop records the presence of threat and the means to contain it. This pattern of aggression and reparation, to invoke the object-relations psychoanalyst Melanie Klein's terms, constitutes the trace of an earlier, formative experience, one that long precedes the composition of the poem. The reiterated representation of this experience, therefore, leads us back to the origins of Bishop's literary creativity and serves as an inscription of the psychodynamics that inform her relation to her own creative process. Here I shall expand on the ideas presented in my book, *Elizabeth Bishop and Marianne Moore: The Psychodynamics of Creativity.*[1] I shall attend to moments in the poems when Bishop introduces and deflects aggression and offer a brief, psychoanalytically inflected interpretation of such moments. My aim is to formulate an approach to address issues pertinent to an understanding of Bishop through the lens of Kleinian theory.

In "Infantile Anxiety Situations Reflected in a Work of art and in The Creative Impulse" (1929) Melanie Klein describes what she considers the "most profound anxiety experienced by girls. ... It is the equivalent of castration anxiety in boys. ... The little girl has a sadistic desire, originating in the early stages of the Oedipus conflict, to rob the mother's body of its contents, namely, the father's penis, faeces, children, and to destroy the mother herself. This desire gives rise to anxiety lest the mother should in her turn rob the little girl herself of the contents of her body (especially of children) and lest her body should be destroyed or mutilated". Klein continues: "In my view, this anxiety, which I have found in the analyses of girls and women to be the deepest anxiety of all, represents the little girl's earliest danger situation".[2] When, later, the

---

1.   Joanne Feit Diehl, *Elizabeth Bishop and Marianne Moore: The Psychodynamics of Creativity,* Princeton, 1993.

2.   Melanie Klein, "Infantile Anxiety Situations in a Work of Art and in the Creative Impulse, (1929)" in *The Selected Melanie Klein*, ed. Juliet Mitchell, Harmondsworth, 1986, 92.

child enters what Klein calls the "depressive phase", she seeks to make reparation to the mother she has destroyed in phantasy. This reparative gesture can take the form of creative work: literary, artistic, musical. This paradigm is complicated, however, by the processes of psychic development, for, as the child matures, she introjects the maternal imago, and thus the assault on the mother is experienced as an attack upon an aspect of the self, reparation, therefore, becomes a self-recuperative gesture. Thus, the self constitutes both the origin of aggression and the capacity to make restitution. And the work of art comes into play as a vehicle for such restitutive desires.

What I find striking in Bishop's poems is the extent to which this dynamic of aggression and reparation plays itself out within the works themselves. The trace of this aggression is most frequently located in a source outside the self, a source, I would suggest, which is invested by the authorial psyche with feelings first experienced by it in a process of projective identification. The external locus thus signifies a projective manoeuvre on the part of the psyche, thereby allowing the psyche to displace aggression, to re-locate it outside the self. Various speakers in Bishop's poems are placed in positions of danger, an aura of imminent threat resides in their world. One hears the words of the dream of the Unbeliever:

> I must not fall.
> The spangled sea below wants me to fall.
> It is hard as diamonds; it wants to destroy us all.[3]

In "Wading at Wellfleet" the sea is "all a case of knives" (7).

On other occasions the threat of aggression is at once more localized and contained. This containment is achieved most frequently through either the willful withholding of action or conversion of the aggressive object into a more benign or sorrowful form. One thinks in this regard of the "empty wasps' nest" of "Santarém" and the "one tear", which, "like the bee's sting, slips", reluctantly proffered by the Man-Moth. In each instance, an object of potential harm is transformed – the wasps' nest now devoid of its wounding inhabitants; the tear, which the simile relates to an instrument of aggression, restored to the benign purity of a sacred gift. A similar neutralization of danger occurs in "The Fish" where the ravishing and magisterial description of the hooked fish climaxes in the speaker's freeing it: "And I let the fish go" (CP, 44). The speaker of other poems is not, however, always so capable of checking aggression. As Crusoe, in "Crusoe in England", recalls, " ... I'd dream of things / like slitting a baby's throat, mistaking it / for a baby goat" (CP, 165). At other times, aggression infuses the processes of the landscape itself as in

---

3. Elizabeth Bishop, *The Complete Poems 1927–1979* , New York, 1984, 22. Subsequent references to this edition are given in the text.

"A Cold Spring", "Greenish-white dogwood infiltrated the wood, / each petal burned, apparently by a cigarette-butt". Or the atmosphere may signal danger – as in the double sonnet "The Prodigal", where we read "But evenings the first star came to warn". By the end of the poem, the paranoid subject is unable to distingish between external circumstance and internal turmoil:

> Carrying a bucket along a slimy board,
> he felt the bats' uncertain staggering flight,
> his shuddering insights, beyond his control,
> touching him. (71)

This touch conjoins outside and inside as the bats are identified *as* the prodigal's private interpretations in a linguistic cross-over that fuses natural and subjective realms.

Throughout Bishop's poems, danger is accompanied by either deflection or containment. From a psychoanalytic viewpoint, this rhetorical phenomenon can be understood as tracing the process whereby the poet acknowledges the presence of aggression in her interactions with the world-as-object and makes restitution to that world by verbally containing this aggression. What is the source of this aggression, and where lie the origins of the desire to make restitution?

According to Klein, aggression plays a primary role in artistic creation. The initial impetus to do violence stems from our earliest, formative experience, the infant's instinctual drive to destroy the mother and all that she contains. In the second stage of development as outlined by Klein, the depressive stage, the child is able to conceptualize the hitherto split images of the good and bad mother as one entity, a presence toward whom the child experiences feelings of guilt that stem from her possessing destructive phantasies. Now the creative impulse is born as the child seeks, through her efforts, to restore the wounded mother of phantasy to her original condition. Klein conceptualizes all later, adult creative endeavours as a reenactment of this desire to make reparation, to restore the mother to her former self. I suggest that this theory of creativity may shed light on poetic analysis, for this very same dynamic of aggression and reparation is rhetorically enacted through the introduction and transmutation of violence, a pattern present throughout Bishop's work. It is, moreover, this movèment between aggressivity and restitution that, along with Bishop's characteristic equivocations, contributes to the uncanny illusion of the reader's witnessing an ongoing, active throught process operating in the poem that evolves simultaneously with the reading of it. The deployment and swift rhetorical containment of aggression endow Bishop's poems with an aura of covert movement and dynamic, albeit submerged, interactivity. Furthermore, poems seemingly remote from the personal come to be infused with language that, according to this analysis, finds its source in the originary infant-mother dyad. The successful containment of aggression ensures the continuance of poetic productivity, the aesthetic accomplishment of a single poem depends, in part, on the author's ability to strike a balance between the energizing, aggressive impulse and restitutive desire.

Tellingly, this dynamic of aggression and reparation plays itself out over a broad spectrum of narrative subjects, whether Bishop's speaker is advocating a costume for the pink dog or describing the rapine desires of the Portuguese conquistadors who chase "those maddening little women ... retreating, always retreating" in "Brazil, January 1, 1502". Indeed, it is the very ubiquitiousness of this dynamic that leads one to speculate that its underlying motivations are related to fundamental feelings associated not with any specific occasion but with the workings of the creative process itself, that there is something inherent in that process which gets expressed through the articulation and silencing of conflict.

In "The Bight" Bishop constructs a scenario laced with an aggression which simultaneously proliferates as it is subordinated to the maintenance of a process of commercial exchange. That process of exchange, moreover, comes to signify the movements that constitute the living of a life. Birth, the passing of time, and the spectre of death are all introduced early on in the poem; witness the title, with its pun on the orally located act of biting (echoed in the poem's closing lines with the dredge's "dripping jawful of marl"), the note between title and text, "On my birthday", accentuating maternal origins, and the "white, crumbling ribs of marl" that resemble skeletal remains. The scene itself is incendiary, for the bight is dangerously dry. This flammable site, where the "boats are dry, the pilings dry as matches", is infused with the expectation of fire. Indeed, a flame does appear, but only as a means to characterize the color of the water which is "the color of the gas flame turned low as possible". This introduction of incendiary possibility ushers in a descriptive process that keeps presenting aggression only to contain it. The "little ocher dredge's" scooping out the water floor itself signifies continued aggressive activity. If the "white, crumbling ribs of marl" recall a submerged skeleton, then the dredge's incursions into the earth may be associated with the exhumation of the dead. This sombre process shadows the purposive and beneficent task of the dredge which must work to keep the bight open to enable the boats' safe passage. The birds that inhabit this place are "outsize", their behaviour characterized as excessively violent: "Pelicans crash ... like pickaxes", yet such aggressive forays usually yield nothing. Both in their contrasting colours and martial name, the "black-and-white man-of-war birds" embody conflict. The birds

> soar
> on impalpable drafts
> and open their tails like scissors on the curves
> or tense them like wishbones, till they tremble. (60)

An open pair of scissors would be poised to cut, to close together to complete its aggressive action; on the other hand, the birds tense their tails "like wishbones", which, if forced together, would snap and break. Hence, the tails are descriptively balanced between incipient aggression and the suspenseful withholding of self-destruction.

When the sponge boats appear, they are represented as being both domesticated and quaint: "The frowsy sponge boats keep coming in / with the obliging air of retrievers". The association of the boats with obedient dogs, eager to please, imparts an aura of controlled, good-natured pruposefulness to the scene. If the sponge boats bristle "with jackstraw gaffs and hooks", instruments for catching fish, this predatory, commercial purpose is contained within the picturesque, for the boats are "decorated with bobbles of sponges". So, too, the "blue-gray shark tails", synechdoches for the most lethal acquatic predator, are rendered harmless; swords converted into "little plowshares", in a gesture at once diminutive and pacific, as the tails are "hung up to dry / for the Chinese-restaurant trade". Danger is transformed into a decorative commodity through its participation in a commercial endeavour. Unlike these sharks' tails, the fate of the "little white boats" piled up against each other, or lying on their sides, is less certain. The victims of the last storm's violence, the question of their being "salvaged" remains unresolved. Indeed, they resemble "torn-open, unanswered letters". The adjectives, "torn-open, unanswered", are especially telling. "Torn-open" would suggest a violence or aggression that might be associated with eagerness on the part of the letters' recipient. What is striking is the apparent contradiction between this implied eagerness and the fact that the letters go "unanswered". Literally, the letters would go unanswered because the boats are stranded on the shore; the venue for commerce stilled. In the subjective realm of feeling, the metaphorical letters may go unanswered for a number of reasons; the letters disappoint or anger the recipient; they admit of no response or the sender has disappeared. Whatever the reason, communication is interrupted. Yet, on shore, the process of metaphoricity continues. "The Bight" Bishop writes, "is littered with old correspondences". While "littered", as a verb, conveys a sense of waste, of the extraneous letters marring the shore, there is also, perhaps, a veiled reference back to those "obliging retrievers" that carry and give birth to litters of pups. What is left on the shore might then be understood both as the remnants of a one-sided correspondence, letters unanswered, reciprocity unsustained, and creatures bearing new life, products of maternity. Whatever the balance struck between these two meanings, the playfulness of the line guards against too gloomy a reading, while suggesting how we might interpret the poem and its psychological correspondences as a whole. Moreover, the figuration of bats as letters, written documents, draws our attention to the writerly process suggesting an analogy between this shipping scene and literary activity. For, in describing life at the bight, by metaphorizing the matter-of-fact, the poem gestures toward a sequence of correspondences between creative and natural processes. The natural processes enacted in the poem and the tenuous reciprocity signified by the bight itself suggest the difficulties of channelling aggression, the need to preserve human currency, and the efficacy of making contact with and freeing oneself from the dead in order to sustain a life-giving exchange. "Click. Click. Goes the dredge, / and brings up a dripping jawful of marl". The dredge, as mouth, bites into the earth and, like the retrievers, brings up its prize, the friable clay and calcium carbonate that remind one of mortal (might they be maternal?) remains. This aggressive yet essential bite into potentially deadly matter is instantaneously subsumed into the larger, panoramic characterization of the simultaneity of a vast range of experience: "All the untidy activity continues, / awful but cheerful". "Untidy", with its gently chastising, domestic connotations, draws us away from the mortal intimations of the "dripping jawful of marl", while the poem's last three words, "awful but cheerful" summing up the scene, preserve as they resolve the tension between the instances of aggression and their submergence within processes that ensure the continuance of life. A birthday poem, "The Bight" delineates a natural scene in which manifestations of aggressivity are controlled through humour, in which the necessity for violence is channelled into images of domesticity. Both humour and the deployment of the domestic act as rhetorical strategies that, if they do not exactly neutralize, nevertheless de-fuse or mask the presence of aggression. Such verbal gestures function as linguistic containers for actions which otherwise might prove destructive of the very system they seek to secure. Translating the rhetorical to psychodynamic terms, aggression, which is everywhere in this poem, can be understood as being handled in ways that contain, modify, or subordinate it to the ongoing process of sustained movement. Along with its brilliant aesthetic effects, the poem could be said to accomplish a fundamental piece of psychological work – the preservation of the life-instinct not through the denial but through the recognition and deployment of aggression. If we recall Bishop's biography and the poem's occasion, we might speculate that the object of aggression is the abandoning mother and that aggressive feelings must be neutralized or deflected in order to restore an image of the good mother into the self, thus ensuring the daughter's safety, her ability to tolerate her own aggressive instincts by rhetorical handling that enables her, through reparation to the mother, to vanquish guilt and so renew her own creative capacities. The "awful" and the "cheerful" are two faces of the same identity, formed by the beholder's imaginative projections onto the scene. Reparation occurs when the imagining self or the creating subject finds a home for its aggressive impulses, thereby accommodating forces that otherwise threaten to destroy the other or the self. It is the modulation of these aggressive impulses through the writerly ego's narrativizing of natural processes that salvages those impulses and enables them to serve an integrated self. In Kleinian terms, the poem articulates the achievement of what I have earlier alluded to as the "depressive" phase of development wherein the child no longer separates the "bad" or destructive object from the "good", but comes to understand that object, preeminently the mother, as containing both negative and positive aspects, of viewing the other, and hence, the self, as no longer either / or, but as a nuanced, modulated, capacious self. "The Bight" locates aggression in a provisional space where incendiary possibility makes way for an always tentative, recuperative alterity.

While "The Bight" may be among the clearest, most sustained instances of the aesthetic containment of the aggressive in the matter-of-fact, elsewhere, in both her poetry and prose, Bishop addresses related processes of the mind's striving to find ways to preserve its equilibrium in the face of inner- or externally-derived attack. The question of the origins of the aggressive impulse and its object is reiterated in both the late poem "In the Waiting Room" and the prose narrative, "In the Village". Although others, most notably Lee Edelman, have written at length on "In the Waiting Room", I wish to focus on the dynamics specifically associated with the handling of aggression. In this poem, the almost-seven-year-old Elizabeth passes the time in the dentist's waiting room reading the *National Geographic* and "carefully" studying photographs that represent various kinds and consequences of aggression:

> The inside of a volcano,
> black, and full of ashes;
> then it was spilling over
> in rivulets of fire.
>
> . . . .
>
> A dead man slung on a pole
> – "Long Pig," the caption said.
> Babies with pointed heads
> wound round and round with string;
> black, naked women with necks
> wound round and round with wire
> like the necks of light bulbs.
> Their breasts were horrifying. (159)

What she witnesses in the magazine is a prelude to what she hears:

> Suddenly, from inside,
> came an *oh!* of pain
> – Aunt Conseulo's voice –
> not very loud or long. (160)

The confusion surrounding the origins of the cry, whether it comes from the girl or the aunt, or both, initiates a vertiginous loss of identity. The cry results from an act of clinical performance that might be construed as a form of prophylactic aggression situated in an oral site. The cry emerges from inside an identification that the girl assumes with the aunt. To offset the vertiginous feelings that issue from this fusion of identities, the girl says to herself, "three days / and you'll be seven years old". She inserts the language of fact between the confusion precipitated by her perceptions of aggression, both visual and aural, and the sense of individuality she strives to maintain. Almost lost to the uncanny experience of merger between herself and her aunt, between herself and the images in the *National Geographic* – something pulls her back – the "cry of pain ... could have / got loud and worse but hadn't". On the verge of being overcome by sensation,

> The waiting room was bright
> and too hot. It was sliding
> beneath a big black wave,
> another, and another: (161)

the self is returned to ongoing reality, to the matter-of-fact. The process of recuperation is silent, transpiring in the space between the poem's closing stanzas:

> Then I was back in it.
> The War was on. Outside,
> in Worcester, Massachusetts,
> were night and slush and cold,
> and it was still the fifth
> of February, 1918. (161)

Whatever psychic processes are enacted within that trans-stanzaic silence, the outcome is a return to the quotidian, the facticity of dailiness that orients the speaker in her world. Aggression and destruction which have carried the speaker to the brink of dissolution are now contained enough to permit the reemergence of identity, the continuation of ordinary consciousness. The mystery surrounding this mental process remains unsolved. What substitutes for that solution is the repetition of a sequence of facts that establishes a reassuring connection with external circumstance. Although the poem excludes any explanation of how this transition is made, the verbal testimony of the final stanza itself offers a kind of answer. For, it is the world of the matter-of-fact that stands in for other, more disruptive, potentially catastrophic realities. Bishop's oft-noted devotion to the matter-of-fact, when contextualized psychoanalytically, might be seen as a willed orientation toward the external as an act of defence against the blurring of ego boundaries. Paradoxically, attentiveness directed toward the external enables the writerly ego simultaneously to align itself empathically with the outer world while the iteration of facts, the very process of naming, inscribes a continual sense of difference btween those facts and the imagining subject. Thus, in an ironic gesture of self-assertion, the poet strengthens self-other boundaries through an investment in attending to outward fact.

A related strategy can be seen operating in "In the Village", where issues of aggression, incorporation, and abandonment coalesce to challenge the emergent self's capacities for survival. I cite only the most overt instances that trace the psychodynamic process of the containment and diffusion of threat that resides beyond and inside the self. I say "inside" as well as "beyond" because from the very first paragraph of "In the Village", we learn that an echo of a scream, this time that of the mother, remains hanging over a Nova Scotian Village, over the speaker's village. All you have to do is "Flick the lightning rod on top of the church steeple with your fingernail and you will hear it".[4] The scream resides, "hangs like that, unheard, in memory – in the past, in the present, and those years between" (Prose, 251). As in "In the Waiting Room", the scream initiates in the narrator-as-child a crisis of identity. "She screamed. The child vanishes" (Prose, 253). Here abandonment itself becomes a form of aggression as the mother's repeated withdrawals from the child's presence would, according to Kleinian theory, create in the daughter a profound sense of guilt, in trying to understand the reasons for the mother's inexplicable disappearances, the daughter would imagine herself as their cause; her aggressive impulses would be felt to have so damaged the mother, or hold the potential to so damage the mother that she must escape from the daughter. The symbiotic relation of mother and daughter, the child's inability fully to distinguish between her impulses and actions, results in the child's overwhelming dependence upon the mother's reactions. In the face of this potentially self-annihilating guilt, the child aligns herself with Nate, with the blacksmith's world, where the "beautiful sounds" from the shop "at the end of the garden" promise immediate gratification and pleasure. But this solace proves insufficient to protect the child from the impact of her mother's vocal expression of distress:

---

4. Elizabeth Bishop, *The Collected Prose*, ed. Robert Giroux, New York, 1984, 251. Subsequent references to this edition are given in the text.

Clang.
The pure note: pure and angelic.
The dress was all wrong. She screamed.
The child vanishes. (253)

In gendered terms the child's alignment with the male and the gratification she receives from him and his actions in the metallic world of work do not suffice fully to assuage the daughter's trauma stemming from maternal abandonment. So great is the trauma associated with the mother's final disappearance, the narrator reiterates it only indirectly: "Now the front bedroom is empty ... The front room is empty. Nobody sleeps there. Clothes are hung there". As throughout the narrative, here external objects continue to participate in the enactment of feeling, to register the consequences of loss. The finality of the mother's absence is conveyed through the fact of graphic indelibility. "The address of the sanatorium is in my grandmother's handwriting, in purple indelible pencil, on smoothed-out wrapping paper. It will never come off" (Prose, 272). Hiding the package and its address from Nate, the child protects the identity of its destination and, hence, the recognition of her mother's incarceration / absence. "Every Monday afternoon I go past the blacksmith's shop with the package under my arm, hiding the address of the sanatorium with my arm and my other hand". "Going over the bridge" the child stops and stares down into the river. What she sees there is not only a natural scene but a projection of the dynamic processes and associated feelings that she has experienced in the traumatic beginnings of her life:

> All the little trout that have been too smart to get caught – for how long now? – are there, rushing in flank movements, foolish assaults and retreats, against and away from the old sunken fender of Malcolm McNeil's Ford. It has lain there for ages and is supposed to be a disgrace to us all. So are the tin cans that glint there, brown and gold. (273)

The fishes darting movements, their "assaults and retreats", can be compared to the mother's comings and goings, to the daughter's Monday afternoon trips to the post office, and to her intermittent visits to the blacksmith's shop. The object of ambivalent attraction and repulsion, "Malcolm NcNeil's Ford" with its alliterative "M's" suggests that other word beginning with M, "mother", as it more prominently signifies a masculine-identified, metallic object that is "supposed to be a disgrace to us all". Its desirability is enhanced by the aesthetically lovely "tin cans that glint there, brown and gold" (Prose, 273). The trace of the female is intensified, for the trout, which look transparent, would, "if one did catch one ... be opaque enough, with a little slick moon-white belly with a pair of tiny, pleated, rose-pink fins on it" (Prose, 274). What moves toward and away from Malcolm McNeil's Ford, submerged symbol of ambivalence is, through the narrator's description, identified as feminine. Now the clang of Nate's hammer enters this scene. "Oh, beautiful pure sound! It turns everything else to silence". But this erasure of other sounds does not silence the river – the body that contains both the maternal and the masculine – which, "once in a while, gives an unexpected gurgle". At the repetition of the *Clang*, the scream only apparently disappears. I say "only apparently" because at this crucial moment of potential resolution, of the potentially complete substitution of the clang for the scream, the language introduces a significant ambiguity. "Now there is no scream. Once there was one and it settled slowly down to earth one hot summer afternoon; or did it float up, into that dark, too dark, blue sky? But surely it has gone away, forever". Doubt appears in the alternative destinations of the scream: the earth, the sky? And in the anxious reassurance of "surely". The clang comes from afar; it emanates from the world: "It sounds like a bell buoy out at sea. It is the elements speaking: earth, air, fire, water" (Prose, 274). And yet this sound does not vanquish the doubt that remains in the narrator's mind:

> All those other things – clothes, crumbling postcards, broken china, things damaged and lost, sickened or destroyed, even the frail almost-lost scream – are they too frail for us to hear their voices long, too mortal? (274)

The question is at once odd and inevitable: are these phenomena, with their vulnerability to the ravages of time and loss, too painful to be heard? The implicit answer is, of course, "yes", as the narrator calls out to Nate, "Oh, Beautiful sound, strike again!" (Prose, 274). The very need for a recreation of that sound, however, forfeits as it asserts the efficacy of the blacksmith's power. The narrator summons the clang to obliterate her doubts, to silence the voices "too mortal" to be sustained. This, I suggest, does not amount so much to the permanence of resolution – to a total silencing – as to an expression of the origins of the child's need to elicit the sounds that emanate from the world of the matter-of-fact, a masculine-identified world that can only intermittently drown out the echoes of the maternal scream which, though apparently dispersed, remains either in the earth or in the sky, absorbed into the very atmosphere surrounding her. In terms of aggression and the related issues we have been addressing, the repeated trauma of maternal abandonment and, by extension, the world of vulnerability to which it predisposes the daughter, are dealt with through her realignment with masculinity. What should not be ignored, however, is that Bishop's own father had died when she was eight months old. Hence, if we read this story autobiographically, the daughter faces not a single, but a double trauma, the absence through illness or death, of both parents. The turn to Nate as a masculine, substitute figure, is a turn away from the originary abandonments of both parental figures to the apparently more secure realm of unambiguous, immediately gratifying action, of clearly visible cause and effect, a world of the male-identified matter-of-fact. yet that alternative world canot finally erase the echo of loss that remains forever present, only to be summoned.

Whether in "The Bight", "In the Waiting Room", or "In the Village", indeed throughout Bishop's work, one witnesses the rhetorical inscription of aggression and commensurate efforts of reparation. This paradigm creates, I suggest, a dynamic scenario in which reparation assumes the form of containment of aggression, sublimation, and gift-giving – the verbal deflection of the aggressive instincts that at once fuel as they threaten to destroy the psyche's creative capacities. Furthermore, the Kleinian theory of the infantile anxiety situation would have been intensified for Bishop, in the absence of both parents, the child's phantasies of having caused them irreparable harm could not be diffused or alleviated by their actual presence. In the face of such extenuating psychic circumstances, the wounded yet brilliant daughter finds a way, through the deployment of various vebal strategies, to make reparation to her phantom-parents, primarily the mother, and, in so doing, to fashion an art not only nuanced and controlled, but profoundly revelatory of the origins of the nascent creative self.

ROMANTIC ENTANGLEMENTS:
ASHBERY AND THE FRAGMENT

BENJAMIN COLBERT

Philosophy is the real homeland of irony, which one would like to define as logical beauty; for wherever philosophy appears in oral or written dialogues ... there irony should be asked for and provided ... Only poetry can also reach the heights of philosophy in this way ... There are ancient and modern poems that are pervaded by the divine breath of irony throughout and informed by a truly transcendental buffoonery ...[1]

Many of the works of the ancients have become fragments. Many modern works are fragments as soon as they are written.[2]

Without ellipses or other marks of discontinuity, the fifty ten-lined stanzas of John Ashbery's *Fragment* are not fragmented in appearance. Despite its internal incoherencies, the poem begins and ends with a satisfying sense of departure and closure. As Charles Berger notes, it is a "whole fragment",[3] defying totality even while presenting itself as a totality, opposing what Rodolphe Gasché, in a foreword to Friedrich Schlegel's *Philosophical Fragments*, calls "the classical, pre-Romantic concept of the fragment".[4] The classical fragment is broken off, incomplete, "structurally linked with the whole or totality of which it would have been, or of which it has been, a part".[5] The Romantic fragment, on the contrary, is an ontological and epistemological statement with roots in philosophical scepticism, but related more intimately to Kantian and post-Kantian idealism. It becomes the only means by which to represent the unrepresentable "transcendental idea of totality", which is to say that, all representation being fragmentary, only the fragment form itself can adequately

---

1   Friedrich Schlegel, *Philosophical Fragments*, trans. Peter Firchow, Minneapolis, 1991, 42.3.

2.   Schlegel, 21.

3.   Charles Berger, "Vision in the Form of a Task: *The Double Dream of Spring*" in *Beyond Amazement: New Essays on John Ashbery*, ed. David Lehman, Ithaca and London, 1980, 190.

4.   Rodolphe Gasché, "Ideality in Fragmentation", in Schlegel, viii.

5.   Gasché, vii.

represent this fragmentariness while at the same time pointing beyond and back to itself in an ironical gesture. As Gasché observes, "its focus lies on an *essential* incompletion, an incompletion that itself is a mode of fulfilment".[6] For the Romantic artist, the fragment offers a form that is philosophical precisely because it reveals the tension between representation and truth, even as it locates or privileges in representation itself the "mode (or mood) of fulfilment" that must stand in place of absolute knowledge.

The philosophical stanzas of Ashbery's *Fragment* (1966) align both poem and poet with the Schlegelian tradition. The poem's ontological preoccupation with "passages of being"[7] is continually involved in self-irony; while presenting passages of text as fragments to be read of an elusive whole, the passages reveal themselves as spaces of transition in which beginnings and endings are by no means fixed or continuous: "And the great flower of what we have been twists / On its stem of earth, for not being / What we are to become" (285). In the important thirteenth stanza, Ashbery imagines the truth of being and its "*whole*ness" as the unrepresentable core of a sphere of psyche, the blood orange. Yet this organic structure provides an unstable metaphor which cannot entirely accommodate the metaphysical and aesthetic ideas superimposed upon it:

> Like the blood orange we have a single
> Vocabulary all heart and all skin and can see
> Through the dust of incisions the central perimeter
> Our imaginations" orbit. Other words,
> Old ways are but the trappings and appurtenances
> Meant to install change around us like a grotto,
> There is nothing laughable
> In this. To isolate the kernel of
> Our imbalance and at the same time back up carefully;
> Its tulip head whole, an imagined good.   (287)

The space delineated by the perimeter cannot be represented as a thing in itself, even though it seems to provide a gravitational core, an inside, a centre of formation, an ultimate referent for all signifiers that the imagination deploys (its "singe vocabulary") or redeploys ("Other words, / Old ways"). The very orbiting of the imagination – which aptly suggest the elliptical circling and play of Ashbery's *oeuvre* – effectively keeps it from penetrating to the sources of its own power. The simile, however, can only go so far, itself a representation of that imagination. "Imbalance" supplements "orbit" as the visceral organicism

---

6. Gasché, xxx.

7. John Ashbery, "Fragment" in *Poetry* (February 1966), 283. While *Fragment* was eventually published as an independent work (with illustrations by Alex Katz, Black Sparrow Press, 1969), I use the earlier text here. All further references will be cited parenthetically.

of the blood orange is transformed. Unable to comprehend its own essential nature and to stabilize its incessant workings, the imagination reconfigures "kernel" and "tulip". The interior is exteriorized, even as a seed contains and expresses a flower, though perhaps not the one we would expect. The tulip's "wholeness" is represented by its "goodness", but ironically, this can only be a fragment of wholeness and an "*imagined* good".

The interpenetration of inside and outside, or self and not self, as well as the inability to comprehend the inside without the outside might be the theme of Ashbery's *Fragment*, even as the poem endeavours to uncover the "outside / Within the periphery" (288) of the imagination's orbit. Like Schlegel, Ashbery seems to recognise the necessary irony, the Romantic irony, of his art, and perhaps more important, of the self-invention this entails. As Anne Mellor has shown, Schlegel's "ironic artist must constantly balance or 'hover' between self-creation ... and self-destruction[,] ... a process in which he simultaneously projects his ego or selfhood as a divine creator and also mocks, criticises, or rejects his created fictions as limited and false".[8] For Ashbery, this process is inseparable from his creation and recreation of a dialogic other, the "you" of *Fragment*. "Thus your only world", writes Ashbery, addressing this anonymous companion, "is an inside one / Ironically fashioned out of external phenomena ..."

> Nothing anybody says can make a difference; inversely
> You are a victim of their lack of consequence
> Buffeted by invisible winds, or yet a flame yourself
> Without meaning, yet drawing satisfaction
> From the crevices of that wind, living
> In that flame's idealised shape and duration. (286)

Ashbery seems to be saying that his dialogic other can never be essentially represented with reference to anything outside the orbit of what makes a subject a subject, and that the attempt to do so is always and necessarily ironic, since the external must be brought into that orbit in the capacity of imagery or figures of speech, always expressing what is other than the thing itself. But a more immediate irony lay in the fact that the "you" is a function of Ashbery himself, perhaps even the "external" representation of Ashbery's self. "Your" only world is "inside" the poem, and the poem itself is "ironically fashioned out of external phenomena" – "Nothing anybody says can make a difference" because everything Ashbery writes does. In this sense the "invisible winds" might represent Ashbery's own creative imagination, exerting dominance over its subject while shifting responsibility for this kind of *subjection* outside the creative process ("You are a *victim* of *their* lack of consequence" [my

---

8. Anne K. Mellor, *English Romantic Irony*, Cambridge, MA, 1980, 14.

emphasis]). Nevertheless, perspective shifts and Ashbery entertains a vision of the subject no longer subjected by creative control or inscription. The dialogic other is refigured as a flame outside of the meanings imposed by what "anybody says", including the artist. The flame comes alive *within* art at the places creativity has no control over ("the crevices of the wind"). The last clause in the stanza, finally, carves out another space for non-subjected life *within* the image-to-be of "that flame's idealized shape and duration". The effect is of a series of Chinese boxes deferring the space of subjectivity while affirming that there is such a space within the forms that contain it. Ashbery creates and modifies his creations with the self-consciousness of Schlegel's ironic artist, a self-consciousness only thinly disguised in its otherness; as Ashbery admits early on in the poem, "You exist only in me and on account of me / And my features reflect this proved compactness" (284). Ashbery's very fragmentation of self, or destruction of self into the fragmented dialogic form, operates simultaneously as self-creation.

Ashbery's image of the self as flame "without meaning" living in the phenomenalism of the flame itself gets to the heart of the poem's ontology, where being itself *is* unmeaning, as suggested in the apposition: "This time ? You get over the threshold of *so much unmeaning, so much / Being*, prepared for its event, the active memorial" (286 – my emphasis). Here Ashbery plays syntactically with a number of interrelated and interchangeable propositions: being's event is active memorial, and without active memorial being can never become event. "Event" and "active memorial" open up a space in the present to give meaning to unmeaning, and foist a potentially fictional becoming onto the very being that would be represented. But "event" is a loaded term, and entails "a meaning which is precisely the function of structural – or structuralist – thought to reduce or suspect", as Derrida points out at the beginning of "Structure, Sign, and Play".[9] This may lead us to suspect a larger awareness in Ashbery's deployment of "event" as another ironic gesture aimed at marrying structuralist suspicion with post-structuralist play, opening up an indeterminate range of Schlegelian, Saussurian, and Derridean possibilities for representing structure.

Yet there are places in *Fragment* where Ashbery hovers uncertainly, almost affectionately, about the "threshold" of meaning. That nexus between inside and outside, kernel and flower, planet and orbit, meaning and unmeaning fascinates him, informs his imagery, but also helps us distinguish his idea of the relationship between the fragment and the whole-as-structure from Schlegel's. Derrida's essay again gives a "model", reminiscent of Ashbery's "blood orange", from which to begin:

---

9. Jacques Derrida, "Structure, Sign and Play", *Writing and Difference*, trans. Alan Bass, Chicago, 1978, 278.

The concept of centred structure is in fact the concept of a play based on a fundamental ground, a play constituted on the basis of a fundamental immobility and a reassuring certitude, which itself is beyond the reach of play. And on the basis of this certitude anxiety can be mastered, for anxiety is invariably the result of a certain mode of being implicated in the game, of being caught by the game, of being as it were at stake in the game from the outset.[10]

For Derrida, the very spirit or mood with which an author's imagination plays with, or deploys images, metaphor, irony, becomes the measure of his stake or lack of stake in the game. For Ashbery, the orbital imbalance in the structure of the blood-orange introduces an anxious note, signalled and only partially allayed by the self-conscious irony of his disclaimer; "There is nothing laughable / In this". The very structures the imagination creates to explain itself almost fail in that task. But imbalance is not free-fall, and though the certitude the imagination stretches after is in the end not completely reassuring, at the same time Ashbery resists the "mode of being ... caught by the game" – implicated, perhaps, but never caught.

Schlegel's own mood might best be summed up in his phrase, "transcendental buffoonery", what Mellor calls "an authorial consciousness that is simultaneously affirming and mocking its own creation".[11] It is anything and everything but anxious, since its ironic play gestures towards the reassuring certitude of a transcendental idealism, an absolute but unrepresentable order. When Schlegel writes that "a fragment, like a miniature work of art, has to be entirely isolated from the surrounding work and be complete in itself like a porcupine", this buffoonery is in full display – the affirmative emphasis on organic completion and fragmented wholeness is nicely mocked by the less than hermetic spiny quadruped.[12] There is nothing in this fragment, nor any of the others, that sounds the melancholy, existentialist note of so much other Romantic poetry (e.g. Hölderlin or Keats).

When compared with the fragments which make up Ashbery's poem(s), the Schlegelian fragment sounds rather *wholesome*. Ashbery's fragments are far more self-consciously speculative, and hold up signposts to their own inadequacy, a form of self-mockery to be sure, but one not without its darker side. One such fragment, very likely on the subject of fragments, makes a fine antithesis to Schlegel's porcupine fragment. For Ashbery, fragments (though he does not use the word) are

---

10. Derrida, 279.

11 Mellor, 17.

12 Schlegel, "Athenaeum Fragments" #206, 45.

> ... the externals of present
> Continuing – incomplete, good-natured pictures that
> Flatter us even when forgotten with dwarf speculations
> About the insane, invigorating whole they don't represent.   (297)

What Schlegel had represented as "complete in itself" is now bluntly deemed "incomplete". The "miniature work of art" has been vulgarised into a "dwarf speculation" – a mirror, as the Latin root implies, but one that distorts. And though this porcupine is good-natured, its deictic quills are turned against those they flatter, not towards the elusive, but "invigorating whole". For Ashbery, finally, the best that can be said about this *whole* is that it is insane, a word that recalls Foucault's *Madness and Civilisation* (1965). Foucault's contention that "where there is a work of art there is no madness" invites us to regard *Fragment* as an attempt to explore the edges of insanity.[13] Ashbery's "unmeaning" is like Foucault's "unreason", the disturbing otherness that is not only reason's negation, but that properly belongs "in the inaccessible domain of nothingness". Of course, Foucault paradoxically offers in madness a "silent transcendence" which is "the truth of madness", but here we veer from Schlegelian affirmation towards another kind of liberation, one that replaces once and for all self-creation with self-annihilation.[14] Altogether, there is something less than good-natured in that good-natured picture.

Harold Bloom, however, has found in *Fragment* the sublimation of another kind of anxiety, the anxiety of influence. But influence itself for Bloom creates an anxiety of "being caught in the game" of substitution at the expense of individuation and originality, and it is in this sense that we are *not* talking about two different anxieties at all. Like Derrida, Bloom speaks of an anxiety over our abilities to construct successfully an essential self, one not based merely on "other words" and "old ways", but that can claim an unrepresentable centre of its own. For Bloom,

> ... the mature Ashbery of *Fragment* subverts and even captures the precursor (Wallace Stevens) even as he appears to accept him more fully ... Stevens hesitated almost always until his last phase, unable firmly to adhere to or reject the High Romantic insistence that the power of the poet's mind could triumph over the universe of death, or the estranged object-world. It is not every day, he says in his *Adagia*, that the world arranges itself into a poem. His nobly desperate disciple, Ashbery, has dared the dialectic of misprision so as to implore the world daily to arrange itself into a poem.[15]

---

13. Michel Foucault, *Madness and Civilization,* trans. Richard Howard, New York, 1988, 288–89.

14. Foucault, 107, 100–01.

15. Harold Bloom, *The Anxiety of Influence*, Oxford, 1973, 145.

But if Ashbery has achieved this *apophrades*, this synthesis of the high Romantic dialectic, it is a kind of equanimity on the other side of anxiety, an equanimity that metonymically suggests the very anxiety it belies. Like Derrida, Ashbery would have merely grown comfortable with the discomfort that the absence of a transcendental signified provides, when "everything becomes discourse".[16]

More than *Fragment*, Ashbery's subsequent work squarely faces the ontological anxiety of the fragment along with the anxiety of influence, and it seems that either Bloom had jumped the gun in declaring *Fragment* the epitome of *apophrades*, or that Ashbery has been and will be haunted by the unfinished, perhaps unfinishable, business of the earlier poem. Thus, the opening poem in *April Galleons* (1988), "Vetiver", combines a nostalgia for and mockery of Romantic unities with an allusion to Schlegel's description of the dialogue as "a chain or a garland of fragments":[17]

> Ages passed slowly, like a load of hay,
> As the flowers recited their lines
> And pike stirred at the bottom of the pond.
> The pen was cool to the touch.
> The staircase swept upward
> Through *fragmented garlands* , keeping the melancholy
> Already distilled in *letters of the alphabet*.[18]

This dialogue with Schlegel takes Schlegel's language over-literally and exchanges epistolary letters for "letters of the alphabet" (Schlegel writes: "A dialogue is a chain or garland of fragments. An exchange of letters is a dialogue on a larger scale"). But the inversion of "garland of fragments" to "fragmented garlands" transforms Schlegel's transcendental buffoonery to something more serious and melancholy: "It had all been working so well and now, / Well, it just kind of came apart in the hand". What had been working so well, the poem suggests, was precisely the lack of the individuation that Bloom celebrates, the Romantic continuity with the Romantic past, "a situation / That has come to mean us to us".

---

16. Derrida, 280.

17. Schlegel, "Athenaeum Fragments" #77, 27. This important fragment reads in full: "A dialogue is a chain or garland of fragments. An exchange of letters is a dialogue on a larger scale, and memoirs constitute a system of fragments. But as yet no genre exists that is fragmentary both in form and content, simultaneously completely subjective and individual, and completely objective and like a necessary part in a system of all the sciences".

18 John Ashbery, "Vetiver", *April Galleons*, New York, 1988, 1 – my emphasis. Further references to poems in this edition cited in the text.

The "fragmented garlands" also announce another kind of fragment, the fragmented dialogue, of which Ashbery's broken, ironic conversation with Schegel is one example, and the conversation with his self-like other, the "you" of *Fragment* as well as of *April Galleons*, is another. But these fragments are tainted with melancholy: the fragmented garlands of fragments speak of lost or unattainable victory. They are fragments which have lost the Schlegelian sense of being complete in themselves. Ashbery's complex allusion emphasizes the incompletion that his own sense of the fragment takes on, even as it places himself still in a Romantic fragment tradition. At the same time, it is important not to miss the self-mockery in the opening lines of "Vetiver", as Ashbery deflates the Romantic imagery by turning it against itself. The mythopoeic, almost Blakean, opening is immediately balanced against the mundane "load of hay", while in the second line Ashbery reduces the passage of an age to the voices of the many flowers that speak throughout Romantic nature poetry (e.g. Wordsworth's "The Waterfall and the Eglantine").

Overall, what *April Galleons* adds to the problem of *Fragment* is the development of a vital temporal element. In *Fragment*, hints Ashbery:

> ... the future, an open
> Structure, is rising even now, to be invaded by the present
> As the past stands to one side, dark and theoretical
> Yet most important of all ...   (294–95)

April Galleons, however, recognizes and makes much of the importance of the past. An ironic nostalgia for a time of transcendental unities seems to underscore many of the poems especially concerned with the problem of influence, priority, and originality: "When Half the Time They Don't Know Themselves", "Posture of Unease", "Vaucanson", "Polite Distortions", "Not a First". "Vaucanson", for example, opens with the cold confidence of the Oedipal poet: "It was snowing as he wrote. / In the gray room he felt relaxed and singular". The poem wryly follows this poet's strategies of forgetfulness, avoidance, misprision, as he attempts to shake the untrustworthiness of this mood. Because understanding "diminishes us / In our getting to know it", the poet maintains his distance even while implying a centre to his authority, the Romantic "muttering kinship: / Things with things, persons with objects, / Ideas with people or ideas". But this "muttering" doesn't really make itself clear. The process of composition continues to defer meaning rather than reveal it, just as the warmth of the sun defers our understanding (and the poet's) of what the snow was all about at the beginning of the poem:

> Ah, this sun must be good:
> It's warming again,
> Doing a number, completing its trilogy.

Life must be back there. You hid it
So no one would find it
And now you can't remember where. (AG, 25)

What seems to be most on Ashbery's mind is the "muttering kinship"
promised by Romanticism – a Romanticism treated with very large brush-
strokes as the connection between mind and nature that has become part and
parcel of language itself – again, what Bloom calls "the high Romantic
insistence" on the poet's power to "triumph over ... the estranged object
world".[19] What rankles the post-modernist Ashbery, who sees his own art
implicated in this kinship, is this Wordsworthian premise that the mind and
nature are exactly fitted to one another, and that here is a "fundamental ground",
a "reassuring certainty" (to remotivate Derrida's phrases) to accommodate the
poet's play of language. Although Ashbery is capable of playfully imitating
this Romantic naiveté in "When half the time they don't know themselves ..."
("There has to be a heart to this. / The words are there already" etc.), he gets to
the crux of a wider problem in "The Romantic Entanglement":

And we can see now how it's impossible
To answer anything and stay unnatural,
Response being, by its very nature, romantic,
The very urge to romanticism. The precise itch. (AG, 72)

If "response" is by its very nature Romantic, Ashbery again implicates the
dialogic voices of his own poetry and his own voice insofar as that can be
termed a response. The only voice that could defy this Romanticism would be
a voice that arises from nowhere and stays "unnatural". It does not respond to
things as they are, nor does it respond at all. It speaks without having been
asked to speak, speaks for the sake of speaking. It must be caught in the act of
speaking, and its speech must take the form of a fragmented dialogue freed
from the melancholy of "Vetiver". It must be a parenthesis, or an excerpt from
an ongoing monologue.

Foucault's "The Discourse on Language" begins with the caveat that he
would wish that he could take up his speech as if it had no beginning or end,
and this as a response to his own anxiety of becoming part of the establishment
(the *Collège de France*) outside of which he had remained for so long.[20] This
seems to be Ashbery's predicament in *April Galleons*, even as he recognises
his own perhaps inevitable participation in the urge to Romanticism. As he
puts it in "The Ice Storm", "I want to cut out of this conversation or discourse".

---

19 Bloom, 145.

20. Michel Foucault, *The Archaeology of Knowledge & The Discourse on Language*, trans.
A.M. Sheridan Smith, New York, 1972, 215.

Beyond conversation, discourse, Romanticism lay the undiscovered, undiscoverable country of a Post-modernism that has defied its own constituent connection with the past, a Post-modernism that abandoned nostalgia and embraced a radically new future. But Ashbery can't just "cut out" of temporality and its constraints, and his gestures at the possibility of a "beyond" can merely signify his own *desire* for the radical position. What best allows him to maintain his positioning on the edges of this Post-modernism, a step away from Romanticism (not Modernism), is his manipulation of ironic fragmentation within a formal whole. His goal is not to make way for Romanticism's optimism, but to undermine its transcendental claims while affirming the will to create.

This also aligns Ashbery with a larger conversation on the boundaries between Romantic, modern and post-modern discourse, although Ashbery's work in effect tends to elide the modern and regard an emerging Post-modernism as an alternative to the Romantic, "the very urge to romanticism". When Lyotard claims that "the essay (Montaigne) is post-modern, while the fragment (*The Athenaeum*) is modern" he too engages in this larger elision.[21] But Lyotard's point is too that the post-modern precedes the modern, as Montaigne precedes Schlegel. It explores, struggles and plays without understanding its own principles, yet in hopes that these will be discovered in their becoming. The modern/Romantic comes later, when "response" has been recovered as a reassuring formalist imperative, though the contents of the response may not offer a position. As Lyotard puts it (and I think we may revealingly read "Romantic" for his "Modern"):

> ... modern aesthetics is an aesthetic of the sublime, though a nostalgic one. It allows the unpresentable to be put forward only as the missing contents; but the form, because of its recognizable consistency, continues to offer to the reader or viewer matter for solace and pleasure. Yet these sentiments do not constitute the real sublime sentiment, which is in an intrinsic combination of pleasure and pain: the pleasure that reason should exceed all presentation, the pain that imagination or sensibility should not be equal to the concept.

> The postmodern would be that which, in the modern, puts forward the unpresentable in presentation itself: that which denies itself the solace of good forms, the consensus of a taste which would make it possible to share collectively the nostalgia for the unattainable ...[22]

---

21. Jean-François Lyotard, *The Postmodern Condition: A Report on Knowledge*, trans. Geoff Bennington and Brian Massumi, Minneapolis, 1984, 81.

22 Lyotard, 81.

I have been proposing that by tacitly exploring the substitution of the Romantic for the modern, Ashbery's work has realigned his aesthetic problem as one of priority rather than future anteriority; that he is much more ready to give Romanticism its due as an ideological force with ongoing repercussions. Moreover, Ashbery does not completely relinquish his Romanticism, or the fragment as he moves beyond *Fragment* into subsequent work. Instead he hovers somewhere between Romanticism and the post-modern condition, neither solaced by Schlegelian buffoonery nor suffering the pain of imaginative ineffectuality.

Finally, in recognising our "romantic entanglements", Ashbery helps define a space for what might be called a post-modern Romanticism (or a Romantic Post-modernism), complementing the meta-criticism inaugurated by Jerome McGann (*The Romantic Ideology*, 1983) in his attempt to separate critical thinking from the Romantic ideologies that it criticises. And it is this that lifts Ashbery beyond the pales of the Bloomian "anxiety of influence" theory that seems to gloss some of his poetry so well. For Bloom's discourse does not succeed in the self-conscious ironisation of itself as Romantic discourse, as does Ashbery's. For his part, Ashbery recognises, with the anxious pleasure of paradox, how complicity with the past and freedom from it are simultaneous gestures that form the fulcrum of his art. "What one is chiefly led to contemplate", he writes in "Polite Distortions" (AG, 62):

> isn't that sensible
> If fragmented discourse, but how, with no children around
> To contest it, the same old story is different
> With each new telling.[23]

---

23 Schlegel, "Critical Fragments" #99, 12: "Whoever isn't completely new himself judges the new as if it were old; and the old seems ever new until one grows old oneself."

"QUESTIONS OF TRAVEL":
ELIZABETH BISHOP AND THE NEGATIVE SUBLIME

HELEN M. DENNIS

> The negative sublime is an aesthetics not of identity but
> of difference, of the gap that opens between the empirical
> subject and the world she perceives.[1]

> (O difference that kills,
> or intimidates, much
> of all our small shadowy
> life!)[2]

Taking "Brazil" as a focus for this essay I explore the "Questions of Travel" it
poses, questions which raise issues about first world / third world tourism, as
well as those which recapitulate issues of human identity in relation to the
"other". I employ romantic definitions of the sublime to highlight the
discontinuities between the poet as speaking subject and the foreign world she
travels to. I argue that this trope of the poet in Brazil is a metonym for the
post-romantic self's relation to the world, in which expectations of discovering
a stable identity through the processes of simile and metaphor are subverted
by shifts in tone towards a more disparate representation of the relation between
the poet and her environment.

Tourists and Indians
I begin by recalling an occasion when the folk-singer Joni Mitchell appealed
to a restless crowd after an interruption on stage at the Isle of Wight Festival in
1970 with these lines:

> And there were tourists
> who were getting into it like Indians,
> and Indians who were getting into it like tourists.

---

1. Linda Marie Brooks, *The Menace of the Sublime to the Individual Self: Kant, Schiller,
Coleridge and the Disintegration of Romantic Identity*, Lewiston, N.Y., 1996, 31.

2. Elizabeth Bishop, *The Complete Poems 1927–1979*, London, 1991, 102. Further
references to this edition are given in the text.

And I think that you're acting like tourists, man!
Give us some respect.

It was the lines "And there were tourists who were getting into it like Indians,
and Indians who were getting into it like tourists" which struck me. In Mitchell's
account of the postcolonial postmodern world there are no tourists who act
like tourists and no Indians who act like Indians. And somehow the audience
knows that tourists who get into it like Indians are judged with approval while
Indians who get into it like tourists are targets of disapproval. My premise is
that by travelling to Brazil into a different culture Bishop is inevitably
constructing herself as a type of tourist. A further premise is that tourism is a
phenomenon associated with romanticism's quest to discover and define the
self through the "other". My definition of romanticism derives from Linda
Brooks study of the sublime in Kant, Schiller and Coleridge since her analysis
highlights a number of the problems of definitions of the romantic self which
we still encounter in the postmodern world.

I shall assume that what drives the tourist is the quest for a coherent sense
of the self. Tourism provides an opportunity to arrive at a stable ego identity
using the unfamiliar landscape or the exotic culture as the other against which
one measures and defines the self. For the romantic poet the exotic foreign
location allows a construction of the self that the familiar and domestic has
apparently denied. Consider for a moment "In the Waiting Room" where the
young Elizabeth does not want to be identified with Aunt Consuela:

> Why should I be my aunt,
> or me, or anyone?
> What similarities –
> boots, hands, the family voice
> I felt in my throat, or even
> the *National Geographic*
> and those awful hanging breasts –
> held us all together
> or made us all just one?   (161)

The quest for a sense of self, or a reassurance that one is anyone, involves an
investigation of the "similarities", that is, what is common to humanity, what
constitutes human identity and in particular, female identity? This poem also
articulates a resistance to female and familial identity: she confuses herself
with her aunt – whose voice screams? – but she does not want to be confused
with her aunt. Nor does she want to be the women in *National Geographic*.
Moreover these lines question the very notion of a unified whole, a common
humanity. I also suggest that the movement of this poem enacts a characteristic
version of the sublime with a three phase progress from an initial state of

equilibrium into a state of terror and confusion brought about by the unsettling eruption of a sublime idea, to end with the mind's reappropriation of equilibrium, though on a higher or transcendent level. "In the Waiting Room" recalls a childhood moment of terror about individual and human identity and shapes it into a characteristic expression of the "sublime".

The negative sublime

I am attempting to draw together a cluster of concepts which I think are related here. First, the concepts of "tourists" and "Indians" and the ways these categories get blurred by the mid- to late-twentieth-century, for the first tourist romanticizes the "Indian" and attempts a cultural identification with him/her. The issue is whether such identification can ever be authentic, but we must also ask why the civilized westerner feels drawn to the rituals and cultural formations of the tribal or third world other? Second, the concept of the "individual self" and of "human female identity" in the modern world has a rich inheritance of philosophical definitions of the self which may be traced back to romantic thought. My third concept is that of the "sublime" which I connect with the issue of how the cultured western consciousness perceives and responds to exotic and unfamiliar landscapes and this is connected to our notions about the formation of individual identity which can be seen to be achieved through a self conscious comparison of the self and its limits with the enormity of that which environs us. Finally, I argue that experiences of the sublime are reflected in Bishop's work and that her characteristic notation of the sublime corresponds to the Kantian or "negative sublime".

I now define my understanding of the sublime and the negative sublime before proceeding to suggest instances of it in Bishop's poetry. Romanticism is a celebration of the imagination's power to spin out the "self-other" parallels that ground human identity. The sublime is a characteristic site of this where the human imagination meets the vast, the overwhelming, the incomprehensible in nature and feels a sense of elevation as the human powers rise to perceive the sublime. In Edmund Burke's account of the sublime the subject encounters the external cause of terror, the subject's imagination "swells" and rises to meet it and feels a triumphant pleasure at having expanded the human faculties to join with it. In Kant, the sublime permits the imagination a merely futile attempt at this union before collapsing, and this failure produces not exaltation in the subject but obedient "respect". After Burke, the sublime is no longer identified with the godhead, so it tends to become a focus of the abyss between subject and object, self and other, poet and world. We cannot help but experience and perceive the sublime but the notion of the incomprehensible, the ungraspable, the infinitudinal no longer shores up the human identity. Instead, it leads to yet more hyperbolic attempts to make the connection, to construct a metaphysical bridge over the abyss. Yet the compulsive attraction of such incomprehensible vistas remains.

Thus the romantic and post-romantic attraction towards the sublime which might appear in theory to contribute to the process of definition of an individual self (either through the transcendent powers of the imagination or the awful power of reason to contain the world in a grain of sand) in practice contributes to an experience of the negative sublime, which subverts the romantic aesthetic of connection between subject and object, self and other, the poet and the world. The self comprehends the vastness but is inadequate in the face of it. Hence the formation of a stable individual self is undermined and a more tenuous and provisional construction of autonomy supersedes it. According to Brooks, because of the tension between what Schiller described as "actuality as a limit and his ideas as infinitude" or what Wilfred Mellers has described as "the incongruence between ... concrete actuality ... and the self's struggle to shape it" the autobiographical project becomes tantamount and doomed since "the negative sublime is an aesthetic not of identity but of difference".[3]

Traces of the negative sublime in Elizabeth Bishop
I began with reference to Bishop's "In the Waiting Room", and I return to that poem for a moment and consider it together with two moments in "Primer Class" and "The Country Mouse" from the *Collected Prose*, where Bishop discusses geography:

> Only the third and fourth grades studied geography. On their side of the room, over the blackboard, were two rolled-up maps, one of Canada and one of the whole world. When they had a geography lesson, Miss Morash pulled down one or both of these maps, like window shades. They were on cloth, very limp, with a shiny surface, and in pale colours – tan, pink, yellow, and green – surrounded by the blue that was the ocean. The light coming in from their windows, falling on the glazed, crackly surface, made it hard for me to see them properly from where I sat. On the world map, all of Canada was pink; on the Canadian, the provinces were different colors. I was so taken with the pull-down maps that I wanted to snap them up, and pull them down again, and touch all the countries and provinces with my own hands. Only dimly did I hear the pupils' recitations of capital cities and islands and bays. But I got the general impression that Canada was the same size as the world, which somehow or other fitted into it, or the other way around, and that in the world and Canada the sun was always shining and everything was dry and glittering. At the same time, I knew perfectly well that this was not true.[4]

---

3. Brooks, 34.
4. Elizabeth Bishop, *The Collected Prose*, ed. Robert Giroux, London, 1994, 10–11.

The perspective here is interesting. Bishop is writing a memoir of the childlike failure to grasp or fully comprehend something. Yet the misunderstanding and confusion are instructive. She cannot see the maps "properly" from where she sits, and if this is because of her age it also suggests that if only she could move like the tourist she could see them properly. She hears about them "only dimly", yet she imagines that the "sun was always shining"; here we see the foundation for the tourist's motivation to get to the place where it is no longer dim, where the sun is always shining, even though we know there is no such place. Then there is the confusion between the map of Canada and that of the world: they are the same size, therefore they are the same size; our "home" is as grand as the rest of the world put together, although we know perfectly well this is not true. There is a fascination with and confusion between the map as emblem and the land and world it represents, which throws into question how we should read the relationship between the figurative and the real in Bishop's work.

The other prose passage I call on is the account of the incident described in "In the Waiting Room":

> After New Year's, Aunt Jenny had to go to the dentist, and asked me to go with her. She left me in the waiting room, and gave me a copy of the *National Geographic* to look at. It was still getting dark early, and the room had grown very dark. There was a big yellow lamp in one corner, a table with magazines, and an overhead chandelier of sorts. There were others waiting, two men and a plump middle-aged lady, all bundled up. I looked at the magazine cover – I could read most of the words – shiny, glazed, yellow and white. The black letters said: FEBRUARY 1918. A feeling of absolute and utter desolation came over me. I felt ... *myself*. In a few days it would be my seventh birthday. I felt *I, I, I*, and looked at the three strangers in panic. I was *one* of them too, inside my scabby body and wheezing lungs. "You're in for it now," something said. How had I got tricked into such a false position? I would be like that woman opposite who smiled at me so falsely every once in a while. The awful sensation passed, then it came back again. "You are you," something said. "How strange you are, inside looking out. You are not Beppo, or the Chestnut tree, or Emma, you are *you* and you are going to be *you* forever". It was like coasting downhill, this thought, only much worse, and it quickly smashed into a tree. *Why* was I a human being?[5]

5. *The Collected Prose*, 32–33.

It seems to me that much of Bishop's mature poetry continues to express these preoccupations with the sense of personal identity which does induce an "awful sensation" when contemplated closely, and with the relation between that sense of the self as too small, too powerless, positioned in dim light on the margins, unable to quite see the full picture face to face and the universe as we represent our knowledge of it, which in 1918 included the confident pink of Empire.

So that travel becomes a quest to resolve questions of positioning and identity through an empirical proof, which is always and inevitably undermined, since the quest is for evidence of the self which the world can never adequately provide. Hence my contention that there are traces of the dilemma of the romantic poets in Bishop's work. As they tried to bridge the abyss between noumen and phenomenon through philosophical contestation, through the esemplastic powers of the primary imagination, through the "glorious realm of *Schein* or aesthetic illusion", so she moves from dimly perceiving the maps to travelling as a means of mapping the self and also as a way of mitigating the "awful sensation" of inevitable human identity.

One of the problems of romanticism is the divide between the phenomenal and the noumenal which I have just referred to, and one of the tasks of the romantic poet is thus to find ways of linking the two. I am not suggesting that this presents such a crisis for the modernist poet, yet traces remain and are clearly visible in Bishop's work of the question of what is heautonomy (autonomy) and how it can be achieved? Even if Bishop's footnote to the "The Man-Moth" implies it is a whimsical, playful poem, based on a "Newspaper misprint for 'mammoth'," it is a poem which plays on the sense of the self and its double. The man-moth foregrounds the "imaginary" identity and plays down the actual, and yet there are moments of linkage:

> Each night he must
> be carried through artificial tunnels and dream recurrent dreams
> Just as the ties recur beneath his train, these underlie his
> rushing brain.   (15)

Here the simile is used in reverse. The fantasy world of the "imaginary" is proffered as the norm, and details from what we normally accept as the "real" world, the world of commuter travel becomes the descriptive figure of speech. The figurative and the real, or the vehicle and tenor have been inverted. The sublime is the locus where phenomenon and noumen should meet, it is an indeterminate space which should act as a bridge between the two; or as a place where the impossible leap can be made to connect the two. "The Man-Moth" articulates the difficulty of this, and does so through allusion to a version of the sublime which emphasizes the trope of the vertical:

> He thinks the moon is a small hole at the top of the sky,
> proving the sky quite useless for protection.
> He trembles, but must investigate as high as he can climb. (14)

There is a desire for security but a compulsive attraction which draws him to the awful elevation. So that this is a type of attempt at aesthetic transcendence, in a modernist parody of what Brooks calls the verticality of sublime landscapes. Yet even in the romantic project the ascent is doomed to a fall.[6] The vertical landscapes of the romantic sublime with their dizzying heights and peaks lost in the clouds emphasize the impossible but ineluctable ascent and the subsequent fall back into the merely human. The pattern of aspiration and falling back is replayed here by Bishop, "But what the Man-Moth fears most he must do, although / he fails, of course, and falls back scared, but quite unhurt" (14). "The Man-Moth" represents the absurd quest for the harmony and totality and the concomitant fall back down in a cartoon version of the modern city-scape. It ends with a tear which becomes a "pearl" of wisdom or exchange with the reader; a tear which reminds us that terror and self-pity are also linked in the romantic landscape of the self. Which brings me finally to "Brazil", and Bishop's "Arrival at Santos".

"Brazil" **and questions of travel**

> Here is a coast; here is a harbor;
> here, after a meagre diet of horizon, is some scenery:
> impractically shaped and – who knows? – self-pitying mountains,
> sad and harsh beneath their frivolous greenery,
> with a little church on top of one. (89)

This is the language of the Primer, or of a child's naive drawing. There is a confusion though, for is it a child's perception represented in her drawing or is it the actual landscape which is "impractically shaped"? And whose are the "self-pitying mountains" dressed in frivolous greenery? The glib answer would be that this is a pathetic fallacy; except that the feminine archetype drawn on to compose the pathetic fallacy here is more conventional and less striking than the actual female figure in the scene. In fact rather than similarity we have disjunctures between the landscape and the arriving tourists. What is clearly

---

6. Demystification, de Man argues, is like Baudelaire's *dedoublement* (the subject's doubling of itself), in which the artistic or philosophical person laughs at herself falling – she laughs at a mistaken assumption she was making about herself and about the myth of totality or meaning that she had believed possible. She must continue to make the assumption, however, knowing that she will relinquish and take up the myth of totality *ad infinitum* (Brooks, 55).

articulated is the "tourist's" desires "for a different world, and a better life, and complete comprehension".

>   Oh, tourist,
>   is this how this country is going to answer you
>   and your immodest demands for a different world,
>   and a better life, and complete comprehension
>   of both at last, and immediately,
>   after eighteen days of suspension?   (89)

Miss Breen's home is Glens Falls, and the poem enacts the word "Falls" with the "s" dropped down onto the next line. But Glens Falls is a site of early nineteenth-century tourism and also of literary romanticism. In *The Last of the Mohicans*, for example, Natty Bumppo describes them thus:

> It falls by no rule at all; sometimes it leaps, sometimes it tumbles; there, it skips; here, it shoots; in one place 'tis white as snow, and in another 'tis green as grass; hereabouts, it pitches into deep hollows, that rumble and quake the 'arth, and thereaway, it ripples and sings like a brook, fashioning whirlpools and gulleys in the old stone, as if 'twas no harder than trodden clay. The whole design of the river seems disconcerted. (*The Last of the Mohicans*, ch.VI).

If this is a typical romantic landscape, depicting a wilderness which is terrifying to his interlocutors, the next move in his speech is also typical, in that he draws a moral analogy between the unruly river which is brought back into contained order and the rebellious man:

> And yet what does it amount to! After the water has been suffered to have its will, for a time, like a headstrong man, it is gathered together by the hand that made it, and a few rods below you may see it all, flowing on steadily toward the sea, as was foreordained from the first foundation of the 'arth! (*The Last of the Mohicans*, ch. VI).

His reasoning by analogy suggests a version of the positive sublime, which is precisely what we do not find in "Arrival at Santos"; but by the worked in allusion to "Glens Fall/s" we have embedded recognition of the trace of the romantic or transcendental tendency to desire to discover or invent correspondences between the human order and the landscape.

The tourist's demands are not meet, so that the poem enacts an initial romantic tendency to interpret and represent the strange landscape according to the tourist's agenda, which is deflated and reflected in the poem's inconsequential humour. By the time we have gone through immigration and customs and dealt with the stamps which do not stick, we are stripped of various cultural assumptions, including the assumption that we are of sufficient significance for the landscape to render up meanings for us:

> We leave Santos at once:
> we are driving into the interior   (90).

The soap and postage stamps also suggest a sense of transience, of not making any lasting impression on the landscape, of letting it slip, or its letting us slip. So that this final line is stripped of metaphoric suggestion, and one feels that the interior is just the interior, alien and resistant to the tourist's quest. Yet the next poem recapitulates the meeting of western, colonizing mind with the "jungle" in a further attempt to find or read significance into the landscape.

However, I think "Brazil, January 1, 1502" re-enacts this attempt in order to reaffirm the difference from and the indifference to the colonial presence:

> Januaries, Nature greets our eyes
> exactly as she must have greeted theirs: (91).

What a wonderfully false naive statement! To put January in the plural immediately posits multiplicity; and we know "Nature" cannot "greet" anyone, unless they are anthropomorphizing their environment. Moreover the epigraph from Kenneth Clark raises the reader's awareness of the tendency of "civilization" to perceive nature as embroidered, tapestried landscape, that is, through its own cultural perceptions. This in turn reminds the reader that different cultures from different eras and locations see differently. So here we have a poem which apparently seeks identification with sixteenth-century Iberian adventurers, and apparently suggests that a mid-twentieth-century tourist and a sixteenth-century Portuguese explorer perceive Brazil in similar ways. I think this is undercut by "Arrival at Santos" with the lines "Oh, tourist, / is this how this country is going to answer you / and your immodest demand for a different world"; but it is also subverted by the final stanza of "Brazil, January 1, 1502" which views the sixteenth-century "Christians, hard as nails" with analytic objectivity as even their desires and lusts are mocked. So I would argue that there is an initial and superficial identification with the early colonial explorers, a recognition of the ways in which the western consciousness tries to read the jungle, seeks to find the fulfilment of its desires in its encounter with a vivid and prolific landscape, a hint of the experience of appreciation of the "sublime", but then a counter movement which "retreats" from enacting in the poetry a moment of unification of nature, landscape, colonizer, tourist and native other, a pulling back to recognize alienation and difference – not blanket harmony.

It seems to me that "Brazil" contains poems where the poet shifts to hyperbole and employs a mode already signalled by "The Man-Moth", that of movement from the actual to the imaginary, and in the case of "The Riverman" an imaginary which is a blend of native belief in magic and a western sense of the fantastic. I sense in this poem, as in the earlier sequence "Songs for a Colored Singer", and as in "The Burglar of Babylon", traces of a colonial mentality, an embedded sense of civilized superiority, yet a fascination with the "other", whether Afro-American or Rio poor. This leads me back to my initial quotation from Joni Mitchell:

> And there were tourists.
> And there were tourists
> who were getting into it like Indians,
> and Indians who were getting into it like tourists.

The best one can do as a "tourist" is get into it "like Indians" – but acting "like" is not the same as "being". In this reading of the Kantian sublime, the sympathetic imagination is no longer a sustainable solution, and we are left only with the recognition of inadequacy and difference. And that perhaps leaves one wondering, why bother? And that, I take it, is precisely the question in "Questions of Travel":

> Think of the long trip home.
> Should we have stayed at home and thought of here?
> Where should we be today?
> Is it right to be watching strangers in a play
> in this strangest of theatres?
> what childishness is it that while there's a breath of life
> in our bodies, we are determined to rush
> to see the sun the other way around?
> The tiniest green hummingbird in the world?
> To stare at some inexplicable old stonework,
> inexplicable and impenetrable,
> at any view,
> instantly seen and always, always delightful?
> Oh, must we dream our dreams
> and have them, too?
> And have we room
> for one more folded sunset, still quite warm?
>
> But surely it would have been a pity
> not to have seen the trees along this road,
> really exaggerated in their beauty,
> not to have seen them gesturing
> like noble pantomimists, robed in pink.

. . .   .

– And never to have had to listen to rain
so much like politicians" speeches:
two hours of unrelenting oratory
and then a sudden golden silence
in which the traveller takes a notebook, writes:

"Is it lack of imagination that makes us come
to imagined places, not just stay at home?
Or could Pascal have been not entirely right
about just sitting quietly in one's room?" (93–94)

Metaphors and similes operate here, but they tend to emphasize difference not similarity. The rain is not like politician's speeches in any fundamental way; trees are not actually noble pantomimists. Her previous assessment of the landscape and all it contains is more accurate: "inexplicable and impenetrable, at any view," pretty much sums it up. The self is not reflected in nature, one does not find confirmation of one's individual identity by travelling the tourist road. Instead, one finds inconsequential disruptions and discontinuities. But the effect of this experience of being alien in an alien landscape is to prompt one to ask, as Bishop does at the end of this poem, "Should we have stayed at home, wherever that may be?" That is to question not only "travel" but its binary opposite "home".

There is the apocryphal story of the Oxbridge philosophy student who received a straight First when everyone else in his class was awarded a Lower Second for a paper where the question was "Why?". His answer, as I am sure is well known, was the single word "Because". In effect, Elizabeth Bishop puts the same question, both to herself and her reader, and finds the same answer. My attempt here to adumbrate the sense of the sublime, the compulsion of the tourist, and the inevitable cultural differences which exist between the United States and Brazil has been a footnote to Bishop's traveller's notebook. And her traveller's notebook is a tiny "Legend" to our map of the world.

JOHN ASHBERY'S "A WAVE" (1983):
TIME AND WESTERN MAN

DENNIS BROWN

I intend to focus on one longer (and later) poem of Ashbery's, "A Wave",[1] which I have elsewhere described as the "Tintern Abbey"[2] of poetic postmodernism. My sub-title indicates a desire to situate the poem within a larger twentieth-century genealogy, including (if only implicitly) the "wave-theory" of physics, free verse, Imagism, and stream-of-consciousness writing – conveniently signalled for instance in Virginia Woolf's *The Waves*, (1931) – as provocatively encapsulated in Wyndham Lewis's largely neglected critique *Time and Western Man* (1927).[3] The "analysis" in Lewis's book will suggest a thematic development linking mainstream literary modernism and postmodernism (and strongly manifested in "A Wave") which is characteristically denied by architectural and philosophical arguments which assert a postmodern "turn" against both modernity and aesthetic modernism.[4] The three terms of Lewis's title will be extrapolated in relation to "A Wave" to help place the poem's own representations of the following three concepts: temporal flux, New World "Centrality", and an imaginary masculinity. Such a discussion will help give contextual justification for my own conviction as to the poem's unique contribution to contemporary literary aesthetics and cultural studies.

By homing in directly on "A Wave" I am not attempting to isolate it from the Ashbery canon: nor am I taking one side in the gender divide. The poem is twenty one pages long and the passages selected for commentary help to anchor my argument. In choosing these I have not been concerned to outline the shape of the poem overall, partly because it seems to me that the wave-aesthetic at issue is only partially reliant on linear ordering. The poem, I suggest, is more

---

1   All quotations from John Ashbery, *Selected Poems*, London, 1987.

2. See, Dennis Brown, *The Poetry of Postmodernity: Anglo/American Encodings*, Basingstoke & New York, 1994, 111–12.

3. Wyndham Lewis, *Time and Western Man*, ed. Paul Edwards, Santa Rosa, 1993. Further references to this edition are given in the text as TWM.

4. *The Poetry of Postmodernity*, 4.

like a mosaic or collage or even mobile. To paraphrase a line from Theodore Roethke, when it moves it moves more ways than one, and like *Finnegans Wake*,[5] its sense of an ending (for there is one) is liable to send us back to the beginning to try it all again:

> We'll
> Stay in touch. So they have it, all the time. But all was strange.   (351)

> To pass through pain and not know it,
> A car door slamming in the night.
> To emerge on an invisible terrain.   (330)

A wave, as figure, suggests a movement constrained and confined only by its boundaries. A round pond creates different wave-effects to the sea's shore or the banks of a river; just so, too, light-waves may be blocked, radio-waves "bent" or radar-waves jammed. In the poem, the typographic reading-flow is hemmed in by margins, and points to one end which is always present. But in my end is my beginning, and as in other modernist texts, the flow of time here facilitates too an unravelling of times past. You never step into the same river twice, but you can swim back upstream and, over time, the very placement of rivers may change: the river presumably alluded to by Heraclitus is now some miles from his native Ephesus – which is why the town died. Time is a funny business – especially in an era when "all that is solid melts into air".[6]

> ... and all of a sudden the scene changes:
> It's another idea, a new conception, something submitted
> A long time ago, that only now seems about to work
> To destroy at last the ancient network
> Of letters, diaries, ads for civilization.
> It passes through you, emerges on the other side
> And is now a distant city, with all
> The possibilities shrouded in a narrative moratorium.   (330)

For all its quasi-poststructuralist scepticism about the possibility of saying anything straight (and it has its own version of Derrida's post-Freudian "mystic

---

5. James Joyce, *Finnegans Wake*, London, 1982, 292. For my discussion of the Lewis–Joyce rivalry see Dennis Brown, *Intertextual Dynamics Within The Literary Group – Joyce, Lewis, Pound and Eliot: The Men Of 1914*, London, 1990, New York, 1991, 125–32 and 158–65 especially. See also Scott W. Klein, *The Fictions of James Joyce and Wyndham Lewis: Monsters Of Nature and Design*, Cambridge, 1994.

6. Karl Marx's phrase, of course, but I also had in mind Marshall Berman's *All That Is Solid Melts Into Air: The Experience Of Modernity*, London, 1983.

writing-pad"[7] – where "the grain of the wood ... pushes through" and "becomes part of what is written" (335), the poem has important things to say about time, partly in intertextual dialogue with such writers as Eliot, Stevens, Woolf, and (I think) Beckett.[8]

Time

Wyndham Lewis was sufficiently neo-Platonic (and indeed Aristotelian) to wish to resist any complicity with a Heraclitean flux. In *Time and Western Man* he polemically positions himself as a "space man", claiming to speak for "the world of classical 'common sense' – the world of the Greeks, the world of the Schoolmen ... the world of nature, too, and ... a very ancient one indeed" (TMW, 177). His position, we might say, is a form of "plastic" (his word) essentialism, postulating both spatial rationality and ultimate self-consistency – as he put it, "the ego" of the "European Enlightenment" (TWM, 289). From this vantage- point he anatomises what he dislikes in modern culture in terms of a "time-school" where "time and change are the ultimate reality" (TMW, 160). Involved here, he writes, is "dispersal and transformation of a space-phenomenon into a time-phenomenon throughout everything" (TMW, 172); hence "you are no longer a centralised self, but a spun-out, strung-along series, a pattern-of-a-self, depending like the musical composition upon time". Such relativity is identified in specifically liquid terms: "Both Einstein and Bergson are river officials of the great River flux" (TMW, 389). So too, I would argue, is Ashbery such a "river official" and the whole thematic of "A Wave" is a fluid representation of postmodern experience in terms of inherent "time philosophy". This is the opposite of Wordsworth's rationally revolving world of "rocks and stones and trees". Everything in Ashbery's poem is shifting, dissolving – appearing only to disappear:

>   ... like jazz music
> Moving over furniture ...   (331)

>   ... the implausible
> Picaresque tale ...   (337)

>   ... swamped
> As though by a giant wave that picks itself up
> Out of a calm sea and retreats again into nowhere ...   (343)

---

7. Jacques Derrida, "Freud and the Scene of Writing", in *Writing and Difference*, translated by Alan Bass, London, 1981, 196–231.

8. See for instance the "translated" mini-narrative on page 347, and especially the reference to Zeno's paradox.

> ... the maelstrom of definition ...
> ... over and over
> In a continuous, vivid present that wasn't there before ...   (346)

> ... the walls, like veils, are never the same, (351).

What Lewis's critique alerts us to in the writing of Stein, Joyce, Woolf and others is a cultural construction of temporal flux which "A Wave" carries forward towards the 1990s.

West world

Where Lewis wants to assert "Western" mind against time-philosophy, in Ashbery as in Joyce the implication is that it is precisely western science, philosophy, aesthetics and experience which have developed a fluxive temporality. Ashbery's "Wave" sweeps through a New World (sometimes, perhaps, New York) scenario of post-industrial detritus and postmodern consumerism:

> ... the quiet time
> In the supermarket, and the pieces
> Of other people's lives as they sashayed or tramped past
> My own section of the corridor ... (334)

This is postmodernism as a mutation in the advance of Western modernity – what Richard Rorty has called the "pageant of historical progress which will gradually encompass all the human race",[9] except that "progress" seems too purposive a word:

> There would be more concerts
> From now on, and the ground on which a man and his wife could
> Look at each other and laugh, remembering how love is to them,
> Shrank and promoted a surreal intimacy, like jazz music
> Moving over furniture, to say how pleased it was
> Or something. (331)

Ashbery's laid-back, wrap-around lines (the tone a kind of poeticized, international airport-controller's drawl) convey an ultimately centripetal force where all "marginal" phenomena (and ideolects) are sucked into a Westernized vortex of global economics and culture. It is Ashbery's linguistic ability to keep the Western centre from falling apart which constitutes, I suggest, his aesthetic authority.

---

9. See Richard Rorty, "Cosmopolitanism With Emancipation: A Response To Lyotard" in *Modernity and Identity*, ed. Scott Lash and Jonathan Friedman, Oxford, 1993, 68.

Yet in Lewis's *post*-Vorticist terms, Ashbery is unmaking or at least remaking, the whole mythos of the "West". Time-honoured categories – such as "nature" and "culture" – are slyly deconstructed within an emergent space-time:

> Orchards where the quince and apple seem to come and go
> Mysteriously over long periods of time; waterfalls
> And what they conceal, including what comes after – roads and roadways
> Paved for the gently probing, transient automobile ... (338)

The terrain is postcolonial as well as postmodern, but one clearly determined by geopolitics generated by westernized schedules: "all games and disciplines" (332), "the headlines and economy" (334), "the dungeon of better Better Living" (337), "our inane rounds" (343). The zone is a hyperreal Nowhere yet as thronged, under "fabrications" which hymn an "anthem to perpendicularity" (345), with the grotesquery as in the street-shots at the beginning of Ridley Scott's *Bladerunner*. This is an ultimately "First World" realm – "our planet, its climate, its sonatinas / And stories" (348) – boasting its contemporaneous relevance beyond any rationale: just the way it is now. And it is precisely this Euro /American feel that gives the poem its simulacrum of "centrality", inscribing intellectual drift and emotive consumerism as New World end-of-history:

> Flares are launched out over the late disturbed landscape
> Of items written down only to be forgotten once more, forever this
> time. (350)

This scenario undoes Lewis's western mind – as it does, surely, such more recent reassertions of post-Enlightenment reason as Fredric Jameson's *Postmodernism, or, the Cultural logic of Late Capitalism*, David Harvey's *The Condition of Postmodernity*, Terry Eagleton's *Ideology: an Introduction*, or Christopher Norris's *What's Wrong with Postmodernism: Critical Theory and the Ends of Philosophy*.[10] "A Wave" works against this grain. Ashbery's world constructs an alogical disorientation of western mind: for without an Eastern "Other", there can be no oriented West. Waves, in short, cannot be "cognitively mapped"[11] for they do not conform to the points of the compass.

---

10. See Fredric Jameson, *Postmodernism, Or The Cultural Logic Of Late Capitalism*, London, 1991, David Harvey, *The Conditions of Postmodernisty: An Enquiry Into The Origins Of Cultural Change*, Oxford, 1988, Terry Eagleton, *Ideology an Introduction*, London, 1991, and Christopher Norris, *What's Wrong With Postmodernism: Critical Theory And The Ends Of Philosophy*, Brighton, 1990.

11. Jameson's phrase in *Postmodernism, Or The Cultural Logic Of Late Capitalism*.

Imaginary masculinities

Ashbery represents a "Modernist Self"[12] by quite continuously evoking a stylistics of "we". Nevertheless, the "amazingly quiet room in which all my life has been spent" (351) constitutes a gendered "room of one's own" which is also a "room with a view" – the "growth of the poet's mind", here, pioneers a postmodern imaginary masculinity. However, it is in strong contrast to Lewis's masculinism in *Time and Western Man* where the male, objectivising gaze, founded in an aggressive/defensive coherent self, masters all space in rational perspective – right up to the vanishing point. In "A Wave" Ashbery is negotiating a modified masculinity in which space itself is surrealistically filmic ("all of a sudden the scene changes") and time a matter of drifting, loops, sudden surges, memory-lapses, rewinds and wave-motion – both space and time dissolved into an inchoate space-time which Lewis abhorred in its stylistic representation as proto-écriture féminine: of Stein he wrote, "this capable, colossal authoress relapses into the role and mental habits of childhood" (TWM, 60): of Joyce, "the method of *Ulysses* imposes a softness, flabbiness and vagueness everywhere in its bergsonian fluidity" (TWM, 101). In this, of course, it is Ashbery not Lewis who is in the modernist and postmodern mainstream – that of Proust, Joyce, Richardson, Eliot, Pound, Woolf, Beckett etc. Yet Lewis's thinking strongly clarifies what is going on – a reactive androgynisation of "Western Man".

For such masculinity had typically been constructed as an end-directed journey through a fixed, if estranged, geography full of forward-pointing symbolic significations: in "A Wave" these are alluded to as, for example, "steeply shelving terrain", the "haunted house", "the place of power", "a ruined fort", a "major/Bend in the swollen river", "the roadblocks", "strangers / in taverns", "the garden", the "old man", "footfalls / of the police" etc. However, Ashbery's postmodern Childe Roland is never impelled to the classical final encounter. Such significations of male purposiveness against external threat remain as faded markers, part of the semiotic haze, in a contemporary "picaresque", ad-hoc nomadism. Where Lewis saw western man undone in the Great War (an experiential reality underlying the endeavour of *Time and Western Man* in important ways), Ashbery represents an uncentred masculinity dissolved into the conurban quotidian banal:

> One is almost content
> To be with people then, to read their names and summon
> Greetings and speculation, even nonsense syllables and
> Diagrams from those who appear so brilliantly at ease

---

12. See Dennis Brown, *The Modernist Self In Twentieth-Century English Literature*, London, New York, 1989.

In the atmosphere we made by getting rid of most amenities
In the interests of a bare, strictly patterned life that apparently
Has charms we weren't even conscious of, which is
All to the good, except that it fumbles the premise
We put by, saving it for a later phase of intelligence, and now
We are living on it, ready to grow and make
mistakes again ...   (338)

On such hypothetical and non-effectual "premises" does the 1980s Prufrock drift ahead.

The overall stylistics of "we" suggests a more diffused selfhood than we are yet used to. From a male point of view this is, no doubt, what Robert Bly would call "soft" masculinity[13] – a nomadic spilling over gender boundaries in search of non-patriarchal commonality:

What were the interruptions that
Led us here and then shanghaied us if not sincere attempts to
Understand and so desire another person, it doesn't
Matter which one, and then, self-abandoned, to build ourselves
So as to desire him fully, and at the last moment be
Taken aback at such luck ...   (345)

However, I don't think we have here merely a generalized renunciation of what R.W. Connell in *Masculinites* satirizes as "searching for a 'true self' or a 'real me' ",[14] but rather a shared unmaking of identities in that "melting pot" which Lewis's disciple Marshal McLuhan was to call the "global village".[15] What breaks down here is any "Western" fixity of definition or coherence of rational mapping:

The complications of our planet, its climate, its sonatinas
And stories, its patches of hard ugly snow waiting around
For spring to melt them. ...   (348)

---

13. Robert Bly, *Iron John: A Book About Men*, Shaftesbury, 1992, 2 and following.

14. R.W. Connell, *Masculinities*, Cambridge, 1995, 139.

15. For a brief discussion of the Lewis–McLuhan reationship see my *Poetry of Modernity*, 2–3. In my view McLuhan and the Toronto based COUNTER-BLAST group helped invent "postmodernity" in all but name. Granted the Anglo-Gallic tensions in Canada, it is interesting that Jean-François Lyotard's highly influential later book *The Postmodern Condition: A Report on Knowledge*, translated by Geoff Bennington and Brian Massumi, (Manchester University Press, 1986) was originally commissioned by "the Conseil des Universitiés of the Government of Quebec", p.xxv.

Perceived from a variable and fluid masculinity, shared humanity is condemned to be free in a wave-like continuum where the ability to surf is more important than the habit of ordnance surveying:

> By so many systems
> As we are involved in, by just so many
> Are we set free on an ocean of language that comes to be
> Part of us ...
> ... and the waves talk to us,
> Preparing dreams we'll have to live with and use.   (333)

"A Wave", then, unsettles (I suspect the political pretensions of the word "subverts") the overt meanings of all three terms in Lewis's 1927 title: "time" is represented in positive not negative terms (as Joyce replied to Lewis: "Your genius it's worldwide, your spacest sublime!/ But, Holy Saltmartin, why can't you beat time?");[16] "Western" is implied as a positioning which can only maintain relevance by assimilating marginalities into a finally un-centred postmodern unfolding; and "Man", as term, becomes androgynised and diffusely socialized into an imaginary post-masculinity. Time, is, apparently, on Ashbery's side not Lewis's.

However, the value of Lewis's critique is that afforded by the suppressed pole in any binary opposition: it illuminates the "other" because the "other" is constructed in opposition to it. *Time and Western Man* saw modern thought as obsessed by flux, marginality, feminisation, sex, jazz, dementia, childishness and inversion. All this has an observable corollary in the postmodern sponsorship of ephemerality, subaltern studies, écriture femininé, sexual fix (Stephen Heath's term),[17] pop-jazz-rap, schizophrenia, youth-culture and queer theory. Without any overtly political allegiances, Ashbery's "A Wave" inherently endorses postmodernism as modernism conducted by other means.

Yet if deconstructionists are right, the ghost of "space man" ought to haunt the "time philosophy" of the poem: and it surely does, as also in Eliot's *Four Quartets* or Woolf's *The Waves*: "the ancient network / Of letters, diaries, ads for civilisation" (330); "one idea is enough to organise a life" (331); "the great chain" (336); "this explicit earth" (338); "the report that will finally be made" (342); "the logic of my search" (347); "Enough to know that I shall have answered for myself soon" (351). "A Wave", I suggest, plays out the tensions between postmodernist arguments and those of anti-postmodernists that have spilt over from the 1980s into the 1990s. To judge by much recent writing in,

---

16. James Joyce, *Finnegans Wake*, p. 419.

17. Stephen Heath, *The Sexual Fix*, Basingstoke, 1982.

for example new social geography, the sociology of identities, poststructural theology or neo-pragmatic language philosophy,[18] the issues now dominate cultural studies in general. However, while aesthetic terms such as "representation", "deconstruction", "irony" or "hermeneutics" are now well to the fore, poetry as a discourse remains a Cinderella waiting to be asked to the ball – the shadow of Plato – patriarchal spatial, western man – with his primal splitting of "dialectic" against poetics still presides over the postmodern academy. For the reasons I have given above, "A Wave" is a fitting exemplum to indicate why, in the end, poetry speaks truer than mere theory.

---

18. See, for random exemplification, Rob Shields, *Places on the Margin: Alternative Geographies of Modernity*, London, 1992, Anthony Giddens, *Modernity and Self-Identity*, Cambridge, 1991, Don Cupitt, *Taking Leave of God*, London, 1980, and Richard Rorty, *Objectivity, Relativism and Truth*, Cambridge, 1991.

"IS ANYTHING CENTRAL?"
ASHBERY AND THE IDEA OF A CENTRE

EDWARD LARRISSY

"Is anything central?" The question occurs at the beginning of "The One Thing that can Save America", in *Self-Portrait in a Convex Mirror*.[1] Unlike some Ashbery questions it is not entirely rhetorical, being quite ostensibly a question about America, as we discover at the beginning of the second stanza. (Like his precursor, Whitman, Ashbery is quite capable of making America represent the world: "This is American calling", as we are told in "Pyrography").[2] The question, being about America, alludes to the title: "The One Thing that can Save America" is the one central thing that can "save the phenomena': that is, act as or be their principle. The answers to the initial question are rhetorical. They are, that is to say, loaded, since we are given a list of things which it is hard to see as central to America:

> Orchards flung out on the land,
> Urban forests, rustic plantations, knee-high hills?   (SP, 44)

Knee-high hills central to America? I think not; and the very quality of oxymoron in that phrase, and in "Urban forests", suggests a multiplicity which includes the paradoxical and the extreme: large enough, like Whitman, to contain contradictions. The next question ("Are place names central?") carries an implication, for it implies the possibility of an originary or quasi-Adamic naming, as befits a poem referring to America. The question raised is not directly answered in the negative. But the place names, redolent of the small and excentric, rush wearyingly by, as if seen from a train or car: they do not seem central, and we are told that, while they are "connected to my version of America", the "juice", a metaphor for the central, is "elsewhere". The question about place names, then, has been raised only as a way of placing the poem as origin-hunting. It proceeds to give us a clue about where to look for the juice,

---

1. John Ashbery, *Self-Portrait in a Convex Mirror*, Harmondsworth,1976, 44–45. Subsequent references in the text will be cited as SP.

2. John Ashbery, *Houseboat Days*, Harmondsworth, 1977, 8. Subsequent references in the text will be cited as HD.

without, of course, being brazenly indicative. There are two classes of event that would, it seems, fit the bill:

> Where then are the private turns of event
> Destined to boom later like golden chimes
> Released over a city from a highest tower?
> The quirky things that happen to me, and I tell you,
> And you instantly know what I mean?   (SP, 44–45)

First of all, these are *events*, and they are events that *happen* to somebody: they are not simply perceptions. They are, however, private – for I think we can safely assimilate "quirky" to the category of private. But they are the private capable of being made public: in the first instance, made public by booming "like golden chimes / Released over a city from a highest tower": that is to say, they are the spiritually central with respect to the polity, a relationship symbolized by their being the chimes of a cathedral. But the events are also "quirky", and capable of being imparted in intimacy so that another will "instantly know what I mean". They are the human universal, but not of a kind whose intelligibility will be assumed: after all, any interlocutor in general might *not* know what was meant. This one, however, does. They are, then, both intimate and universal and, furthermore, sacralized by being capable of falling under the same category of what is chimed over the city. We have, then, in this one poem, a tentative suggestion that private human intimacy may be regarded as universal and may be tinged with the sacred.

Details

Any suggestion that Ashbery values a universal or central principle, however tentatively it may be described, has to contend with much that asserts the irreducibility of details:

> To be able to write the history of our time, starting with today
> It would be necessary to model all these unimportant details
> So as to be able to include them; otherwise the narrative
> Would have that flat, sandpapered look the sky gets
> Out in the middle west toward the end of summer
> The look of wanting to back out before the argument
> Has been resolved, and at the same time *to save appearances*
> So that tomorrow will be pure.   (HD, 9–10. My emphasis.)

This "saving the appearances" (a recurring concept in Ashbery) is guilty and superficial because it shows too much alacrity in constructing a narrative. But that Ashbery prizes details that are, or seem, unassimilable to a well-rounded narrative, or a brisk history, is well known. Or that contrive to be left out of a conventional film narrative, as in "Forties Flick":

Why must it always end this way?
A dais with women reading, with the ruckus of her hair
And all that is unsaid about her pulling us back to her, with her
Into the silence that night alone can't explain.
Silence of the library, of the telephone with its pad,
But we didn't have to reinvent these either:
They had gone away into the plot of a story,
The "art" part – knowing what important details to leave out
And the way character is developed.   (SP, 5)

So well is the point about details known, that I would rather allude to the ways in which Ashbery intimates the multiplicity of the world other than by simply referring to it, or drawing up lists, which, as everybody knows, is one of his modes. I refer to Ashbery's habit of qualificatory supplementation: a technique whereby clauses shade and cross-hatch the main clause so that it can hardly be discovered: concessive clauses, subordinate clauses. To these are added the simpler supplementation of mere apposition. In sum, the centre of the sentence is buried under qualification:

> Although we mattered as children, as adults we're
>   somehow counterfeit
> and not briefed as to what happened in the intervals to which the longing
>   led us,
> which turns out to be not so tragic after all, but merely baroque, almost
>   functional.
> Yet there can be no safety in numbers: each of us wants and wants to be
> in the same way, so that in the end none of us matters, and in different
>   ways
> we cannot understand, as though each spoke a different language with
>   enough cognates
> to make us believe in deafness – their deafness – as well as in our own
>   reluctance
> to dramatize, leaving our speech just sitting there, unrinsed, untasted,
>   not knowing us,
> or caring to.[3]

The subject, then, is qualified grammatically as if in imitation of the assertion that one should not be making a pocket history of the world. As I write, however, there is the added interest of noting that Ashbery's work of the Nineties has started to employ a parodic foregrounding of the technique of supplementation. This is not to say that the old technique of shading has been reliquished. Far from it: one can find it on almost every page:

---

3. John Ashbery, *Flow Chart*, Manchester, 1991, 77. Subsequent references in the text will be cited as FC.

> We began to tire of his ravings, but (as so often happens)
> it was just at that point that a salient character trait
> revealed itself, or rather, manifested itself within him.[4]

So the old pedantry is maintained. But one also finds more apparently frivolous supplementation, as if Ashbery were adding words suggested by sound only: take this example from "Andante Misterioso":

> Nowadays people have cars for things like that,
> to carry them away, I mean,
> I suppose.
>   And wherever man sets his giant foot
> petals spring up, and artificial torsos,
> dressmaker's dummies. And an ancient photograph
> and an ancient phonograph, that carols
> in mist.   (CHYB, 10)

In other words, in the nineties Ashbery is returning to a classic surrealist technique of letting the sound breed the sense: there is another good example earlier in the same poem:

> The symphony at the station
> then, and all over people trying to hear it
> and others trying to get away. A "trying'
> situation, perhaps, yet no one is worse off than before.

Ashbery is paying a more obvious tribute to the materiality of language than he has done since *The Tennis-Court Oath*. This fact is symbolized in the way the poems from *Can You Hear, Bird* are arranged alphabetically, in a manner that bears a superficial resemblance to Neruda's *Elemental Odes*: superficial, because Neruda's odes are a celebration of the world, a discovery of the wonders of the mundane, rather than an inquiry into the mysteries of the relationship of word and world, as in Ashbery. His new kind of associationism is even more daunting to the expectation of coherence than his more established manner of the seventies and eighties.

The bad Centre
Alongside examples of the hard-to-assimilate detail and complexity of the world one must place the many references to "the bad centre': the centre that would presume too easily to overmaster and fix detail. In what follows, I

---

4.   John Ashbery, *Can You Hear, Bird*, Manchester, 1996, 26. Subsequent references in the text will be cited as CYHB.

assimilate the idea of a centre to that closely-related category "the whole" –
that is, what is organized, at least for Ashbery, around a centre. There is the
potted history, already referred to. There is, in *As We Know* the "Histoire
Universelle":

> As though founded by some weird religious sect
> It is a paper disk, partially lit up from behind
> With testaments to its cragginess, many of them
> Illegible ... [5]

It is a

> View of the universe pinned on the midnight-blue
> Backcloth of the universe that can't understand
> Who all these people are, and about what so much fuss is being
> made.

More recently we have the idea of the panopticon. Thus, in *Flow Chart*, part
III

> it wasn't until you found yourself inside a huge pen
> or panopticon that you realized the story had disappeared
> like water into desert sand,   (FC, 84)

– another example of the centre leading away from the life, which trickles
away uncontrollably. And in "A Waking Dream", from *Can You Hear, Bird*,
we are roused from vaguest surmise by the opening question: "And the failing
panopticon?" it is important to realise that a panopticon is bound to be failing
in Ashbery.

Perhaps the most obvious examples of the bad centre, however, are to be
found in *Three Poems*, where, among various examples, there are both The
Tower of Babel[6] and Childe Roland's Dark Tower, with an affinity suggested
in the juxtaposition. The Tower of Babel links up to a whole range of passages
about interpretation, including one in which it can seem blessed to be reciting
"the only alphabet one knows" (11) in an enchanted room with the beloved.
Yet the danger of such recitation is presented in "this horrible vision of the
completed Tower of Babel, flushed in the sunset as the last ceramic brick was
triumphantly fitted into place, perfect in its vulgarity". This malign fixity recalls
the "rigidity" of those with mind and eye focused on "a nonexistent center, a
fixed point" (74). Childe Roland (92) figures in this internalized quest romance

---

5.   John Ashbery, *As We Know*, Manchester, 1981, 104.

6.   John Ashbery, *Three Poems*, Harmondsworth, 1977, 50, 92. Subsequent references in
the text will be cited as TP.

as a reminder of the possibility of seeing the rage for meaning as destined to disappointment through the agency of some inscrutable malevolence. Thus one can gloss the mention of Browning's hero with a later passage which makes this theme explicit:

> There is no spiritual model for our aspirations, no *vademecum* beckons in the light around us. There is only the urge to get on with it all. It is like the difference between someone who is in love and someone who is merely "good in bed": there is no vital remnant which would transform one's entire effort into an image somewhat resembling oneself. Meanwhile everything conspires to protect the business-as-usual attitude of the diurnal scenery – no leaf or brick must be found out of place, no timbre ring false lest the sickening fakery of the whole wormy apparatus, the dry rot behind the correct facade suddenly become glaringly and universally apparent, its shame at last real for all to see. Appearances must be kept up at whatever cost until the Day of Judgment and afterward if possible.   (TP, 111–12)

The passage does not present a direct parallel with Browning's poem, for the "business-as-usual attitude of the scenery" does not function like the pock-marked wasteland to be found there. Yet the conviction that the apparatus is indeed wormy, and that it proffers a pretence of coherence and value until the Day of Judgement, does suggest an analogue with Browning's poem. ("Appearance must be kept up", by the way, is another version of an idea we have already come across twice – "saving the appearances": providing a delusive centre for phenomena.)

There is also an analogue with the two poles of a characteristic alternation in Browning, of which Childe Roland is one. For if, as we are most memorably reminded in "Two in the Campagna", the attitude that brings us closest to heaven is a kind of scatter-brained benediction that quests unsystematically from moment to moment, "Childe Roland" is the negative obverse if not of that attitude, at least of the universe it beholds: detailed but horrid; open-ended, but only with the queasy open-endedness of a fragment of nightmare. The Dark Tower is the absent centre or the sham centre.

And indeed, the sham centre can be seen as related to the bad centre. Thus, in "The Wrong Kind of Insurance", from *Houseboat Days*:

> Yes, friends, these clouds pulled along on invisible ropes
> Are, as you guessed, merely stage machinery,
> And the funny thing is it knows we know
> About it and still wants us to go on believing ...
>   ... so we may know
> We too are somehow impossible, formed of so many different things
> Too many to make sense to anybody.   (HD, 50)

The sham centre is a function of the pervasive doubt, shared by Ashbery, as to whether there is or could be a centre. This mere doubt is not in itself malignant, even though it may be melancholy, and it can be referred to in quite humorous terms:

> Without further ado bring on the subject of these
> negotiations. They all would like to collect it always, but since
> that's impossible, the Logos alone will have to suffice.
> A pity, since no one has seen it recently.   (FC, 33–34)

If not a Centre, a principle that allows us to behave as if there were one
In *A Wave*,[7] Ashbery reminds us of the "great chain that manages only with difficulty to connect earth and sky together", and we have seen that sometimes "difficulty" is putting it mildly. Yet readers of Ashbery will be familiar enough with the image of the sky as representing an aspiration towards however evanescent and humble a sense of transcendence. The sky, as the night sky, provides a backdrop for much of the first of the *Three Poems*, which is called "The New Spirit". In particular, the Tower of Babel is seen against the night sky:

> In the other direction [from the Tower] one saw the desert and drooping
> above it the constellations that had presided impassively over the building
> of the metaphor that seemed about to erase them from the skies. Yet they
> were in no way implicated in the success or failure, depending on your
> viewpoint, of the project, as became clearer the minute you caught sight
> of the Archer, languidly stretching his bow, aiming at a still higher and
> smaller portion of the heavens, no longer a figure of speech but an act,
> even if all the life had been temporarily drained out of it.   (TP, 50–51)

The constellations are the interpretive sign or alphabet writ large enough not only to encompass something of the cosmos, but to dare to order and explain the apparent ambitiousness of the scattering of stars. At this level of interpretation they recall the extraordinary ending of the fourth and last of Mallarmé's *Plusieurs sonnets* ("Ses purs ongles très haut dédiant leur onyx …"), where at night a mirror in the empty room reflects the seven stars of the Great Bear:

> dans l'oubli fermé par le cadre, se fixe
> De scintillations sitôt le septuor.

("In the forgetfulness enclosed by the frame is fixed at once the septet of scintillations.") Here the seven stars are the world of time – the seven days of

---

7.   John Ashbery, *A Wave*, Manchester, 1984, 74.

the week and of Creation, the seven lower lamps of the Cabalistic tree –
interpreted in the reflective human mirror. Ashbery's image, however, is,
perhaps surprisingly to some, more vitalist than Mallarmé's: the Archer's
motion is an *act* , and if the "life" has been drained out of it, it is only
temporarily. The difference is reflected in the constellation: the idea of the
Archer possesses an unambiguously existentialist resonance. The echoes of
Nietzsche are especially strong: thus, the first section of *Twilight of the Idols*
is "Maxims and Arrows". Admittedly, for Nietzsche the arrow is destructive,
where it is not clear that for Ashbery it is. In Maxim 36, for instance, Nietzsche
playfully reminds us: "Moral: one must shoot at morals".[8] Nevertheless, this
notion is comprised in the larger notion of transcendence of the given, in which
Ashbery does share. Nietzsche formulates such transcendence in terms of a
telos : "Formula of my happiness: a Yes, a No, a straight line, a goal ...".[9] Is
the religious language of *Three Poems* the atheist and transvalued residue or
transformation of Christianity? Or is there something substantial in its Christian
references? The religious language of *Three Poems*, as of other of Ashbery's
work, has been trenchantly addressed by Geoff Ward in these terms in *Statutes
of Liberty*:

> John Ashbery, for all the becalmed artifice and irony of his poetry,
> anchors his thought in Christian perceptions ... Those critics, such as
> Harold Bloom, or David Shapiro, who finds "parodies of spiritual
> progress" in Ashbery's *Three Poems*, have missed the wood for the
> trees.[10]

This runs against conventional wisdom, as expressed by Donald Davie in *Under
Briggflatts*.[11] But I think that, to put the matter in rather Ashberyan terms, it
points accurately to a complicated state of affairs which itself forms a significant
part of the truth. First, however, and not least because of the trajectory of my
own argument hitherto, I must take account of what might tell against such a
conclusion, tentative though it be. For Nietzsche's image of the Archer can be
seen as a progenitor of Camus's Sisyphus, finding the courage to roll the stone
up the hill again in an absurd universe. The road to Christianity is hardly direct
if one sees Ashbery's Archer only in the light of Nietzsche's.

---

8. Friedrich Nietzsche, *Twilight of the Idols and The Anti-Christ*, trans. R.J. Holingdale,
Harmondsworth, 1968, 26.

9. *ibid*, 27.

10. Geoff Ward, *Statutes of Liberty: The New York School of Poets*, Basingstoke, 1993,
168.

11. Donald Davie, *Under Briggflatts: A History of Poetry in Great Britain, 1960–1988*,
Manchester, 1989, 143.

Reading the passage from the first section of *Three Poems*, however, has to be guided by the title of that section: "The New Spirit". The New Spirit is a reference to a central concept of Gérard de Nerval. It can be found, for instance, in the sonnet "Horus", from *Les chimères*, in which the goddess Isis, having disposed of her old, lame and presumably impotent old volcano god of a consort, Kneph, announces:

> l'espirt nouveau m'appelle.
> J'ai revêtu pour lui la robe be Cybèle.
> C'est l'enfant bien-aimé d'Hermès et d'Osiris.

More generally, the "New Spirit" for Nerval represents the likelihood of a new religious dispensation in which the sensuality of paganism and the moral seriousness of Christianity would both be resumed and find new expression in a fresh synthesis. This synthesis, scarcely Joachimite, but definitely influenced by Joachimite ideas in its tripartite temporality, was bred of a quasi-millenarian outlook, appropriate enough to post-revolutionary France, and it seems to me that Ashbery found in the idea a suggestive parallel with his own attempts to isolate the postmodern religious sensibility.

Religion, perhaps, then. But Christian? Nobody can deny that there are many references to Christianity and to Christian structures of feeling in Ashbery. The question is, how to take them. Consider these lines from *Flow Chart*:

> and so get over feeling oppressed, so as to be able to construct the small
> song,
> our prayer
> at the center of whatever void we may be living in: a romantic nocturnal
> place
> that must sooner or later go away.
> At that point we'll have lived, and the having done so would be a passport
> to a permanent adjacent future, the adult equivalent of innocence
> in a child,
> or lost sweetness in a remembered fruit:
> something to tell time by. (FC, 76)

Time regained, or time redeemed: the recovery of the child's innocence after a Fall. Such a schema can easily be paralleled in the very movement of many of Ashbery's poems. But it is some years now since Marjorie Perloff pointed to the link between the movement of Ashbery's poems and that of the Romantic meditative effusion.[12] The systolic motion of a Coleridge conversation poem

---

12. Marjorie Perloff, "'Fragments of a Buried Life': John Ashbery's Dream Songs", in *Beyond Amazement: New Essays on John Ashbery*, ed. David Lehman, Ithaca and London, 1980, 74, 76.

such as "This Lime-Tree Bower My Prison" – the start, fall, rise pattern – was self-consciously modelled on the Christian redemptive schema. But Perloff uses the "Instruction Manual", and of course, as she herself admits, this is a very straightforward poem compared with much of Ashbery, where syntheses break down as soon as they are achieved, to be replaced by another problem. Nevertheless, patterns such as this are recurrent within Ashbery's poems, even if they do not structure a whole poem, and they are often associated with spiritual imagery.

Another aspect of the lines quoted is highly significant: their distinctively human, as well as spiritual, resonance, which is consonant with a Christian spirituality. And this is especially telling: for such a combination of the sacred and the human is also characteristic of Ashbery. In this connection, it is appropriate to return to "The One Thing that can Save America". It will be recalled that the private turns of event "Destined to boom like golden chimes" (the cathedral) are capable of being equated with "The quirky things that happen to me, and I tell you, / And you instantly know what I mean". The cathedral bells chime out these things: therefore they are sacred. But they are also experienced as intimate, valued the more for their mutuality, but at the same time as universal. This tender, sacralized human is, to put it no more strongly, the product of a Christian or recently Christian culture.

Of course, Ashbery is notably inexplicit, not least because he is trying to do something entirely different from Christian apologetics, which is to isolate the intentionality which could transcend the given: to equate that intentionality with creativity, and to connect that creativity with what he often calls the sky, and in *Three Poems* calls the stars. At the very least in a Christian or post-Christian culture Ashbery has no other language for such an endeavour than a Christian one.

When I say "isolate the intentionality", I mean that the old chestnut about abstract expressionism must be cooked more slowly. Let me explain. An Ashbery poem may sometimes read like a vaunting, late Romantic lyric in everything but its mysterious inexplicitness. An opening of fine address, sententious and finely-modulated periods, and an ending which snaps shut with an effect of closure. An abstract movement, as with music, as Ashbery himself has said. But this movement, this adumbration of structure, is not so much a fine flurry *around* a void, as the first movement *beyond* the void: the Archer. It is an originary movement: the first stirrings of the poetic spirit. All those poststructuralist interpretations that codify variants of semiotic disruption and deferral undoubtedly have much material to work on. But they miss the main point. Ashbery is asking not so much about the thrilling mismatch of world and poetic sign, for rather he is putting a question such as this: What must the poetic sign be such that it can be auratic in a way that recalls us to the possibility of going beyond, a going beyond which cannot be even hinted at in abstract terms? And since they must be concrete, has to be conveyed in terms of the imagery and traditions of the poet's culture – indeed, is conceived within those terms.

Ashbery's interest in naming as Adamic and originary is part of that tradition, but it would be hard to make this on its own a pointer to an importance for Christianity any greater than that which is to be found in many another post-Romantic American poet, for whom this theme often has a special significance. Nevertheless, it is arguable that there is a philosophical influence that is congruent with this theme: Ashbery's undoubted awareness of the European philosophical tradition, and his sojourn in Paris in the later Fifties and early Sixties, suggest that phenomenology, especially as developed in the work of Maurice Merleau-Ponty, is just as likely an influence as the structuralism and nascent post-structuralism of that period. All attempts to tie the works of poets to secure philosophical anchors are probably doomed to a high degree of failure; influence here is not a matter of signing up for a list of propositions. Merleau-Ponty attempted to isolate the character of perception as an originary moment in the consciousness of a physical being endowed with a unique perspective on the world.[13] The only claim I am advancing here is that there is a degree of consonance between this attempt and Ashbery's attempt to depict what I have called "the first movement beyond the void". There is nothing intrinsically Christian about this attempt; the other claim advanced here is merely that in Ashbery, nevertheless, this movement is frequently given Christian connotations.

---

13. Maurice Merleau-Ponty, *Phénoménologie de la perception*, Paris, 1945, first English translation, 1962.

ELIZABETH BISHOP AND THE ORIGINS
OF NARRATIVE POSTMODERNISM

THOMAS TRAVISANO

Drawing the circle

In February 1966, following the sudden tragic death the previous October of their close mutual friend Randall Jarrell, Elizabeth Bishop wrote to her intimate correspondent and long-standing artistic ally Robert Lowell:

> I read my class your wonderful piece on Randall one day – I had missed that copy in Brazil, of the NY Review – and they were very moved by it, obviously. I have also read them a lot of Randall's poems ... . He doesn't seem very well known here, so I am bringing him in – and Berryman – and a few others every chance I get.[1]

Bishop, who was always cautious about being labelled and thus reluctant to list her favourite contemporaries publicly, here draws a circle, quite casually – and some may feel surprisingly – in a letter to a trusted confidant, around an intriguing quartet of midcentury American poets who are not commonly seen as a coherent group – Lowell, Jarrell, Berryman, and, of course, Bishop herself.

Here I draw on the materials of a further study that proposes to uncover and explore the underlying network of literary relations linking this quartet of American poets around whom Bishop casually drew her circle in 1966 – Robert Lowell (1917–77), Randall Jarrell (1914–65), John Berryman (1914–72), and Bishop (1911–79). This network grew, persisted, and thrived for forty years just a layer below the journalistically-constructed map of contemporary American poetry, and its influence abides to this day. Yet its operations remain, at best, a semi-open secret two decades after Bishop's death. This midcentury quartet, operating along the margins of, or even in flat contradiction to, those categories most commonly applied by conventional literary histories, left a compelling record of their interchange scattered across a wide range of published and unpublished sources. This essay seeks to combine the best elements of aesthetic and cultural criticism in order to uncover and retrace the making of their flexible, influential, artistically compelling, and surprisingly

---

1. Elizabeth Bishop to Robert Lowell, 23 February, 1966, Houghton Library, Harvard University.

coherent postmodern aesthetic. What follows is a reading of the interconnecting life-texts and literary texts of these four poets as they engage in an ongoing four-way public and private dialogue about what poetry was and could be.

The aesthetic towards which this quartet worked – and the many inventive techniques they evolved in its pursuit – gradually took shape as an incompletely formulated but coherent and powerful set of intuitions: intuitions about which they did not choose to be entirely forthcoming, nor even, perhaps, entirely conscious. This aesthetic's authors were remarkably consistent in their refusal, in the face of persistent demands by interviewers, editors, and anthologists, to voice an aesthetic doctrine. One searches in vain for a single manifesto outlining their individual or group intentions, and indeed, the flexible, practice-centered intuitive aesthetic that they finally achieved resists explicit articulation. Until she became the recent focus of intensive critical attention, Bishop had remained the most elusive of the four. But historians have found each of these four poets "hard to place",[2] and they have found the aesthetic principles of each hard to characterize, both because their artistic strategies were flexible and complex and because each so consistently avoided stating a systematic poetic doctrine. As early as 1940 Bishop, Berryman and Jarrell found different ways to frustrate James Laughlin's demand for a prefatory essay in *Five Young American Poets* defining each young poet's artistic principles. Berryman was acknowledging a shared disposition when he praised Jarrell's famous essay collection *Poetry and the Age* (1953) in a review, for "his neglect to theorize about poetry". Berryman found this "one of the most agreeable features of a prepossessing and engaging book … The point is to deal with the stuff itself, and Jarrell does, nobody better". In 1967, Lowell commonsensically cut through the ongoing – and even then highly ritualized – formalism versus open forms debate with the remark that "I can't understand how any poet, who has written both metered and unmetered poems, would be willing to settle for one and give up the other". Lowell adds, significantly, that "I have never worked my intuitions on this subject into a theory. When I drop one style of writing, it is usually a surprise to me".[3] Bishop's enigmatic, yet powerfully inclusive phrase "it all depends" – her terse and now famous reply to a mid-century questionnaire about poetic theory and practice – might serve as a motto for each member of this circle, as would her continuation, "It all depends on the particular poem one happens to be trying to write, and the range of possibilities is, one trusts, infinite. After all, the poet's concern is not consistency".[4] But despite their

---

2. David Kalstone's phrase describing Bishop in his *Five Temperaments*, New York, 1977.

3. Robert Lowell, "On Freedom in Poetry", in *Naked Poetry: Recent American Poetry in Open Forms*, eds Stephen Berg and Robert Mezey, New York, 1969, 124.

4. Elizabeth Bishop, "It All Depends", in *Mid-Century American Poets*, ed. John Ciardi, New York, 1950, 267.

insistence on retaining the mobility to respond to the demands of the particular poem and their consequent refusal to articulate a formally theorized poetics, if one reads with sufficient care their published poems, essays, and interviews in the context of the unpublished documentary record – if one deals that is "with the stuff itself" – then the active principles of a flexible but surprisingly coherent aesthetic begin to emerge.

They cared intensely about what their fellow quartet members said and thought. Thus, Bishop would write to Lowell in 1951, as she sailed on the freighter *Bowplate* toward her long, unexpected sojourn in Brazil, "With me on the boat I brought your review of Randall['s *Seven League Crutches*] and Randall's review of you[r *The Mills of the Kavanaughs*] ... & I've been brooding over them both".[5] Ten years later Bishop wrote to Lowell, "I have had you on my mind all this time and yesterday morning when I woke up I had been having a long dream about you".[6] In 1957 Lowell wrote excitedly to Bishop – whose own example helped Lowell find the style of *Life Studies* (1959) – announcing that several poems from his new sequence-in-the-making had been praised in manuscript by Jarrell and by Philip Rahv, the influential editor of *Partisan Review*. Bishop replied, "I am so pleased Randall liked the poems – also Philip, but Randall's liking them really means infinitely more" (348). These poets were lifelong learners about their art who studied and learned in particular from one another in a process of flexible, ongoing mutual interchange. Each evolved a personal voice and style, a personal sense of scale, but in the process each looked steadily at the others as they engaged in an extensive, devious, and multifaceted process of literary exploration.

The problem of selfhood in the postmodern world
Like the grouping itself, the term "postmodern" applied to the aesthetic of this quartet of poets may surprise some readers – but this epithet is not chosen lightly. One aspect of this quartet's claim to being termed postmodern is historical priority. As we shall see, the term "post-modernist" was first used extensively in a published and private dialogue between Jarrell, Lowell and Berryman as early as 1947, as they were reviewing one another's early books, and responding to the post-war cultural and poetic scene. Paul Hoover notes the moment when "Charles Olson used the word 'postmodern' as early as an October 20, 1951, letter to Creeley from Black Mountain" as a founding date for the postmodern canon enshrined in his 1994 anthology *Postmodern*

---

5. Elizabeth Bishop, *One Art The Selected Letters*, ed. Robert Giroux, 1994, 225. Subsequent references to this edition are cited in the text as OA.

6. A letter from Bishop to Lowell, [1961].

American Poetry.[7] Hoover adds that "as used here, 'postmodern' means the historical period following World War II", and insists that "Postmodernist poetry is the avant-garde poetry of our time".[8] Donald Allen and George F. Butterick assert in the introduction to their 1982 anthology *The Postmoderns: The New American Poetry Revised* (whose canon of "the postmoderns" reads like a blueprint for Hoover's anthology) that "Postmodernism is not simply after, in time, the modernism of Pound and Eliot, Auden and Stevens, and their younger successors such as Berryman and Lowell, Bishop and Sexton".[9] For Allen, Butterick, and Hoover such poets as Bishop, Lowell, Berryman – and by extension Jarrell – are mere "successors" to modernism and must be excluded by name from their postmodernist canon. But, as I have just suggested, an extensive, and largely neglected, published dialogue in which Jarrell, Lowell and Berryman applied the term "post-modernist" to one another occurred in 1947–48, immediately following World War II and several years prior to Olson's letter. Moreover, as I shall be demonstrating in this essay with particular reference to Bishop, their poetry and criticism both for several years before and several years after that postwar period explores, often quite deliberately, the problem of writing "the poetry that replaces modernism". More importantly, their poetry in the years before, during, and just after World War II deals ever more decisively and powerfully with themes now widely considered postmodern. Despite their constant subtle innovations in subject matter and form the label "avent-garde" does not really fit this midcentury quartet, but John Ashbery once noted of Bishop that she is "somehow an establishment poet herself, and the establishment ought to give thanks; she is proof it can't be all bad"[10] – a remark that might well be extended to the other members of her quartet. Hoover acknowledges "The risk ... that the avant-garde will become an institution with its own self-protective rituals.[11] And Language poet Michael Palmer acknowledges that "Each time one replaces a given model with another model, a theoretical model, whatever, you are inscribing yourself in the larger myth of innovation (and / or myths of recovery, renascence, et al.)". Poets such as Lowell, Jarrell, Bishop and Berryman, though actively innovative in matters of form and content, resisted inscribing themselves within particular

---

7. Paul Hoover, "Introduction", to *Postmodern American Poetry*, New York, 1994, xxv.

8. Hoover, *ibid.*

9. *The Postmoderns: The New American Poetry Revised*, eds Donal Allen and George F. Butterick, New York, 1982.

10. John Ashbery, "Elizabeth Bishop: The Complete Poems", in *New York Times Book Review*, June 1, 1969, 8.

11. Paul Hoover, *Postmodern American Poetry*, xxv.

theoretical models or particular myths of innovation or recovery, and in doing so each remained at the service of the particular poem he or she was trying to write. They also resisted what Palmer describes as the tendency of "avant-gardism" to become "so clearly commodified now, so clearly and simply a matter of what perfume or what soap you're selling".[12] I will be making the case that the literature of postmodernism has produced a range of postmodern aesthetics too dynamic and too various to be limited to a protectively canonized and commodified "avant-garde". And I will be arguing further that the particular aesthetic embodied in the poems of Lowell, Jarrell, Bishop and Berryman is one of the earliest, most flexible, most powerful, and most influential of all of postmodernism's diverse aesthetics.

Their post-war dialogue suggests that by the mid-1940s poets like Lowell, Jarrell and Berryman had already begun to recognize in one another – and were already attempting tentatively to characterize – a shared, complex, and still emerging aesthetic agenda that they saw as significantly different from the modernism of Pound and Eliot, Auden and Stevens. Moreover, this new aesthetic, especially when articulated in prose, encountered significant resistance from their own immediate modernist mentors including Allen Tate, John Crowe Ransom, and Marianne Moore. Indeed, in 1941, still earlier than this just-cited postwar dialogue – in what appears to be the first use, ever, of the term in a literary context – the conjunction "post-modernist" was applied to one of this quartet's young members in a review by a famous, powerful (and disgruntled) modernist mentor. The young poet under review, Randall Jarrell, had gone so far as to acknowledge, in the sole statement about his *own* intentions he allowed himself in his reluctant self-introduction to James Laughlin's 1940 New Directions anthology *Five Young American Poets* his as yet unrealized dream to write "the sort of poetry that replaces modernism".[13] And this confession, in turn, provoked an early and irritated recognition of his incipient postmodernism by his reviewer John Crowe Ransom, Jarrell's former teacher and the powerful editor of *Kenyon Review*. From lessons like this, in part, these poets learned to embody their innovation in their poetry and avoid theoretical formulations. Jarrell, Bishop, Berryman and Lowell were drawn so magnetically, and lastingly, to one another's work because (despite obvious differences in temperament, artistic manner, gender, sexual orientation, and so on) each consciously or unconsciously recognized in the others a shared determination to bypass or unmake modernism's impersonal aesthetic and to

12. Michael Palmer, "An Interview with Michael Palmer", in *Contemporary Literature*, Vol. 30 No. 1, 1989, 10.

13. Randall Jarrell, *Kipling, Auden & Co*, New York, 1980, 51.

create amongst themselves a new aesthetic that would empower them to address the problem of selfhood in the postmodern world.

In their recent survey of the theoretical discourse of postmodernism, Stephen Best and Douglas Kellner assert that "there is no unified postmodern theory, or even a coherent set of positions. Rather, one is struck by the diversities between theories often lumped together as "postmodern" and the plurality – often conflictual – of postmodern positions".[14] Perhaps the single facet of postmodernism on which its shrewdest recent commentators agree is that this phenomenon is, by its nature, multivalent. Certainly, despite their own significant claims to historical priority, what this quartet of poets eventually created was not "the" postmodern aesthetic but "a" postmodern aesthetic. Their particular postmodern aesthetic concerns itself principally with exploring the vicissitudes of the individual human self – the denied or threatened child, the embattled adolescent, the bereaved, imperilled, or disordered adult – dramatizing that individual's problems of knowledge, identity, traumatic loss, and repressed or otherwise unresolved feelings of displacement, confusion, anger and grief.

In his influential characterization of the postmodern self, Fredric Jameson wrote in 1984 of "the 'death' of the subject itself – the end of the autonomous bourgeois monad or ego or individual – and the accompanying stress, whether as some new moral ideal or as empirical description, on the decentering of that formerly centered subject or psyche". And Jameson adds, by way of explanation:

> Of the two possible formulations of this notion – the historicist one, that a once-existing centered subject, has today in the world of organizational bureaucracy dissolved; and the more radical poststructuralist position, for which such a subject never existed in the first place but constituted something like an ideological mirage – I obviously incline toward the former; the latter must in any case take into account something like a "reality of appearance".[15]

Curiously, Jameson neglects to entertain a third possibility: that the embattled, decentered ego, the threatened and possibly traumatized individual human self – of whatever social class, gender, race, age, ethnicity, nationality, or sexual orientation – lives on in the postmodern world, in the midst of what Bishop

14. Stephen Best and Douglas Kellner, *Postmodern Theory: Critical Interrogations*, New York, 1991, 2.

15. Frederic Jameson, *Postmodernism or, The Cultural Logic of Late Capitalism*, Durham, 1991, 15.

called "our worst century so far",[16] struggling toward survival, toward self-knowledge, and even toward tentative or contingent forms of recovery.

Jameson's insistence on an "impersonal" postmodern aesthetic would sound curiously "modernist" to this particular foursome, who, long before Jameson's particular attempt at definition, created their own aesthetic field of action in that neglected – but vitality important – third realm, the realm of the embattled self. The aesthetic that Lowell, Jarrell, Bishop and Berryman worked so hard to create has emerged as one of the most artistically successful and pervasively influential of postmodernism's many lines of development. But given the refusal of its authors to write manifestos or to indulge their editors and readers in extended discursive commentary on their intentions, this remains perhaps the least explicitly theorized of any of America's poetic postmodernism. As I have suggested, in order to articulate the key operating features of this quartet's aesthetic, one must identify and explore the key emotional, intellectual and cultural issues of the poems, while piecing together, from their running commentary in letters, interviews, reviews and prefaces, an understanding of the aesthetic's distinguishing literary techniques and characteristics.

Mature poems engaging originally with such core issues as the individual's problems of knowledge, identity, grief and loss, placed in the context of a detailed yet conflicted map of social and cultural history include Bishop's "The Man-Moth", "At the Fishouses", and "One Art", Jarrell's "Losses", "Protocols", and "The House in the Wood", Berryman's *Homage to Mistress Bradstreet*, and his *Opus Posthumous* and final *Dream Songs*, or Lowell's "Falling Asleep Over the Aenied", "Skunk Hour", and "For the Union Dead". Bishop, Berryman, Jarrell and Lowell shared a preoccupation with loss and with the uncertain process of coming to know the traumatic past – of exploring and coming to terms with unresolved or repressed feelings of loss, grief, abandonment, and personal or cultural dislocation. In their poems and stories, I will be suggesting, these four epistemologists of loss, even those such as Lowell and Berryman, most commonly labelled "confessional poets", are not primarily engaged in a process of revealing the self. Rather they are engaged in a process of exploring the self, of reaching back through a consideration of surviving artifacts, documentary records, lingering memory traces, dreamlike recurrences, symptomatic behaviours, and verbal slippages – that is, through tangible cultural markers and through the intangible and unreliable but powerful messages of the unconscious – toward the elusive junctures of the traumatic past. Their poetry places the present self among these elusive, ambiguous, but naggingly insistent knowledge-sources as it probes for insight into the causation of present dismays and disorders. In short, these four poets are exploring lost worlds.

---

16. Elizabeth Bishop, dust jacket to Robert Lowell's *Life Studies*, New York, 1959.

Bishop and the origins of narrative postmodernism

One of the last poems Elizabeth Bishop published during her lifetime, "Santarém" (1978) begins with an idiomatically convincing, but syntactically curious sentence: "Of course I may be remembering it all wrong / after, after – how many years?". Bishop's sentence starts out tentatively as a declarative, only to trail off, into still greater uncertainty, as a question. Such self-interruptions and self-questionings, common enough in Bishop, have generally been read as disarmingly candid off-the-cuff disclaimers, dropped into descriptive lyrics by a modest poet obsessed with factual precision. But an alternative reading might perceive in this opening sentence a slyly sophisticated postmodern gambit, embodying a tactic whose appealing modesty is slyly disingenuous, quietly subversive, deflecting modernist conceptions of the poet as ordering self. According to this alternative reading, Bishop deliberately breaks through the just-emerging narrative frame of "Santarém", in order to slightly – but effectively – de-center the authority of each detail in the vivid stream of apparently uncalculated recollection that follows. According to his reading, Bishop's subtle, unobtrusive opening calls into doubt not just the modernist poet's aspirations to an ordering vision but even those more modest claims to exactitude of recollection and observation that critics both friendly and unfriendly had long since granted to be Bishop's forte.[17]

I will be arguing for the validity of *both* these lines of interpretation. The tactics embodied in Bishop's opening gesture meld a seductively direct casualness with a quite uncanny level of self-consciousness and sophistication, creating an artistic resource of great subtlety and surprising power. And the tactics represented here have been employed, not just by Bishop, but by a diverse range of poets who came of age artistically both before and after 1945, many of whom remain on the scene, still actively producing poetry. Langdon Hammer has recently claimed that "No poet has more widely or powerfully influenced current poetic practice than Bishop"[18] – yet the basis for Bishop's pervasive current influence seems to leave most commentators puzzled. But if one examines Bishop's originating role in the important and still influential line of poetic development that I have begun to sketch, the reasons underlying the depth and breadth of her current influence becomes clear. I suggest that we name this line of development "narrative postmodernism". Jay Clayton has recently argued in *The Pleasures of Babel* for the operations of narrative in postmodern fiction, but he does not carry his analysis into poetry, where the

---

17. James McCorkle, *The Still Performance: Writing, Self, and Interconnection in Five Postmodern American Poets*, Charlottesville, 1989, 40, where McCorkle sees this opening as evidence that Bishop "further dislodges the authority of art".

18. Langdon Hammer, "The New Elizabeth Bishop", *Yale Review*, Vol. 82, No.2, 1994, 137.

resurgence of postmodern forms of narrative has been similarly striking. What I am here naming "narrative postmodernism" operates as a multi-layered matrix of dialectics, employing conventional narrative elements, dream textures, temporal shifts, and various de-centering tactics to raise questions about centrality and marginalization, knowledge and power, the unitary and the divided self, epistemology and authorial privilege. But the characteristic techniques and thematic implications of narrative postmodernisms, though they have been widely exploited by successive generations of poets, have so far been more or less elided from literary history. In part, this is because of that answer "it all depends" that Bishop made to the battery of questions about poetic technique and structure that John Ciardi also posed to Randall Jarrell in 1950 for his anthology *Mid-Century American Poets*.

Bishop is here resisting a process of critical appropriation that, in the years since midcentury, has become an almost inevitable consequence of literary fame. In fact, Bishop rejects the assumption of the poet's conscious command of artistic processes implicit in every one of Ciardi's questions, while she politely but firmly insists on the broadest possible latitude for technique and for subject matter ("there are no restrictions"). What matters most, for Bishop, are the requirements, not just of the individual poet, but of "the particular poem one happens to be trying to write". While her Vassar classmate Muriel Rukeyser asserted a universal psychology of poetic composition in her response to Ciardi's questionnaire, Bishop expresses grave doubts about the means by which aesthetic theory might actually shape practice:

> No matter what theories one may have, I doubt very much that they are in one's mind at the moment of writing a poem or that there is even a physical possibility that they could be. Theories can only be based on interpretations of other poets poems, or one one's own in retrospect, or wishful thinking.[19]

Ironically, however, Bishop, like Jarrell, had in fact formulated a rather elaborate theory of poetic form, as well as a partial theory of creative psychology, as far back as the mid-1930s, based largely on her own reading and experimentation, while she was still at Vassar. (She uses the word "theory" when alluding to her approach in a letter to Moore – without describing the theory.) But Bishop, like the other members of what would become her informal artistic circle, remained extremely guarded about revealing in public that their work might be supported by an even partially formulated set of cognitive principles. And if one analyzes Bishop's privately held ideas about the dynamics of poetic construction, one finds that they bear a striking family resemblance to Jarrell's own emerging ideas about poetic structure, as they appear in the long-lost

---

19. John Ciardi, *Mid-Century American Poets*, 267.

1942 lecture "Levels and Opposites: Structure in Poetry", which I recently rediscovered and had published in the Winter 1996 *Georgia Review*, though neither could have read the other's views, and they did not sit down to share ideas about the writing of poetry until January of 1947.

"It all depends" remained a characteristic Bishop phrase, one she would revert to again in 1966 in reply to interviewer Ashley Brown's question about the need to have "a 'myth' – Christian or otherwise – to sustain" the work. Bishop responded:. "It all depends – some poets do, some don't. You must have something to sustain you but perhaps you needn't be conscious of it. Look at Robert Lowell; he's written just as good poetry since he left the Church. Look at Paul Klee: he had 16 paintings going at once; *he* didn't have a formulated myth to look to, apparently, and his accomplishment was very considerable".[20] When Brown rejoined, "But some poets and critics have been terribly concerned about this, haven't they?", Bishop replied, simply, "Some people crave organization more than others – the desire to get everything in place".[21] Bishop was joined in her insistence on freedom in the choice of technical resources and subject matter by her friend Lowell, cited above, as well as by her colleagues Jarrell and Berryman. Even when they were partly conscious of principles that sustained them, they were reluctant to admit these principles in public, a reluctance hardly shared by most of their poetic contemporaries and elders, who as a rule were bristling with principles, and would state them at the drop of a hat. Starved for freedom of action in their youth, these poets went to extraordinary lengths to maintain the freedom of the poem to become itself on its own terms.

Bishop's private experimentation with the dynamics of postmodern voicing can be traced through the documents as far back as the mid-1930s, when she was a senior at Vassar College and her poems were just beginning to appear in national magazines. Working alone, Bishop described features of her new aesthetic in such Vassar essays as "Time's Andromedas" (1933) – an essay which, in many ways, anticipates contemporary chaos theory – and "Gerard Manley Hopkins: Notes on Timing in His Poetry" (1934), as well as in a series of 1933–34 letters to her generally uncomprehending contemporary Donald Stanford. If we look at Bishop's emerging aesthetic during this period, she is speaking concretely and locally, about the problems of timing and diction in the poems she was then attempting to write and in the process thinking about the principles of a dynamic poetic structure. Bishop, like her future friend Jarrell in the 1942 "Levels and Opposites", was piecing together the features of the new aesthetic I term narrative postmodernism.

---

20. Ashley Brown, "An Interview with Elizabeth Bishop" in *Shenandoah*, 1966, 295.

21. *ibid.*, 296.

Given the refusal of the originating narrative postmodernists to formalize their aesthetic position, given their indifference to founding a publicly recognized school of poetry, given the wide and eclectic reach of their technical apparatus, and given wide-spread assumptions that narrative and postmodernism are mutually exclusive, it is by no means surprising that this remarkably extensive line of poetic development has been largely overlooked or misplaced by literary historians. Hence, though this line of development has been much read and widely discussed, and it has created a most impressive body of poetry across four or five poetic generations, its aesthetic characteristics remain poorly defined and fragmentarily understood, more than sixty years after this aesthetic first began to emerge in the mid-1930s. This is in part because of the reluctance of pioneers like Bishop, along with Lowell, Jarrell and Berryman, who were working under socially conservative modernist mentors, to open to public discourse the complex, powerful, and carefully worked out aesthetic positions (now recoverable in archival manuscripts), that served as the cognitive wellsprings of their poetry; in part because those easy, conflicting, and misleading labels – "confessional" and "impersonal" – that literary journalists pasted on the careers of these four close friends while they lived still continue partially to obscure intriguing parallelisms in their literary and personal development; and in part because of lingering uncertainties about the denotative and connotative import of that damned elusive term, postmodernism. Yet the power of this line of development derives precisely from its ability to merge elements of postmodern skepticism, indeterminacy or heterogeneity, with techniques and attitudes pioneered by their modernist mentors in their earlier and more experimental phase, and with more commonplace narrative elements, drawn from the rich world of social and cultural markers, creating what Bishop called, in a now famous phrase, "the always more successful· surrealism of everyday life".

Yet the devices of narrative postmodernism, even at their most radical and effective, have most often been examined in isolation – and, because they frequently disguise themselves under a disarmingly casual surface, they are not infrequently condemned as insufficiently new or experimental, as in the dismissive portrait of "the apparent defeat – the absence" of Bishop and the other middle generation of poets in James E.B. Breslin's 1984 survey *From Modern to Contemporary*.[22] Bishop's tactics for de-privileging the poet, for example, were noted by earlier critics often enough, but until recently, at least, these de-privileging tactics have generally been cited as evidence of Bishop's lack of importance. Thus, in 1973, five years before the publication of "Santarém", Jan B. Gordon complained that Bishop gains "a certain surface tension" by

---

22. James E. B. Breslin, *From Modern to Contemporary*, Chicago, 1984, 298.

the loss of poetic *privilege* in every sense of the word: the narrator's sense of an advantage to perspective; an access to secrets, unknown to the protagonists of her poems; or even the subtlety of an untrustworthy vision which might confer aesthetic advantage by granting the reader the right to acknowledge a false subjectivity.[23]

By assuming a "loss" of privilege (how was it lost?), rather than a renunciation, Gordon makes Bishop's technique sound passive, even weak. Yet, from the start of her career, this renunciation of privilege functioned as a key feature of Bishop's elusive style, allowing her to explore perspectives of outsiderhood or marginalization, including the outsiderhood of lesbian identity identified by Rich, along with the outsiderhood of the denied child, the provincial, the colonial subject, the observer, the dreamer, the endangered animal, neglected art object, the disparaged cultural position – in poems that do their subjects the honour of close attention while refusing to claim the privileges of prescriptive ethical authority.

While the poets of high modernism struggled, in the 1920s, to reassert a vanishing cultural, spiritual, or metaphysical order, proclaiming with Eliot at the end of *The Waste Land* that "These fragments I have shored against my ruin", the poets of the later generation to which Bishop belonged found themselves, by the early 1930s, already living among those ruins. In Yeats, in Eliot, in Pound, in Stevens, and even Williams, in *Paterson*, when he posits "that a man is himself a city, beginning, seeking, achieving and concluding his life in ways which the various aspects of a city may embody",[24] represent the last brilliant re-conception of the notion, romantic in origin, of the poet as imaginative centre, as unacknowledged lawmaker, as imperial self. Even when the modernist poet acknowledged, with Stevens, that, "I cannot bring the world quite round, / Although I patch it as I can", or when he acknowledges, with Pound, in his last fragmentary Canto that "I cannot make it cohere", the expectation that the poet make an order remained. Even in her earliest poems, Bishop never tried to present herself as such a privileged observer, and she sustained the stance of an observer without claims to privilege. By the mid-1930s, Bishop was already writing from her lonely, painful and fragmentary inner world with a combination of wit, mystery, narrative surprise, metrical invention and dazzling imagistic virtuosity. Hence, in the poem "Cirque d'Hiver", an observer studies a "mechanical toy", a "Little circus horse with real white hair" who "bears a little dancer on his back". Is this toy an object or an emblem? When we learn that the horse's "mane and tail are straight from Chirico" or that: "He has a formal, melancholy soul" or that:

---

23. Jan B. Gordon, "Days and Distances", 60.

24. William Carlos Williams, "Preface" to *Paterson, Book 1*, New York, 1946.

> He feels her pink toes dangle toward his back
> along the little pole
> that pierces both her body and her soul
> and goes through his, and reappears below,
> under his belly, as a big tin key.[25]

it is hard to avoid the emblematic reading. Yet the direction in which this reading leads remains curiously inconclusive, even in the poem's final five line stanza:

> The dancer, by this time, has turned her back.
> He is the more intelligent by far.
> Facing each other rather desperately –
> his eye is like a star –
> we stare and say, "Well, we have come this far."   (CP, 31)

Rather than claiming the privilege of normative interpretation, this poem ends on a note of dogged persistence: all the elegance and charm of the toy, all the probing of its soul, all the emblematizing skill of the poet, have produced a startlingly inconclusive, yet effectively desperate conclusion: an ending that one could not have predicted when the poem began, and that still surprises after many readings.

When Bishop was a senior at Vassar in the fall of 1933, Yvor Winters, acting as a regional editor of *Hound and Horn*, noticed Bishop's work (submitted for a contest) and suggested that she correspond with another protégé of his, Donald Stanford, then a budding poet and scholar doing graduate work at Harvard. Bishop revealed some of the most important features of her early aesthetic in letters written to Stanford from Vassar. After the startling early achievement of "The Ballad of the Subway Train" in 1927 for North Shore Country Day School's *The Owl*, Bishop's high school poems for *The Blue Pencil*, written under the influence of the sentimental Miss Eleanor Prentice, are notable for their smoothness, their conventional lyric polish, their adherence to what Cheryl Walker has recently termed "the nightingale tradition". After four years of poetic silence following Walnut Hill, when she seemed to be quietly distancing herself from this pre-modernist aesthetic, Bishop began to publish poems again in 1933, and these poems, "A Word With You", "Hymn to the Virgin", and "Three Sonnets for the Eyes", which appeared unsigned in the April and November issues of the renegade Vassar school magazine *Con Spirito*, read like a series of deliberate experiments with the extremities of poetic voice. Bishop acknowledged in a November 1933 letter to Stanford:

---

25. *Elizabeth Bishop, The Complete Poems 1927–1979*, New York, 1989, 31. Subsequent references in the text will be cited as CP.

If I try to write smoothly I find myself perverting the meaning for the sake of the smoothness. (And don't you do that sometimes yourself?) However, I think that an equally great "cumulative effect" might be built up by a series of irregularities. Instead of beginning with an "Uninterrupted mood" what I want to do is to get the moods themselves in the rhythm. This is a very hard thing to explain, but for me there are two kinds of poetry, that (I think yours is of this sort) *at rest*, and that which is in action, within itself. At present it is too hard for me to get this feeling of action within the poem unless I just go ahead with it and let the meters find their way through. (OA, 11)

Bishop's remarks suggest that her achievement, two years later, in 1935, of an active poetic voice that gets "the moods themselves into the rhythm" in two poems that Berryman admired on their first publication, "The Map" and "The Imaginary Iceberg", was the result of conscious, deliberate and lonely effort – effort, it is worth noting, that had already begun before she met her mentor Marianne Moore in 1934. In a letter to Stanford, Bishop relates her notion of a poetry that is "in action" to Gerard Manley Hopkins, a poet whose influence she would soon find means to successfully internalize, and thus disguise. Bishop also cites the writings on baroque prose of the scholar M. W. Croll:

But the best part, which perfectly describes the sort of poetic convention I should like to make for myself (and which explains, I think, something of Hopkins), is this: "Their purpose (the writers of Baroque prose) was to portray, not a thought, but a mind thinking ... They knew that an idea separated from the act of experiencing it is not the idea that was experienced. The ardor of its conception in the mind is a necessary part of its truth." (OA, 12)

Displaying one of his many points of affinity with Bishop, Lowell – another poet who invented his own poetic conventions and learned quite well how to dramatize the mind thinking – chided Tate in a letter of 11 October, 1936, "How can you dismiss Donne's prose in so offhand a manner, incidentally – I love the stuff".[26] Lowell's proclivity for the intricate syntax of baroque prose and verse, syntax that could capture the "ardor of conception in the mind" and maintained a sense of action, helps to explain his promptness to "admire and love" Bishop's early work.

Bishop would write to Stanford, "Have you ever noticed that you can often learn more about other people – more about how they feel, how it would feel to be them – by hearing them cough or making one of those innumerable inner noises, than by watching them for hours? ... Do you know what I'm driving

---

26. Robert Lowell to Allen Tate, October 11, 1936. Princeton.

at. Well ... – that's what I'm trying to get into poetry" (OA, 26). Berryman, who later wrote the words "Starts again always in Henry's ear / the little cough somewhere, an odour, a chime[27] certainly would have known what Bishop was driving at. On the other hand, Stanford, the recipient of these early confidences was not prepared to sustain a true exchange with Bishop: he later distinguished himself as a scholar as Louisiana State University and edited the *Southern Review* for two decades from 1963 to 1983, and retired as Alumni Professor Emeritus. Bishop's letters to him make clear that she hardly expected him to comprehend much of what she said and that she distrusted many of his more or less conventional assumptions about art – and about her. Hence, she wrote, "And one more thing – what on earth do you mean when you say my perceptions are 'almost impossible for a woman's'. 'Now what the hell,' as you said to me, 'you know that's meaningless.' And if you really do mean anything by it, I imagine it would make me very angry. Is there some glandular reason which prevents a woman from having good perceptions, or what?" (OA, 12). Bishop, though painfully shy, did not suffer fools gladly, and she knew how to nail interlocutors firmly to the wall. Bishop needed to find her true artistic peers, and her correspondence with Stanford soon came to a close. Significantly, Bishop did not directly explore these ideas with Marianne Moore, in the correspondence that began with her in 1934, perhaps because she may have wanted to preserve her autonomy in the face of this established elder while developing her aesthetic.

As the years passed, working first in parallel, and later in conversation with Robert Lowell, Randall Jarrell and John Berryman, Bishop wrote the poems that quietly established narrative postmodernism as one of the most influential contemporary modes of poetic discourse – as she was all the while refusing to explicitly state a poetic doctrine. John Crowe Ransom, in the process of labelling Jarrell as an incipient postmodernist in 1941, regretted his protégé's inclination to think "about all the technical possibilities at once". But this very tendency to consider "all the technical possibilities at once", which may be taken as the defining characteristic of this quietly experimental mode of writing, has consistently created fresh and surprising poems, poems that seek an original synthesis of imagist, surrealist, modernist, objectivist and / or formalist elements. Narrative postmodernists who have specifically acknowledged Bishop's importance include James Merrill, John Ashbery, Adrienne Rich, Amy Clampitt, Frank Bidart, Robert Pinsky, Dana Gioia, William Logan and Gjertrud Schnackenberg.

Bishop's particular contribution to postmodern narrative grew out of her extraordinary early focus on the poem as a dramatization of "the mind in action", and her experiments with timing, with the balancing of realism and abstraction,

---

27. John Berryman, *The Dream Songs*, New York, 1969, No. 29.

and with the stripping away of authorial privilege, experiments that began as early as 1933, combined with her uncanny ear for the right diction and her early mastery of the intricacies and uncertainties of a convincing postmodern voice.

The extraordinary descriptive paragraph that follows Bishop's disarmingly ambiguous opening in "Santarém" sets a scene bathed in stately romantic aura, and it seems, for the moment, that despite the opening disclaimer, to be recalling the scene with great and authoritative precision while summoning echoes of earlier literary convergences:

> That golden evening I really wanted to go no farther;
> more than anything else I wanted to stay awhile
> in that conflux of two great rivers, Tapajós, Amazon,
> grandly, silently flowing, flowing east. (CP, 185)

Here Bishop evokes a moment of numinous tranquillity echoing many generations of romantic river literature. American readers might link this moment to the flowing of the Missouri and Ohio rivers into the Mississippi. The narrator seems not entirely in control of her journey. But this sense of tranquillity, and these associations, are almost immediately disrupted:

> Suddenly there'd been houses, people, and lots of mongrel
> riverboats skittering back and forth
> under a sky of gorgeous, under-lit clouds,
> with everything gilded, burnished along one side,
> and everything bright, cheerful, casual – or so it looked. (CP, 185)

For now the frame of reference veers away from that romantic literature of the river toward Bishop's own previous writings about disorderly water scenes. This scene, with its "mongrel / riverboats skittering back and forth" is reminiscent of "The Bight", with its "frowzy sponge boats" that "keep coming in / with the obliging air of retrievers". Each scene is characterized and personalized, but in the context of a recognition that this is just one person's rather external view of the scene, one person's way of recalling a particular moment:

> I liked the place; I liked the idea of the place.
> Two rivers. Hadn't two rivers sprung
> from the Garden of Eden? No, that was four
> and they'd diverged. Here only two
> and coming together. Even if one were tempted
> to literary interpretations

such as: life / death, right / wrong, male / female
– such notions would have resolved, dissolved, straight off
in that watery, dazzling dialectic. (CP, 185)

The authority of the poet is undercut by her inability to accurately remember
her allusions (imagine T.S. Eliot or Marianne Moore misremembering their
carefully documented sources?). While Eliot, Pound and Moore each make a
point of the fact that they are citing from a printed source, Bishop, although
she no doubt checked her reference at some point in the writing process, makes
it seem as though she is thinking, imperfectly, aloud. And she undercuts
traditionally dyadic structures, those weary old dualisms rehearsed in the poem,
showing these as merging in a "watery, dazzling dialectic" that leaves all the
components mixed together both dazzlingly and inextricably: one can not
distinguish Amazon from Tapajós. Such a stress on the dynamic intersection
of a multi-planar dialectic shows Bishop's sympathy for the conception of
poetic structure articulated by Jarrell, who insists in his 1942 lecture that "there
are no things in a poem, only processes" and who argues that:

> Poetry is interested in communicating extremely complicated systems
> of thoughts, perceptions, and emotions, which have extremely
> complicated non-logical structures; for this, logical structure is
> pathetically inadequate. In poetry we are trying, often, to do things which
> logic cannot do, which can be done only in defiance of logic: to reconcile
> the individual to both sides of an inconsistent world order, to console
> him for the inconsolable, to unify things which cannot be unified and
> which any submission to reality should make us differentiate.

Bishop's characteristically prismatic imagery, which, due to its multi-planar,
de-centred character, seems in this sense quite deftly postmodern, runs
throughout her poetic oeuvre, from "Florida" where "After dark, the fireflies
map the heavens in the marsh / until the moon rises", (CP, 33) through the
"rainbow, rainbow, rainbow" that glows in the oily pool of bilge in the bottom
of the boat in "The Fish", through the fighting cocks of "Roosters", who, as
they do battle, display "all that vulgar beauty of iridescence", through "Over
2,000 Illustrations and a Complete Concordance", where:

> The eye drops, weighted, through the lines
> the burin made, the lines that move apart
> like ripples above sand,
> dispersing storms, God's spreading fingerprint,
> and painfully, finally, that ignite
> in watery prismatic white-and-blue. (CP, 57)

Bishop's prismatic images, as we have already seen, have quite different tones and feels, quite different emotional weights, but they emerge as products of a dynamic way of looking, conveying her sense both that the ordinary can suddenly blaze out with surprising beauty and complexity, and that nothing is reducible to plain, schematic black and while. In fact, what appears to be mere black ink may not actually be, as one watches the engravings in an old family Bible finally and painfully ignite "in watery prismatic white-and-blue". For this prismatic imagery is associated with movement, with the unpredictable, and thus with surprise and change. Hence, in "Quai d'Orleans",

> We stand as still as stones to watch
>   the leaves and ripples
> while light and nervous water hold
>   their interview.
> "If what we see could forget us half as easily,"
>   I want to tell you,
> "as it does itself – but for life we'll not be rid
>   of the leaves" fossils."   (CP, 28)

Bishop's lifelong absorption in the complexities of perception, like her fascination with shifting lighting effects, show how consistently she was engaged with a postmodern reconfiguration of the problem of "the mind in action". And they are subtle marks of her role, from the mid-1930s onward, in the origins of narrative postmodernism, an influential aesthetic that links her, as a founding member and innovative source, with a midcentury quartet of poets that she herself defined in 1966 to include Lowell, Jarrell and Berryman.

THE "UNFAMILIAR STEREOTYPE": REPETITION IN THE POETRY OF JOHN ASHBERY

KRYSTYNA MAZUR

So I cradle this average violin that knows
Only forgotten showtunes, but argues
The possibility of free declamation anchored
To a dull refrain ...[1]

"We see that there really is nothing left to write about" says Ashbery in "Late Echo". "[O]r, rather, it is necessary to write about the same old things / In the same way, repeating the same things over and over ..."[2] Rather than demand to "make it new" Ashbery's poems often prefer to present themselves as the "late echo" of the poem's title. The notions of repeating or "recycling" have become crucial for Ashbery's readers, be it as forms of "belatedness" in Harold Bloom's theory of poetic influence, or as the target of criticism, when his readers complain of Ashbery repeating himself. An examination of Ashbery's repetitive strategies reveals, however, that to say (or read) again (in the sense of the discovery of sameness) is something of an oxymoron; and to repeat oneself or someone else, desirable as it may seem to some, and redundant to others, is in fact never possible. Repetition, Ashbery seems to argue, is never a return of the same, or, as Gertrude Stein has put it, there may be "no such thing as repetition".[3]

The two poems I examine below – Ashbery's long, meditative "Self-Portrait in a Convex Mirror", and a pantoum, "Hotel Lautréamont" – engage in two very distinct models of poetic repetition. While in the former, repetition is present as a recurrence of motif, pattern and figuration, in the later, exact repetition of whole lines is dictated by convention which calls for a kind of mechanical iteration. In the former repetitions seem to be generated by the

---

1. John Ashbery, *Houseboat Days*, London, 1977, 1.

2. John Ashbery, *As We Know*, Manchester, 1981, 88.

3. Gertrude Stein, "Portraits and Repetition", *Lectures in America*, New York, 1957, 166. Stein essentially argues for repetition as the principle of gradual change; Ashbery's poem is a brilliant echo of Stein's argument.

poem's thematic concerns, in the latter repetition itself seems to generate the poem.[4] In both cases, however, repetition is a principle of change. In both poems repetition performs the task of making the familiar unfamiliar again, of revitalizing calcified structures.

In "Self-Portrait in a Convex Mirror" repetitions are apparently contingent upon the poem's themes. Announcing itself as a "Self-Portrait in a Convex Mirror / As Parmigianino did it",[5] and thus a kind of poetic duplicate of the painter's work, the poem is, on a certain level, a poem *about* repetition. The ambiguity of its opening lines allows us to read the poem also as its speaker's own self-portrait: a poetic self-portrait which is like that of the painter's, or, to use the poem's favourite metaphor, which "mirrors" the painter's work. This double task of reproducing Parmigianino's self-portrait and producing its own is grounded in another set of repetitions or series of copies which are shown to have generated Parmigianino's painting itself. Repetition is thus a recurrent pattern which structures the poem's unfolding. And yet, despite the poem's apparently symmetrical structure, to try to map out the poem's progress is to find oneself caught in a series of mirrorings which are very unstable, in which originals and copies tend to exchange positions (so that repetition becomes the source of what it attempts to duplicate) and which demonstrate that an act of mirroring always involves change. An attempt to define the sources and effects of such repetitive slippage is one of the poem's concerns: it argues that the painter's and the poet's perspectives, their tools, their moments of attention (and inattention), their memory, as well as the shifting contexts of their work, all intrude upon the copies they produce.

As soon as we are taken into the world of the painting we discover that Parmigianino's self-portrait involves more than just one copy:

> Vasari says, "Francesco one day set himself
> To take his own portrait, looking at himself for that purpose
> In a convex mirror, such as is used by barbers ...
> He accordingly caused a ball of wood to be made

---

4. For a discussion of the two types of repetition see Barbara Johnson's "Strange Fits: Poe and Wordsworth on the Nature of Poetic Language", where Wordsworth's fiction of the "natural" repetition of "emotion recollected in tranquility" is juxtaposed with Poe's model of mechanical iteration. Johnson observes how essential the distinction between the two models is for both poets and demonstrates how difficult it is, at the same time, to sustain that very distinction. See Barbara Johnson, *A World of Difference*, Baltimore, 1987, 89–99. J. Hillis Miller makes a similar argument in relation to fiction in his *Fiction and Repetition*, Cambridge, MA 1982, 1–21.

5. John Ashbery, *Self-Portrait in a Convex Mirror*, Harmondsworth, 1976, 68. Hereinafter references to this edition are given as page numbers in the text.

By a turner, and having divided it in half and
Brought it to the size of the mirror, he set himself
With great art to copy all that he saw in the glass."
Chiefly his reflection, of which the portrait
Is the reflection once removed. (68)

The poem's ironic qualification of the Vasari quote is a first hint that the gaze of the copyist is necessarily selective. The quotation marks themselves are in fact an apt typographical image for the mechanism of self-portraiture: translated into verbal terms that mechanism could be illustrated as a proliferation of quotation marks: Parmigianino's face is already "Parmigianino's face" when reflected in the mirror, and becomes "Parmigianino's face" when painted on the ball of wood, and so on. The number of quotation marks the image acquires by the time it reaches us (via the painting, via Vasari, via Ashbery's poem, and so on) is uncountable. To use quotation marks is to claim to cite word for word, to repeat exactly. But it is also to suggest a doubling of voices: what were once somebody else's words are now also mine, and thus necessarily different. As the poem demonstrates, slippages have to occur in the course of quoting (in the course of mirroring or repeating). "... as in the game where / A whispered phrase passed around the room / Ends up as something completely different" (80). These slippages are the marker of the difference repetition makes; and, as "the principle that makes works of art so unlike / What the artist intended" (80), they are crucial to Ashbery's definition of the creative process.

By resorting to a quotation in order to describe the painting's history the poem reminds us also that any knowledge of the painting's origins has to be necessarily second-hand and therefore subject to its own distortion. In fact, the most straightforward descriptions of the painting, which apparently aim at producing its faithful poetic duplicate, testify to the difficulty in containing such record to the purely descriptive. A description will always necessarily be also about something else – be it the context of the painting's reception or the speaker himself. What the poem achieves as it aims at a reproduction is, rather, a collage of perspectives, none of which is given precedence over the others.

Interestingly, the speaker's own self-portrait emerges most clearly out of such considerations of the painter's work, and thus indirectly, the poem indeed mirrors Parmigianino's self-portrait but this task of mirroring is achieved as a kind of side-effect: a contemplation of another's art lends materials for a self-portrait. The contemplation of the self, in turn, will yield elements other than the self:

... This otherness, this
"Not-being-us" is all there is to look at
In the mirror ... (81)

The notion of a "mirror reflection" fails to signify exact repetition. The poem's "accumulating mirror", rather than guarantee a faithful copy tends to shuttle the image through a series of distortions. This very lack of control over our copy, the "surprise and novelty" of the discovery that the "end result" is never what we planned (a discovery that "… A ship / flying unknown colors has entered the harbor" (81)) become the grounds for the formulation of the speaker's own poetics. Repetition defined as difference is repetition of a creative kind: rather than reproduce the same, it constructs a new presence.

Such oblique, accidental repetitions result and are inseparable from the desire to repeat exactly, to produce a faithful copy. Parmigianino's attempt to "embalm" his own image, to shield it from the intrusions of the other in the "bubble chamber" of the painting, "to perfect and rule out the extraneous" (72) may at first seem naive or too premeditated in the face of the poem's own skepticism. And yet, as the poem soon recognizes, Parmigianino's desire for his portrait to exist in a space which freezes the present and locks out change may spring from his very awareness of the illusory control the artist has over his materials:

>   … Often he finds
> He has omitted the thing he started out to say
> In the first place. Seduced by flowers,
> Explicit pleasures, he blames himself (though
> Secretly satisfied with the result), imagining
> He had a say in the matter and exercised
> An option of which he was hardly conscious,
> Unaware that necessity circumvents such resolutions
> So as to create something new
> For itself, that there is no other way,
> That the history of creation proceeds according to
> Stringent laws, and that things
> Do get done in this way, but never the things
> We set out to accomplish and wanted so desperately
> To see come into being. Parmigianino
> Must have realized this as he worked at his
> Life-obstructing task.   (80)

In these lines the poem simultaneously defines its own poetic principles and gives a powerful motivation to Parmigianino's attempt to shield his own portrait from the vertiginous context in which it resides. In these lines the poem also completes a loop in its "argument": what has defined the speaker's poetics now also defines the painter's; and vice versa: the poem's critique of Parmigianino's project is a self-critique. Indeed, the poet shares his tools with the painter; in what are possibly the most frequently quoted Ashbery lines:

> The words are only speculation
> (From the Latin *speculum*, mirror):
> They seek and cannot find the meaning of the music. (69)

These lines resonate with all of the qualifications the mirror has acquired as the painter's tool, with its luring yet never fulfilled promise of faithful recovery or perfect repetition. This circular, accretive gesture is very characteristic of Ashbery's poem whose structure – a peculiar mise en abyme- allows for such an interplay between the painting and the poem which never allows one to be grounded in the other. "Self-Portrait's" mise en abyme is at once a simple duplication: a self-portrait "as Parmigianino did it"; an aporetic duplication; it is impossible to tell which of the two self-portraits is the embedding and which the embedded work; and an infinite duplication: the process of mirroring it has put in motion can be defined as infinite regress. By engaging the device in all of its forms simultaneously, the poem not only highlights the ambiguity of the mirror reflection, but also refuses to give priority to any of its manifestations.[6]

The mediation between the two creative acts, the poet's and the painter's, is thematized as the poem (repeatedly) comments on its own moments of attention to, and forgetting of, the painting:

> As I start to forget it
> It presents its stereotype again
> But it is an unfamiliar stereotype, the face
> Riding at anchor, issued from hazards, soon
> To accost others, "rather angel than man" (Vasari).
> Perhaps an angel looks like everything
> We have forgotten, I mean forgotten
> Things that don't seem familiar when
> We meet them again, lost beyond telling,
> Which were ours once. (73–74)

Forgetting or loss, moments of inattention, the inability to hold a meaning intact, englobed, allows objects or words to become meaningful again. Whether it be due to the "injected urgencies" of the other, the intrusions of other contexts, other objects or words, or the simple fading of attention, the words we once possessed slip out of our control. The coming back to our "stereotypes" already makes them "unfamiliar", that is, meaningful again.

The making of the "unfamiliar stereotype" is one of Ashbery's most characteristic (and most celebrated) preoccupations: the recycling of the cliché,

---

6. For an insightful, lucid discussion of the painterly and literary uses of mise en abyme, see Lucien Dallenbach's, *The Mirror in the Text*, Cambridge, 1989, 7–38.

of the metaphor which has "gone stale" as it became all too familiar, of the word which has lost its meaning through our appropriation. Ashbery stays with them just long enough to give them a new context, but never so long as to allow them to "lock into place" (for "locking into place is 'death itself', / As Berg said of Mahler's Ninth" (76), as Ashbery quotes, unlocking the old phrase in a new context) – thus the characteristic breathless succession of disparate images, clashing observations, unlikely combinations of words in his poems which always impart "a sense of novelty and amazement" to the reader.

"Hotel Lautréamont" differs radically from "Self-Portrait" as far as the function of poetic form is concerned: in a pantoum repetitions are generated mechanically; they are a formal requirement, a function of a convention. The writing of a pantoum is an exercise in feeding words into a ready pattern, or, to use Ashbery's phrase, a "paint-by-numbers".[7] While repetitions in "Self-Portrait", however disruptive, *may* be read as a way of organizing the poetic materials (at least that is the fiction any long, meditative poem will work with), in a pantoum (or a sestina, or a villanelle) repetitions are manifestly present as the structure which exists prior to the poem, a type of formal limitation. Since in a pantoum every line is repeated in a tight symmetrical grid the poet's task is to devise lines which could be readable in two different contexts: an attempt to wrest meaning from a particularly rigid structure. At the same time, the very fact that each line is repeated makes it necessarily ambiguous. And since each of the immediate two contexts of each line are similarly doubled, what we witness when we try to anchor a reading of the poem in some single stable element is a type of infinite regress: the more we retrace our steps, the more the proliferating meanings elude our grasp.

While in the case of "Hotel Lautréamont" it seems almost impossible to say what the poem is "about", it is possible to discern certain recurrent thematic clusters. I will attend here to those of the poem's "themes" which seem directly related to its structural pattern. Taking Ashbery's suggestion, I will use one of the poem's own metaphors – the "hotel" of its title – as a way into the poem. In response to an interviewer's question about the title "Hotel Lautréamont", Ashbery says:

> there is something very attractive about a hotel because it has got so many rooms, and so many different kinds of people all doing different things. ... I wrote the poem "Hotel Lautréamont" because I found a photograph of Lautréamont. ... He seemed to be in a hotel room, and of course he lived in small hotels during his brief career ... . And then I

7. David Herd, John Ashbery "In Conversation", *P.N.Review*, 99, 21, i, (September–October 1996), 35.

8. Herd, 36.

thought of the four sections of four stanzas each as being like four floors of a hotel, like the boxes behind the desk where the keys are hung.[8]

The attractiveness of "hotels" (in both literal and figurative senses of the word) seems to be that of a structure (architectural, poetic) which can simultaneously contain different "rooms". The structure itself is permanent, its elements identical and symmetrically aligned, yet it may be inhabited by different presences, different voices. A "hotel" poem is, then, a structured way of letting rooms to different voices.

The image of the key boxes complicates matters considerably as it introduces an element of mise en abyme into the simple symmetrical pattern: the grid of the key boxes is contained by and reproduces the structure of the hotel, but at the same time contains the "keys" to each of the hotel rooms, so that access to the whole structure leads through the box, and, consequently, through each of the hotel rooms (or voices). Thus a pattern (of the hotel) which could produce a sense of structural closure is undone from within. (Ashbery's hotel metaphor is, of course, a perfect definition of a pantoum.)

In the same commentary Ashbery suggests that Joseph Cornell's "boxes called hotels" have been a parallel inspiration: "the fact that his [Cornell's] collage, which I chose for the book jacket seemed to be looking out of a window – or into a window, you can't tell which – had a hotel-like feel".[9] In a hotel room you don't feel "at home": you are not in possession of the room (or voice) you inhabit: you do not feel "inside" even as you are looking outside from its window. Cornell's collage has a chilling quality: in place of an interior warmth / light we are given the image of snow falling in the dark. This estrangement – like that of Lautréamont, a stranger in the places he inhabited, literally and poetically[10] – a sense of not knowing whether one is inside or outside, defines precisely the instability we witness as readers of a pantoum: repeatedly, we feel to be in possession of meanings which then stubbornly escape us.

Lautréamont's name in the poem's and book's title makes him the presiding ghost of the whole collection. An analysis of this resonant allusion goes beyond the scope of my immediate interests here (and may well be a false path to follow, considering Ashbery's often whimsical employment of quotation and allusion). It is worth noting, however, the unlikely juxtaposition between the name "Lautréamont" and the form of the pantoum used as a mode of allusion. Lautréamont's single long prose poem, variously praised and criticized for the violence of its subject matter and equally violent manipulations of poetic form

---

9. Herd, 36.

10. Comte Lautréamont, the pseudonym of Isidore Ducasse, the 19th century French author of *Songs of Maldoror*.

relies on abrupt and often shocking juxtapositions which deprive it of any sense of continuity or even coherence. Lautréamont's readers describe the principle of his work as the "principle of endless change". As Gaston Bachelard has put it, "with Lautréamont comes a participation in a discontinuity of acts, in the expressive joy of the moment of decision. But these instances remain unpremeditated; they are savored in their isolation. They are lived out in rapid and uneven succession ... Ducasse's poetry is an accelerating cinema from which the indispensable intermediate forms are deliberately eliminated".[11] Any order that exists in the poem which has earned Ducasse the label of a "proto-surrealist" is a violent and unpredictable one.

The relationship Ashbery's "Hotel Lautréamont" sets up with its predecessor is thus from the outset a paradoxical one. "Lautréamont" and "pantoum" are not likely to find their way into a single entry of a poetic dictionary, yet Ashbery's poem suggests some striking parallels between the violence of chaos untamed by poetic convention and the violence of a rigid pattern of poetic convention itself, parallels between the violence of disorder and the violence of order. The rigid order of a pantoum (not unlike what "Self-Portrait" calls "the chaos" of Parmigianini's organizing mirror) puts such a strain on language that, paradoxically, it may yield meanings which verge on the unintelligible.

The inside / outside dynamic of "Hotel Lautréamont" is thematized in the poem in the way it speculates about enclosures and escape, about being "indoors" and "trying to leave". Interestingly, the poem places those concerns in relation to speculations on the conditions of literary creativity. The poem begins and ends with references to the history of a literary form, the ballad. Its opening lines produce a mock version of a literary historian's text:

> Research has shown that ballads were produced by all of society
> working as a team. They didn't just happen. There was no guesswork.
> The people, then, knew what they wanted and how to get it.
> We see the results in works as diverse as "Windsor Forest" and "The
>   Wife of Usher's Well".
>
> Working as a team, they didn't just happen. There was no guesswork.
> The horns of elfland swing past, and in a few seconds
> We see the results in works as diverse as "Windsor Forest" and "The
>   Wife of Usher's Well",
>   or, on a more modern note, in the finale of Sibelius violin concerto.[12]

---

11. Gaston Bachelard, *Lautréamont*, Dallas, 1986, 9.

12. John Ashbery, *Hotel Lautréamont*, New York, 1992, 14. Hereinafter references to this edition are given in the text.

Unlike the model of "lyric subjectivity" ("the enchantment of self with self"),[13] ballads are a collective enterprise. Designed as if according to a plan ("The people ... knew what they wanted") the ballads are a predictable outcome ("they didn't just happen"). "The results" of this reliable enterprise are manifest in "Windsor Forest" and "The Wife of Usher's Well". This seems to be the "argument" of the first stanza of the poem. As soon as we enter the poem's second stanza, however, and are confronted with the first repetitions, the initial sense of control over the poem's "meanings" (demonstrable in our ability to paraphrase) is lost.

The same "results" seem to entirely slip out of (the ballad-makers', the speaker's, our own) control in the second stanza where "[t]he horns of elfland swing past", and, as if by magic, "in a few seconds" (and not ages of accretion as one would expect) the result is produced in the form of, again, "Windsor Forest" and "The Wife of Usher's Well". The same whimsical "horns of elfland", which the poem invites us to read as an alternative origin of ballads will seem to trigger the disintegration of the world when provided with a new context in the third stanza, "The horns of elfland swing past, and in a few seconds / The world as we know it sinks in dementia".

The conflicting readings of the quoted "results", that is, the incompatible accounts of how ballads are made, are further complicated by the indeterminacy of the context in which they reappear. To try to arrive at a solid grasp of that context is to encounter more of the same difficulties, more lines which appear in two contexts and whose meaning is, therefore, necessarily indeterminate. The coherence of paraphrase must be lost here. Any attempt to describe the poem's progress will merely highlight the arbitrariness of the poem's juxtapositions which do not yield an overriding logic.

The question implicitly raised by this kind of investigation is, again, the question of origins: to what extent a poetic line is a "result" of the line which precedes it? In a pantoum, a poem in which the order of the lines is pre-established according to a conventional pattern, the meanings generated by the repetitions are to a large degree a matter of accident: "the horns of elfland" appear in those places in the poem which the convention of the pantoum calls for and not as a logical extension of the preceding line: the "results" the poem produces seem to be a product of a mechanical repetition as opposed to an expression of a continuing thought. The difficulties I encountered in my reading came from the presupposition that the poem will follow a linear progression, that one line will feed into the next, that continuity and development are the grounds on which poetic meaning rests. What the poem insists on, however, is a subversion of linearity. Meanings emerge as the result of repetitive accretion, rather than progression. Additionally, the mixed registers of the poem's opening

---

13. *Self-Portrait in a Convex Mirror*, 73.

stanza not only prevent us from locating anything like the poem's "speaker" in its opening lines, but also, by nature of their grammatical structure, complicate the very issues of origin and authorship they address. "Ballads were produced by all society": this wonderfully familiar use of the passive voice combined with the somewhat vague, undefinable agent – "research" – make for a telling mismatch between the implicit argument of the first stanza and the grammar which carries it. The collective agent which hides behind "research" is an uneasy echo of the "collectivity" which produced the ballads. To complicate matters, Ashbery may be simultaneously forging his own version of "collective writing" here, by echoing Ducasse's "Poetry should be made by all. Not by one".[14]

The highly controlled form of precisely recurring repetitions is likely to produce meanings which are absurd or unintelligible. One may expect a pantoum to be conditioned by a tension between an attempt to control and a slipping out of control, and indeed the terms of entrapment and escape surface in the poem in a series of related images. The poem's collective subject, the speaking "we", choose the categories of entrapment and escape as a means of self-representation:

> In troubled times one looked to the shaman or priest for comfort and
>   counsel
> Now, only the willing are fated to receive death as a reward,
> and night like black swandsdown settles on the city.
> If we tried to leave, would being naked help us?
>
> Now, only the willing are fated to receive death as a reward.
> Children twist hula-hoops, imagining a door to the outside.
> If we tried to leave, would being naked help us?
> And what of the older, lighter concerns? What of the river?   (15)

The speaker(s) of the poem seem to be hindered by what they possess or are possessed by: "If we tried to leave, would being naked help us?" Burdened by the immediate, material or older, immaterial concerns – the heaviness of what can be carried on, as well as the "older, lighter" luggage – they are immobilized, yet impatient to move on. The poem later returns to this motif: "Small wonder that those at home sit nervous by the unlit grate"; ready to leave, yet unable to, stationary but restless: the condition of the poem's speaker(s) reproduces the poem's own tension between its static symmetries and restless motion. This dynamic – suggested by the thematic and formal aspects of the poem – is nowhere more dramatic than in the imperceptible shifts the meanings undergo as they stubbornly reappear yet always escape the grasp of any given context.

---

14. Comte Lautréamont, *Les Chants de Maldoror*, New York, 1965, 33.

The reversal in "the willing are fated" – was it not the fated (to live an afterlife?) that used to be willing to die (when the shaman and priest were there to counsel?) – may be one of the possible answers to the poem's question, figuring "death" as a potential, though apparently no longer satisfying, solution, or means of escape. The children of the following stanza provide us with an alternative:

> Children twist hula-hoops, imagining a door to the outside,
> when all we think of is how much we can carry with us.
> And what of older, lighter concerns? What of the river?[15]
> All the behemoths have filed through the maze of time.   (15)

The children lend the hula-hoop image to the poem – an apt figuration for the dynamic of its vertiginous motion. It is again the power to imagine (this time, "a door to the outside") that figures the desired exit. One is invited to believe that, to be like the children who are still capable of conceiving an "outside", it would help to forget what one "carries" (it would help to be "naked"). That is indeed a formidable task for a reader of a pantoum, "when all we think of is how much we can carry with us" from one line to the next.

The emerging into the open – prepared for in the third and enacted in the fourth section of the poem – suggests, however, that in order to "leave" one needs more than a willingness to imagine or have faith. The concluding stanza of the third section prepares for this breakthrough:

> Small wonder that those at home sit nervous, by the unlit grate.
> It was their choice, after all, that spurred us to feats of the imagination.
> If remains for us to come to terms with our commonalty
> And in so doing deprive time of further hostages.   (15)

Paradoxically, it is what others have determined ("their choice") that provides the necessary imaginative stimulus ("Spurs us to feats of imagination") and prepares for the recognition of "our commonalty". That very recognition, in turn, allows the breakthrough, allows to "deprive time of further hostages". Apparently it is the very weight of what we "carry", the burden of our "commonalty" that allows the escape.

The long-awaited movement into the open is silent: "Now, silently as one mounts a stair we emerge into the open". The poem addresses this blockage by going back to its old question: "To end the standoff that history long ago began / Must we thrust ever onward, into perversity?" And as the poem again turns

---

15. "Poetry is no more tempest than it is cyclone. It is a majestic and fertile river" Ducasse, *Poésies*, 306. Ashbery may be alluding to, or testing this proposition by Ducasse.

back upon itself for answers its movement is indeed that of a "thrust into perversity" – from the Latin *pervertere*, to overturn (related to verse).

The pantoum writer's burden are the already made formal "choices" he has to work with, his limitation the rigidity of form imposed on poetic materials, the closure of a tight structure which has to be undone from within to yield meanings. It is not, however, just the poet's ingenuity (his "feats of the imagination"), but also the form itself, ("steeped in the nostalgia of a collective past")[16] that puts the poem in motion. The recognition of the "commonalty" is made possible through the recycling of an old form which carries echoes of other voices. The internal repetitions which construct the form itself allow the poem's voice(s) to be echoed and extended in turn.

Repetition highlights ambiguities inherent in language itself. Ashbery discusses the nature of such ambiguity in his commentary on Raymond Roussel:

> Sometimes he would take a phrase containing two words, each of which had a double meaning, and use the least likely meanings as the basis of a story. ... Elsewhere he would transform a common phrase, a book title, or a line of poetry into a series of words with similar sounds. A line of Victor Hugo, *"Un vase tout rempli du vin de l'espérance"* was denatured by Roussel into *"sept houx rampe lit Vesper,"* which he developed into a tale of Handel using seven bunches of holly tied with different colored ribbons to compose, on a banister, the principal theme of his oratorio Vesper.

> Just as the mechanical task of finding a rhyme sometimes inspires a poet to write a great line, Roussel's *"rimes de faits "*(rhymes for events) helped him to utilize his unconscious mind. Michel Leiris says, "Roussel here rediscovered one of the most ancient and widely used patterns of the human mind: the formation of myths starting from words. That is (as though he had decided to illustrate Max Müller's theory that myths were born out of a sort of "disease of language"), transposition of what was at first a simple fact of language into dramatic action". Elsewhere he suggests that these childish devices led Roussel back to a common source of mythology or collective unconscious.[17]

To paraphrase the opening of "Hotel Lautréamont", "language is produced by all society".

Ashbery's commentary on Roussel's experiments suggests that the power of language to create its own meanings, as well as the ambiguities and surprises it has in store can be traced to the very "collective" nature of linguistic creation.

---

16. *Self-Portrait in a Convex Mirror*, 77.

17. John Ashbery, "On Raymond Roussel" in Michel Foucault, *Death and the Labyrinth*, Berkeley, 1986, xxiii–xxiv.

Roussel's mechanical doubling of phrases or sounds, or "the mechanical task of finding a rhyme" are thus a way of exploring these common sources which lay beneath the calcified linguistic structures. The usefulness of such experiments lies in their power to defamiliarize, to "denature" what has been familiar and natural, and thus make it meaningful again. The "unfamiliar stereotype" gives back the same words but endows them with new meanings.

Repetition engenders sense which may otherwise be inaccessible to the speaker. The example Ashbery chooses to demonstrate the generative power of Roussel's "denatured" phrases is very telling: for Roussel to develop a tale of the origins (of a musician's work) with sounds borrowed from words (of another writer) is a particularly sharp instance of origins played out by mechanical iteration.

In "Hotel Lautréamont", as in "Self-Portrait", repetition is both a limitation and a source of surprise. The more exact the repetition, the more powerfully it demonstrates that meanings will not be held intact. As it proves the failure of mimetic representation, repetition is simultaneously celebrated for its power to extend, to make new meanings. The surprising turns repetition takes subvert the logic of linearity and progression, "derail" the poem's argument in rich and unpredictable ways, so that what gets "achieved" is never, and more than, "what the artist planned". It is the very failure of repetition to enact the return of the same that makes it meaningful: meanings reside in the difference repetition makes.

THE "HYBRID MIX" OF ASHBERY'S
THREE POEMS OR, HOW NOT TO BE FRENCH

JOHN PILLING

In his study of *Paris and the Nineteenth Century*,[1] a contribution to the series "Writing the City", Christopher Prendergast suggests that:

> [d]espite various, more or less sophisticated, neo-formalist attempts to "define" the prose poem as a genre, it is best thought of as a hybrid mix, irreducible to analytical definition, and, on a historical view, reflecting that tendency from the early nineteenth century onwards to break the traditional hierarchy of genre, in particular the distinction between the high "poetic" and the low "prosaic".

Prendergast's target here, or rather targets, are (as his footnote reveals) the contributors to a volume called *The Prose Poem in France*, edited by Mary Ann Caws and Hermine Riffaterre; and I think – in spite of the merits of that collection – his conclusion is incontrovertible. Prendergast explores "the prose poem" as "hybrid mix" in connection with Baudelaire's *Spleen de Paris*, an acknowledged (if still somewhat neglected) masterpiece of the genre. I wish to adopt the description "hybrid mix" to pursue lines of inquiry relative to the "ugly duckling" in John Ashbery's oeuvre which John Shoptaw has revealed to be the poet's favourite among his many books – *Three Poems* (1972), arguably the most neglected of them.

Three Poems pretty obviously satisfies anyone's minimal requirements for a "hybrid mix" at first glance, by using "poems" in the title and then by manifesting itself / themselves as predominantly written in prose, with the second and third poems wholly in paragraphs. The disjunction is, at the simplest level, not so much an invitation to consider the prose/poem boundary as a demonstration that no such boundary, for this poet, exists. In this connection it seems perfectly reasonable that Ashbery should not have called the book *Three Prose Poems*, which would have obliged him, presumably, to have come closer to "analytical definition" (as Prendergast puts it) than the spirit of the enterprise warrants. Such a title could also have misled Ashbery's readers – many of

1   Christopher Prendergast, *Paris in the Nineteenth Century*, Oxford, 1992, 157.

them aware that he spent a decade living in Paris and had translated from the French – into thinking that there were closer links between *Three Poems* and the "prose poem in France" than in fact obtain. As Stephen Fredman has very helpfully shown, there is actually surprisingly little profit in aligning *Three Poems* with, say, Max Jacob's *The Dice Cup*, or even with a text that Ashbery is known to admire, the "novel" *Hebdomeros* written (in French) by the Italian painter Giorgio de Chirico. One influence upon *Three Poems*, as Fredman demonstrates, is very much closer to home: Gertrude Stein's *Stanzas in Meditation*, reviewed in *Poetry* magazine by Ashbery in 1957. Fredman is, however, very sparing in quotations from Stein's *Stanzas*, and understandably so, since you do not have to read very far into them to see that they are quite unlike *Three Poems* in matter and manner, and since in any case the principal point that Ashbery is making in his review of the *Stanzas* is that they offer "a general, all-purpose mode which each reader can adapt to fit his own set of particulars". Even though Ashbery uses the word "model" – in part, perhaps, to surprise those who would never have believed that Gertrude Stein could be a "model" – I take it that what he really means is that the *Stanzas* open up possibilities, and specifically for writers who, like himself, are interested in a "way of happening". This phrase, "way of happening" recurs in a comparison that Ashbery subsequently makes between Stein's *Stanzas* and Henry James's *The Golden Bowl*, but on their first occurrence the words are in quotation marks, inviting any interested party to register that the phrase in question has been silently adopted from W.H. Auden's "In Memory of W.B. Yeats":

> For poetry makes nothing happen …
> … it survives,
> A way of happening, a mouth.

Irrespective, however, of whether we adopt the Steinian or the Audenesque perspective, *Three Poems* is or are very much concerned with "[a] way of happening". And on numerous occasions, poetic or discursive, Ashbery has vigorously demonstrated or defended his view that what happens is invariably a hybrid mix, and that there is not so much one way in which things happen, but several, even though he likes to quote the Robert Graves line "There is one story, and one story only". *Three Poems* offer three perspectives on the way what happens happens, yet the three obviously belong together rather than with other "poems in prose" which from time to time appear across Ashbery's massive oeuvre. Each is in itself a hybrid mix, all three together are a hybrid mix, and yet the book as a whole tells "one story".

The "one story" told is made up of many stories, or – shall we say? – many stories of stories. The second of the three poems, "The System", is a kind of philosophical investigation; the first, "The New Spirit", a kind of *ars poetica*; the third, "The Recital", an attempt at fusion; and overarching the whole enterprise, as Ashbery has very helpfully indicated, is a love affair, which may or may not justify our recalling a remark of his, about "Fragment" (in *The Double Dream of Spring*), to the effect that "like maybe all of my poems, it's a love poem". Traces of this love affair are visible as early as the second page of "The New Spirit":

> You are my calm world.
> This is my happiness. To stand,
> to go forward into it.[2]

Thereafter the traces remain what they are, mere traces, discernible in the paragraph on self-laceration in "The New Spirit" (11), the passage that compares the beloved to a star (23), and indeed throughout the first of the three poems. The second poem buries the love affair as deep as it can, leaving only a few markers of the beloved's presence (the "invisible web" (95); the "scene in the little restaurant" (101). En passant Ashbery observes, no doubt mindful of Matthew Arnold's "The Buried Life", that "it is best then that the buried word remain buried". The third poem, "The Recital", buries the word – the love which either will not or dare not speak its name – even more deeply. Ashbery's rationale for so doing occurs very close to the end of "The System", where he asks whether "this word", the word he has not uttered, "could possibly be our salvation" and decides that:

> ... we are rescued by what we cannot imagine: it is what finally takes us up and shuts our story, replacing it among the millions of similar volumes that by no means menace its uniqueness but on the contrary situate it in the proper depth and perspective.   (104–05)

The implications of this judgment are manifold: the word, whether uttered or left unuttered, heard or not heard, clearly enough exists in order to end up, as Mallarmé might have said, in a book. Yet the "millions of similar volumes" mentioned are not so much to be read as to be seen; the emphasis falls on a situational scenario constructed complete with "depth and perspective". What we have here is of course in no way original to Ashbery himself, although in his capacities as both poet and "art chronicler" he has been unusually well-placed to explore the matter. Here, perhaps, we have an example of *ut poesis pictura*, in which connection it may be useful to quote again from Ashbery's review of Stein's *Stanzas* in which he says that they are "like certain monochrome de Kooning paintings in which isolated strokes of color take on a deliciousness they never could have had out of context". One striking feature

---

2.   John Ashbery, *Three Poems*, Harmondsworth, 1977, 4. Subsequent references to this edition are given in the text.

of *Three Poems*, parts of which are certainly somewhat "monochrome", is that each poem ends with a visual referent: the constellation of Sagittarius in "The New Spirit", the film show of "The System" and the performance/spectacle of "The Recital".

Ashbery's conjuring of "millions of similar volumes" must, one supposes, have been undertaken in full consciousness that there were not millions of volumes similar to *Three Poems*, the very "uniqueness" of which was guaranteed by both the influences it had sloughed off and those which it had, apparently effortlessly, absorbed. As we know, Ashbery had found the French prose poem, together with his own earlier efforts in the mode, too "rhetorical", too much a matter of "posture". As we also know, Ashbery had decided that Gertrude Stein's attempt, as he puts it, "to create a counterfeit of reality more real than reality" had failed, for the very good reason that "it is still impossible to accomplish the impossible". Indeed, whilst it would be natural to suppose, in part on the basis of *Three Poems* (but perhaps with more confidence on the basis of "Self-Portrait in a Convex Mirror") that America and American writing had served Ashbery's purpose in saving him from a French fate, I think that most of the indicators in and around *Three Poems* point us, perhaps paradoxically, in the direction of English literature. There are, it is true, moments in *Three Poems* where we are effectively invited to recall to mind classic America motifs and, beyond them, the works that contain them. In speaking, in "The System", of "a fork in the road (where) you followed what seemed to be the less promising", a memory of Robert Frost's "The Road Not Taken" seems to swim into view; in the same poem, the mention of a "scarlet thread" points obliquely towards Hawthorne's *The Scarlet Letter*: in "The Recital", the image of "a boat crossing a harbor" looks like a conscious remembrance of Whitman's "Crossing Brooklyn Ferry", Ashbery having recently taken up a teaching position at Brooklyn College. No doubt there are other distinctively American resonances that I have either missed, or not recognized; and there are certainly actual or virtual invocations of such great European reference points as Dante (47, 76), Pascal (57, 69), Cervantes (68), Goethe (92), and Proust (81, 85), with perhaps other, lesser figures also to be detected. But the literary ambience of *Three Poems*, un-English as the book looks, is essentially English, even where (as I shall be obliged to concede) it might more accurately be called "Anglo-American".

My first example is of this latter type. Early on in "The New Spirit", in what is effectively the first of five bursts into verse, Ashbery speaks of "not wanting to 'presume' ". The quotation marks point, I take it, towards one of the unanswered question of J. Alfred Prufrock. However, the Eliot who seems to matter most to Ashbery is not the American of "Preludes" and *Prufrock* but the naturalized Englishman of *Four Quartets*. Throughout *Three Poems* Ashbery moves recurrently close to, or into the same stream as, Eliot in *Four*

Quartets, perhaps inevitably given their common interest in how time passes and whether it passes. Half-way through "The System" for example, Ashbery pauses to observe that "we have as it were boarded the train but for some unexplained reason it has not yet started", which is a kind of backhanded compliment to *The Dry Salvages,* section III; later, in "The System", Ashbery decides that "the place of joining" is the "very place you set out from", in another adaptation of *Four Quartets* material, this time from the fifth and final section of *Little Gidding.*

Early on in "The New Spirit" Ashbery decides that "we must learn to live in others" because "they create us". This is Ashbery's version of Eliot's "Tradition and the Individual Talent" in which "the dead writers" become "that which we know". Ironically, at least two of the dead writers who supplied Ashbery with both stimuli and a modicum of spiritual sustenance during the composition of *Three Poems* – John Clare and Thomas Traherne – have only become known, *where* they have become known, long after their deaths, such that both of them still arguably belong more to "the other tradition" (as Ashbery sees it) than to the mainstream of English literature. At no point in *Three Poems* does Ashbery oblige his reader to register the existence of Clare's autobiographical prose writings and Traherene's *Century of Meditations* behind the scenes; but then neither does Ashbery point his reader explicitly in the direction of W.H. Auden's *The Sea and the Mirror* (1948), the long central section of which ("Caliban to the Audience") must also have acted, at least in part, as an example of what sophisticated prose – very sophisticated indeed by the standards of Clare and Traherne – could achieve as poetry, and as a commentary on the poetic impulse. The ecumenical aspect of *Three Poems,* which begins with "examples of leaving out" (3) the better to let everything and everyone back in, could perhaps hardly be better illustrated than by Ashbery having found new stimulus from his readings in Clare and Traherne, but without prejudice to his old and long-lasting interest in Auden, who in interviews Ashbery has always cited as of more importance than the poet his critics want him to prefer, Wallace Stevens.

With Auden, Clare and Traherne attendant on, if not visibly present in, *Three Poems,* nothing would be easier than to identify Auden as of primary importance at the aesthetic level, Clare at the narrative level, and Traherne at the spiritual level. But such neat distinctions would, I think, be alien to Ashbery's intentions in *Three Poems.* All three of these writers are, after all, casualties of a "leaving out" process above and beyond the one that Ashbery chooses to illustrate at the outset, and I think that it is part of Ashbery's point in writing *Three Poems* to show that readers do not have to have these figures identified, appropriated and insisted upon in a context so flexible and so open-ended that at times it seems as if there is scarcely a context either. Much of what Traherne says on the subject of Love of God, for example, is congruent with what Ashbery says on the subject; yet Traherne is himself not striving to be thought original, his overwhelming purpose being to animate time-honoured commonplaces in a book of meditations designed to stimulate an active and vigorous response in a reader's soul. This is surely also Ashbery's principal purpose, and nowhere more obviously that in the second of the *Three Poems*, "The System", where unusually – if one is misled by the title, as one may well be – the emphasis falls on such an "old-fashioned" notion as the soul.

Ashbery did not need to wander far from the mainstream of American literature to find guidance on the subject of the soul: Whitman and Emerson would have been quite sufficient in this connection. But I think there is telling evidence that, not long after having returned to New York and taking up a position as a teacher of English, Ashbery decided he could best continue in the American grain by reverting to some seminal English texts. Commentators have perhaps been understandably reluctant to pursue this when Ashbery has seemed content to make the whole Anglo-American issue a matter of differential spellings (as in "Tenth Symphony" from *Self-Portrait*). And even in *Three Poems* there are some wry moments – the sudden reminder that "it is never too late to mend" (the title of a largely forgotten Victorian novel by Charles Reade) – which seem to suggest the English may not be much more cute than the Americans. But *Three Poems* is framed by two classic poems in the English tradition. In asking on only the second page of "The New Spirit" "Have I awakened? Or is this sleep again" (4), Ashbery is re-animating the question Keats asks himself at the end of "Ode to a Nightingale". And five paragraphs from the end of "The Recital" Ashbery speaks explicitly of " 'a timorous capacity', in Wordsworth's phrase", the phrase in question being taken from the opening, or prelude to Wordsworth's *Prelude* (Book 1, line 241 in the 1850 version; Book 1, line 243 in the 1805 version.)

In an interview for the *New York Quarterly*[3] conducted shortly before the appearance of *Three Poems*, Ashbery stated that he "want[ed] the reader to be able to experience the poem" – any poem of his – "without having to refer to outside sources to get the complete experience as one has to in Eliot sometimes or Pound". In his recent study *On the Outside Looking Out*, however, John Shoptaw has put the contrary view, with the suggestion that "Knowing what Ashbery's poetry 'means' means knowing where it comes from and how it works". I think it is possible to respect Ashbery's view of "outside sources" as ideally absent from the surface of a given text, whilst nevertheless preferring Shoptaw's approach, which is strong on aetiology and archaeology whatever else it may fail to deliver. It is in this latter spirit that I have sought to trace and identify a reference to the *Prelude* that even a Wordsworth scholar might justifiably have forgotten, or struggled to place, since *Three Poems* is itself a

---

3   *New York Quarterly*, (Winter, 1972, No. 9), 23.

kind of *Prelude*, and arguably a more propitious one than Wordsworth's proved to be, "Self-Portrait in a Convex Mirror" following so close upon it. Although there is no named dedicatee for the book, it is to, and for, a Friend, a specific addressee any one of us could, if we so wished, become; and – even with the huge number of interviews with Ashbery offering important illuminations – still arguably the most intimate and revelatory document on the growth of this poet's mind that we possess, which is no doubt why, or at least one reason why, it remains Ashbery's own favourite among his books.

"THE BLISS OF WHAT?"

PETER ROBINSON

One

Elizabeth Bishop didn't much like England. In March 1936, she sent a postcard of Piccadilly Circus to Frani Blough: "Since last week your fondness for England has made me feel a little suspicious of you".[1] Twenty-eight years later, writing on 19 June from the Hotel Pastoria, London, Bishop describes some Crusoe-in-England-like experiences to her doctor, Anny Baumann. Her companion Lota Costellat de Macedo Soares, had recently returned to Rio de Janeiro after their visit to Italy:

> I did want her to see a bit of England, too – but she was finally so depressed by the high state of agricultural cultivation in Italy, the advanced "civilization", the huge trees in the parks, etc. – as compared to Brazil – that perhaps it's just as well she didn't come. They're all even bigger and better here. (I really prefer something a bit harsher, I confess.)

Then there's the weather in June: "It is terribly cold – or else my blood is thinned by the tropics – and raining, naturally. Although I like the tea very much, I'm already beginning to feel hysterical when I see those *biscuits*".[2] Her "my blood" and "I like the tea" echo towards the close of "Crusoe in England":

> Now I live here, another island,
> that doesn't seem like one, but who decides?
> My blood was full of them; my brain
> bred islands. But that archipelago
> has petered out. I'm old.
> I'm bored, too, drinking my real tea,
> surrounded by uninteresting lumber.
> The knife there on the shelf –
> it reeked of meaning, ... [3]

---

1   Elizabeth Bishop, *One Art: Selected Letters*, ed. R. Giroux, 1994, 39.

2.   *ibid.*, 426

3.   Elizabeth Bishop, *The Complete Poems: 1927–1979*, New York, 1983. Subsequent references to this edition are given in the text.

Iain Crichton Smith's Robinson foresees his return from the island as an emergence "from the world of sparse iron into the vast cinema of sensation";[4] Similarly,, when interviewed by Edward Lucie-Smith on that same 1964 visit for the London *Times*, Bishop joked that "being in England is rather like going to the movies after you've read the book".[5]

Practising poets have to like their own company. A familiar dilemma in the poetic calling is that the solitude it requires is frequently just what the poet engaged in trying to write can barely endure. Frank O'Hara, one of the most sociable of poets, touches on such a conflict of impulses more than once. He has a "weekend coming up / at excitement-prone Kenneth Koch's", though

> I wish I were staying in town and working on my poems
> at Joan's studio for a new book by Grove Press
> which they will probably not print
> but it is good to be several floors up in the dead of night
> wondering whether you are any good or not

Elsewhere, he writes "but I didn't really care for conversation that day / I wanted to be alone", and a line later, "now I am alone and hate it".[6] Furthermore, the solitary devotion to writing is often consciously associated for the writer with an indirect self-therapy. The solitude of someone engaged in writing is then an aspect of the illness and a necessary context for its treatment. Trying to effect a cure can aggravate the disease. Adam Phillips has observed that "turning pain into meaning … is usually itself construed as a painful and often ascetic process. Like crime and punishment, that is to say, the cure can seem a mirror-image of the disease".[7] A fix of this order lies close to the heart of Elizabeth Bishop's life and writing.

Two

Bishop would never have allowed herself to describe the situation of her art in these terms. However, when asked late in life the classic question ("Why do you write poetry?"), she did say: "I was very isolated as a child and perhaps

4.   Iain Chrichton Smith, *The Notebooks of Robinson Crusoe*, 1975, 91.

5.   *Conversations with Elizabeth Bishop*, ed. G. Monteiro, 1996, 13.

6.   Frank O'Hara, *Collected Poems*, ed. D. Allen, 1995, 328. Bishop thought his poetry "mostly bad in the surrealist way – but I think he's improving …". (*One Art: Selected Letters*, 371). As for his sociability, Robert Fitzdale reports: "Frank called in the morning after the party and wanted to see Elizabeth again, and she said, 'I think we've had enough of Frank O'Hara' ". See Gary Fountain and Peter Brazeau, *Remembering Elizabeth Bishop: An Oral Biography*, 1994, 155–56.

7.   Adam Phillips, "Guilt", *On Flirtation*, 1994, 144.

poetry was my way of making familiar what I saw around me". Bishop also made a number of comments on the relation of solitude to writing which suggest her awareness of the dilemma I have outlined above. In the same 1978 interview, Alexandra Johnson said: "A luxuriant romanticism has grown up around how a poet should live and work. How necessary is that quiet, circumscribed life?" To which Bishop replied:

> Well, you get a place all set up, as I've done only one time in my life, which was in Brazil. You have your books and pencils and papers ready. Then you find yourself writing some of your best lines standing up in the kitchen putting them on the back of an envelope.

Interviewed twelve years earlier in that study, she made fun of its suitability for a poet: "Everybody who comes here asks about the view; is it inspiring? I think I'll put a little sign saying 'Inspiration' on those bamboos! Ideally, I suppose any writer prefers a hotel room completely shut away from distractions". Well, "Ideally", perhaps; but in practice it seems likely that what was so beneficial about her "place all set up" with Lota Soares was, at best, not only that she had a separate study, but also that there were other people around for company and support, though not too often: "I was able to work in Brazil because I had no distractions. For the first time in my life I had a study of my own, one that was peaceful, holding all my books, in the middle of a grove. Only on weekends did we have visitors".[8]

The relation of solitude to writing also involves the negotiation between the private and public in a poem's behaviour. In a letter to Robert Lowell about a typescript of *For the Union Dead*, she addressed the problem in the light of an obligation to tell the truth. She has two "minor questions but, as usual, they have to do with my George Washington handicap – I can't tell a lie even for art, apparently; it takes an awful effort or a sudden jolt to make me alter facts".[9] Yet can there be art if you don't alter the facts? Quite rightly, Bishop made a great thing of her devotion to accurate detail: "For 'Crusoe in England' ... Miss Bishop had a friend visit a goat farm to find out how goats open their eyes". Yet when George Starbuck enthused about the same poem ("I suppose Crusoe was a city kid. It's such fun, the accuracy with which you borrow flora and fauna for his little island"), Bishop replied: "It's a mixture of several islands".[10] This implies the condensation of experience needed for art, and Bishop's reluctance to allow such inner processes supremacy.

---

8. *Conversations with Elizabeth Bishop*, 98, 104, 18, 79.

9. *One Art: Selected Letters*, 408.

10. *Conversations with Elizabeth Bishop*, 73,86.

She hated Lowell's use of others' words, writing most forcefully about *The Dolphin* on 21 March 1972:

> I'm sure my point is only too plain. Lizzie is not dead, etc. – but there is a "mixture of fact & fiction," and you have changed her letters. That is "infinite mischief," I think ... One can use one's life as material – one does, anyway – but these letters – aren't you violating a trust? IF you were given permission – IF you hadn't changed them ... etc. But *art just isn't worth that much* .[11]

Lowell countered that it was his way of telling the truth, though George Oppen points to how such an aim can itself underline a poet's social isolation: "Not, perhaps I should add, that I take truthfulness to be a social virtue. I think it very probably is not. But I think it is poetic: I think really that nothing else is".[12] Bishop was perfectly able to see the comic possibilities in a dependence on social conventions, as in "Manners", subtitled *"For a Child of 1918 "*:

> When automobiles went by,
> the dust hid peoples's faces,
> but we shouted "Good day! Good day!
> Fine day!" at the top of our voices.   (121)

Nevertheless, manners and discretion, whatever else they may be, are a social filter for the ghastly truth. This social filter – like the "joking voice, a gesture / I love" (178) in "One Art" – is a form of respect for others and defence of the self. Defences, for Bishop, are not to be scorned or dismissed: "Do I have too many defences?" Wesley Wehr asked her; she answered: "Too *many* ? Can one ever have *enough* defences?"[13] This fundamental conflict in poetry, and not only poetry, between a need for truth-telling and for respectful social presentation, makes completing poems and publishing them extremely difficult. It focuses on the dilemma of the solitary imagination's relation to society, and also the self. Bishop's criticism of *The Dolphin* has Lowell's relations to both in mind: "I don't want you to appear in that light, to anyone – Elizabeth, Caroline – me – your public! And most of all to yourself".[14]

---

11. *One Art: Selected Letters*, 562. For further exploration of the issues involved here, see David Kalstone, *Becoming a Poet: Elizabeth Bishop with Marianne Moore and Robert Lowell*, 1989, 239–47, and Peter Robinson, *In the Circumstances: About Poems and Poets*, 1992, 83–104.

12. George Oppen, *The Selected Letters*, ed. R. Blau DuPlessis, 1990, 82. He is writing to Charles Tomlinson on 5 May, 1963.

13. *Conversations with Elizabeth Bishop*, 44.

14. *One Art: Selected Letters*, 562.

Bishop did not like critics foisting philosophical readings onto her work. Speaking to Wehr in 1966, she said: "Some of our critics can find something in common between just about anything. Comparing me with Wittgenstein! I've never even read him. I don't know *anything* about his philosophy".[15] However, as reported by Regina Colônia in 1970, she gives an account of poetry for her which, whether influenced by Wittgenstein or not, describes something of what could be meant by the art as a "form of life". Needless to say, she uses a less claim-making phrase:

> Writing poetry is a way of *life*, not a matter of testifying but of experiencing. It is not the way in which one goes about interpreting the world, but the very process of sensing it. When one is "on the move," one obviously *discovers* things, but that is merely part of the process. That's why poetry can eventually transmit some sort of experience to the reader, but that is far from being its purpose.

Here, Bishop is commenting on the role poetry plays in a person's life. The "process of sensing" involved finding moments in which objects and events became outward criteria for the isolated and unspeakable inner life. Here, too, is a Wittgensteinian aspect to Bishop's art, for her loathness to "put her feelings" into poetry meant that reading her involves an understanding of the works' surfaces as alive with implication for a consciousness experiencing life, but one which can only be understood in the terms of art, of the poem itself. Bishop's poetic strategies require readers to be tipped-off about the realm "Whereof one cannot speak", as in "The Bight", subtitled for this purpose "[*On my birthday*]", in which abandoned, stove in boats are "like torn-open, unanswered letters" and an earlier reference to Baudelaire is picked up by "The bight is littered with old correspondences" (60). Like a good symbolist poet, she does not allude to what the littering of the bight corresponds in the poem, though her liking for its closing phrase speaks volumes: "awful but cheerful".

Later in the same interview, Bishop turns to the place of poetry in the life of a reader. She has been expressing a fear that the "age we live in, with its terrible *boom* in mass communications, has things about it that endanger poetry

---

15. *Conversations with Elizabeth Bishop*, 43, and similarly 65. Millier gives a poised context for these remarks: "Anne Stevenson had sent the manuscript of the Twayne Series book for approval, and even though Elizabeth carried it with her everywhere she went, it was six months before she could bring herself to comment on it and grant her permission. Stevenson had remarked on some similarity of Bishop's philosophy to Wittgenstein's, and Elizabeth took pleasure in the idea that like M. Jourdain, who found he had been speaking prose all his life, she had 'a philosophy' despite her inability to describe it. Stevenson sent her a copy of one of Wittgenstein's books, which Elizabeth read haltingly but faithfully". Brett C. Millier, *Elizabeth Bishop: Life and the Memory of It*, 1993, 366.

as we know it", but then reflects that it is the place of the art in life which may ensure its survival:

> Down through the ages, poetry has been expressly spared for two good reasons. First, writing poetry does not pay, or when it does pay, it pays little. (The result is that only those who want to write poetry for its own sake continue with the genre.) Secondly, very few people read poetry, something which has enabled it to escape popularity and vulgarization. Thus poetry has evaded the distortions that it might have undergone.

> And even in the event that the modes of mass communication were to spread poetry as widely as they have popular music, there would emerge in all probability an underground – as in the seventeenth century – in which poems would once again be written on single sheets of paper to be distributed to a limited number of readers.[16]

Bishop's account of poetry as a *"way of life"* is Wittgensteinian not because she knows something about his philosophy, but because his later philosophy is an attempt to describe better how language, including the languages of the arts and art appreciation, ordinarily function in the lives of those who are taking part in the relevant "games", as when, for example, he is recorded as saying: "What belongs to a language game is a whole culture. In describing musical taste you have to describe whether children give concerts, whether women do or whether men only give them, etc. etc."[17] Elizabeth Bishop's "Crusoe in England" is about poetry as a *"way of life"*.

Three

The situation of Robinson Crusoe was an occasion and theme that Bishop meditated intermittently through much of her writing life. As early as July 1934, on the island of Cuttyhunk, she wrote in a notebook:

> On an island you live all the time in this Robinson Crusoe atmosphere; making this do for that, and contriving and inventing. [...] A poem should be made about making things in a pinch – & how it looks sad when the emergency is over.[18]

Twenty-two years later, in a letter from Brazil to Pearl Kazin on 30 November 1956, Bishop wrote:

---

16. *Conversations with Elizabeth Bishop*, 51–52.

17. Ludwig Wittgenstein, *Lectures and Conversations on Aesthetics, Psychology and Religious Belief*, ed. C. Barratt, 1966, 8.

18. See Victorian Harrison, *Elizabeth Bishop's Poetics of Intimacy*. 1993, 190.

We've had a terrific four-day storm here and there wasn't a scrap of airmail at the P.O. – perhaps the planes have been held up. Lota was away in Rio and I was all alone with the servants and the toucan (who has a sore foot) & the cat (who was being wormed) and the *roaring* waterfall. I feel as if I'd undergone a sort of Robinson Crusoe experience.[19]

We learn from Victoria Harrison that her poem was begun in 1963. Millier tells us that a draft called "Crusoe at Home" was close to being included in *Questions of Travel* (1965), and that the poem was "granted new life when she visited Darwin's house in Kent, took on considerable depth of feeling in the next six years and became "Crusoe in England".[20] This "considerable depth of feeling" foresees the death of Lota, the end of another relationship through mental instability, and the break up of her life in Brazil. Bishop seems to have returned to the drafts in the spring of 1970, and completed "Crusoe in England" during the summer of the following year.

The poet described herself in a 1951 letter to Lowell as a "minor female Wordsworth", but the allusion to "Daffodils" in "Crusoe in England", far from suggesting that it is a Wordsworthian poem of the imagination,[21] indicates a quarrel with such a view of her as a blithe nature poet:

> the poems – well, I tried
> reciting to my iris-beds,
> "They flash upon that inward eye,
> which is the bliss ..." The bliss of what?
> One of the first things that I did
> when I got back was look it up.

Lorrie Goldensohn notes: "What else does the insertion of that anachronism do for the poem but once again illustrate how exactly limited is the medicinal value of art ... Crusoe cannot verify that *solitude* is bliss until he returns to human society".[22] "Crusoe in England" has more affinity with Coleridge, as David Kalstone proposed, it being "a kind of 'Dejection Ode' countered by the force and energy that memory has mustered for the rest of the poem".[23] In

19. *One Art: Selected Letters*, 332.

20. Millier, 366–67.

21. See Bonnie Costello, *Elizabeth Bishop: Questions of Mastery*, 1993, 203–05.

22. Lorrie Goldensohn, *Elizabeth Bishop: The Biography of a Poetry*, 1992, 251.

23. David Kalstone, *Five Temperaments*, 1977, cited from *Elizabeth Bishop: Modern Critical Views*, ed. H. Bloom, 1985, 71.

her 30 November 1956 letter, Bishop moves from "the *roaring* waterfall" to "a sort of Robinson Crusoe experience" and immediately to "I kept reading Coleridge's letters". The "*roaring* waterfall" is also an S.T. Coleridge experience, combining the "mighty fountain" that "momently was forced" in "Kubla Khan" with its "woman wailing for her demon-lover!" and the storm with its "little child / Upon a lonesome wild" evoked in part VII of "Dejection: an Ode".[24]

Bishop's habitual self-denigrations are also present in the letter, when she concludes "I feel as if I could scarcely be said to exist, beside C". Kalstone's evoking Coleridge aptly isolates two strands in the poem, but I doubt that "Crusoe in England" has this "force and energy that memory has mustered", for it also deploys a Coleridgean irony by which its power and failure are inextricably intertwined.

In her conversation with George Starbuck, Bishop underlines the divergences between her poem and the original narrative:

> GS: I forget the end of *Robinson Crusoe*. Does the poem converge on the book?
> EB: No. I've forgotten the facts, there, exactly. I reread it all one night. And I had forgotten it was so moral. All that Christianity. So I think I wanted to re-see it with all that left out.[25]

"Crusoe in England" ends with an interjected aside: " – And Friday, my dear Friday, died of measles / seventeen years ago come March". Starbuck could have easily found out that Friday does not die at the end of the first *Robinson Crusoe*. Nor does he die of measles. He is killed by a force of "warlike savages" when trying to mediate between them and Robinson's ship in *The Farther Adventures of Robinson Crusoe*.[26]

Differences such as these make it difficult to credit the assertions of those, like David Lehman, who would read the poem as no more nor less than a monologue dramatizing Crusoe himself. In 1966, Ashley Brown asked the poet: "What do you think about the dramatic monologue as a form — you know, when the poet assumes a rôle?" Bishop replied:

---

24. S.T. Coleridge, *The Complete Poems*, ed. W. Keach, 1997, 251, 310.

25. *Conversations with Elizabeth Bishop*, 88.

26. Crusoe orders his man on deck to speak to the savages: "Friday cried out they were going to shoot; and unhappily for him, poor fellow, they let fly about three hundred of their arrows, and to my inexpressible grief killed poor Friday", and Robinson observes: "I was so enraged with the loss of my old servant, the companion of all my sorrows and solitudes, that I immediately ordered five guns to be loaded ... ", Daniel Defoe, *The Life and Strange Adventures of Robinson Crusoe*, Part II, 1903, 179. It seems likely that Bishop was unaware of this, and the *Robinson Crusoe* she read in a night is almost certainly the first volume only.

I suppose it should act as a sort of release. You can say all kinds of things you couldn't in a lyric. If you have scenery and costumes, you can get away with a lot. I'm writing one right now.[27]

"Crusoe in England" begins with memories of scenery and comes towards its close with bits of costume. It is likely that the dramatic monologue she alluded to in 1966 is the early draft, "Crusoe at Home", that almost went into *Questions of Travel*. Bishop discusses the benefits of the form not as allowing the poet, playwright-like, to dramatize the life of a character, but, rather, to extend the possibilities, or escape the limits of lyric. The ventriloquising of Robinson in her poem is a transparent device: "Crusoe in England" *is* readable as a retelling of the Crusoe story, but, as a mode of indirection for Bishop to meditate upon her own experience without the burdens of supposed truthfulness and inevitable exposure entailed by the then-fashionable "confessional" poem, it comes into focus (like Cowper's "Verses, Supposed to be Written by Alexander Selkirk") as a Wittgensteinian double-aspect text. We read it as Robinson, but understand it, metaphorically, as a commentary on Bishop's own creative life: "And this is how it is: if only you do not try to utter what it unutterable then *nothing* gets lost. But the unutterable will be − unutterably − *contained* in what has been uttered!".[28]

Four
"In Prison" is a short story driven by the assumption that unchosen solitude and isolation would prove to be the makings of a person, a person curiously like a writer. The speaker begins "I can scarcely wait for the day of my imprisonment. It is then that my life, my real life, will begin". Towards the story's close there is a long paragraph devoted to "Writing on the Wall":

I have thought of attempting a short, but immortal, poem, but I am afraid this is beyond me; I may rise to the occasion, however, once I am confronted with that stained, smeared, scribbled-on wall and feel the stub of pencil or rusty nail between my fingers. Perhaps I shall arrange my "works" in a series of neat inscriptions in a clear, Roman print ... [29]

The treatment of solitude in *Robinson Crusoe* has an autobiographical source in Defoe's imprisonment for debt. Paul Valéry imagines his Crusoe as an author

27. *Conversations with Elizabeth Bishop*, 26.

28. Paul Engelmann, *Letters from Ludwig Wittgenstein with a Memoir,* ed. B.F. McGuinness, trans. L. Furtmüller, 1967, 7.

29. Elizabeth Bishop, *Collected Prose*, ed. R. Giroux, 1984, 188–89.

with the "Oeuvres complètes de Robinson".[30] David Lehman draws upon a likely similarity between Bishop's story "In Prison" and her later poem: "like Crusoe on his island, he will attempt to convert an alien landscape into one that responds to his humanity".[31] Yet Bishop's account of life on the island in "Crusoe in England" is a return upon the insouciance of this assuming that all a writer needs for self-realisation is the condition of doing time. Her poem is a demonstration of how the imagination cannot be "sufficient unto itself".[32]

"Crusoe in England" begins with the appearance of a new volcano, and "an island being born", but this leads quickly to rather jaded nostalgia for the lost island, a sense of the jaded which is sharpened by something like resentment at the inaccuracy of other accounts, of other books. The imagination lives in a conflictual world of other imaginations:

> They named it. But my poor island's still
> un-rediscovered, un-renamable.
> None of the books has ever got it right.

This note returns towards the end of the poem when the relationship between Robinson and Friday is touched upon: "(Accounts of that have everything all wrong.)" Thus Bishop's Crusoe is not only isolated by his experience of solitude on the island and his sense of not fitting when he returns to "another island, / that doesn't seem like one", but from the start by the sense that his version of this pastoral exclusion is at odds with those of others who take it upon them to retell or interpret events. If Bishop's poem is read as an indirect account of her life in Brazil and with Lota de Macedo Soares, then it is difficult not to sense that these comments in the poem were not partly shaped by such experiences as the conflict with Time/Life over the book about Brazil; the difficulties with Lota's relatives and friends after her death in New York; and perhaps even having the young Anne Stevenson writing to her while researching the first book devoted to Bishop's work.

Similarly, the treatment of Robinson's imaginative activities on the island hardly adds up to an endorsement of Andrew Marvell's "Two Paradise "twere in one / To live in Paradise alone". The waterspouts on the island are imagined as

---

30. Paul Valéry, 'Histoires Brisées', *Oeuvres* vol. 2, ed. J. Hytier, 1960, 414.

31. David Lehman, "'In Prison': a Paradox Regained", cited in *Elizabeth Bishop: Modern Critical Views*, 142.

32. *ibid.*, 139

> Glass chimneys, flexible, attenuated,
> sacerdotal beings of glass ... I watched
> the water spiral up in them like smoke.
> Beautiful, yes, but not much company.

What kind of a writer would it be who could be satisfied with reading his or her own work in place of any communication with others? The sense of creation with and for no social end reaches to terrifying proportions just before the arrival of Friday. Robinson has "nightmares of other islands" and these "infinities / of islands, islands spawning islands" are particularly fearful because he knows

> that I had to live
> on each and every one, eventually,
> for ages, registering their flora,
> their fauna, their geography.

The mention of geography, Bishop's admiration for Darwin's prose, and her own visit to the Galapagos islands would be enough to suggest that this nightmare is interwoven with the poet's own creative temperament, and a knowledge that the registering of natural details, for which she was praised in her lifetime (see letters), could be viewed as a burdensome obligation, especially if such description could not be freighted with a humanly communicative purpose. In an interview in the *Christian Science Monitor* of 1978, Bishop admitted that there was "a certain self-mockery" in this passage that suggested to the interviewer, Alexandra Johnson, "the poet's duty or his burden",[33] and Travisano makes a similar point, calling this "a nightmare version of her life of observations: a career of infinite but barren travel".[34]

Much the same can be said about time, solitude, and what Marianne Moore famously calls "things that are important beyond all this fiddle"[35] in Bishop's poem. Her Crusoe attempts to capture the ambiguous emotions of his situation in puns:

> I'd heard of cattle getting island-sick.
> I thought the goats were.
> One billy-goat would stand on the volcano
> I'd christened *Mont d'Espoir* or *Mount Despair*
> (I'd time enough to play with names),
> and bleat and bleat, and sniff the air.

---

33. Cited in Marilyn May Lombardi, *The Body and the Song: Elizabeth Bishop's Poetics*, 1995, 140.

34. Thomas J. Travisano, *Elizabeth Bishop: Her Artistic Development*, 1988, 181.

35. Marianne Moore, *The Complete Poems*, ed. C. Driver, 1982, 226

The hill has only the one name in Defoe. This is an instance of poetic technique appearing to lack purpose without communicative urgency – prompting wit for its own sake, but a wit that somehow does not come over as funny, or helpfully playful, merely a futile pastime. The underlying, communicative purpose of the lines is to register precisely this problem.

"Crusoe in England" is a poem about the damaging consequences of thinking that the imagination will naturally thrive in the purity of isolation from society. Her Robinson, like Valéry's, attempts the transition from achieved practical well-being to spiritual self-sufficiency, but it does not seem to work:

> Home-made, home-made! But aren't we all?
> I felt a deep affection for
> the smallest of my island industries.
> No, not exactly, since the smallest was
> a miserable philosophy.

This self-correction, a characteristic of the Bishop style, leads into a stanza of self-criticism that makes good sense as an account of a poet agonizing over writers' block:

> Because I didn't know enough.
> Why didn't I know enough of something?
> Greek drama or astronomy? The books
> I'd read were full of blanks …

Indeed, Bishop's biographer, Brett C. Millier, notes that such questioning "does not occur to Defoe's Crusoe, whose great island discovery is the utter sufficiency of the Bible; his books are not 'full of blanks' ".[36]

Five

In recent years, many have been tempted to see "Crusoe in England" as a poem about Bishop's lesbianism, and, more particularly, about her relationship with Lota de Macedo Soares.[37] The editors of *Remembering Elizabeth Bishop*, for example, locate a date of completion for the poem as spring 1970, after the departure from Ouro Prêto of the poet's "secretary" from Seattle: "she found

---

36. Millier, 448.

37. See, for example, Joann Feit Diehl, *Elizabeth Bishop and Marianne Moore: The Psychodynamics of Creativity*, 1993, 104–05; Goldensohn, 250–51; Harrison, 191–93; Lombardi, 37; Travisano, 182.

herself suddenly writing again, for the first time in months, and finished 'Crusoe in England', her lengthy autobiographical poem about the loss of Lota".[38] Elsewhere in the same volume, Frank Bidart speculates that: "she was able to cut off parts of her mind in order to make the poem. For example, someone once said something to her about how 'Crusoe in England' is a kind of autobiographical metaphor for Brazil and Lota. She was horrified about the suggestion. And obviously the poem is".[39] Leaving aside Brazil for the moment, I think Bishop might have had reasons other than self-repression for being horrified at the suggestion. After all, the poem is 182 lines long; of these, only 13 are about Friday.

James Merrill, by contrast, notes that "the poem must have been written off and on in Brazil. A 1965 letter to Howard Moss says that it needs 'a good dusting' ".[40] He later goes on to speculate:

> Was Friday then neither soulmate nor servant, lover nor cannibal – just another teenager cavorting on the beach at Rio? I once idiotically asked the author, on being shown this poem before publication, if there couldn't be a bit more about Friday? She rolled her eyes and threw up her hands: Oh, there used to be – *lots* more! But then it seemed ... And wasn't the poem already long enough?

> Despite its concluding lines, "Crusoe in England" is an elegy less for Friday than for the young imagination that running wild sustained itself alone. Friday's role is to put an end to the monologue. Until he appears it is chiefly resourcefulness and bravado ... that keep Crusoe going in his solitary realm.[41]

This is a good suggestion. It vaunts the possibility of "Crusoe in England" being a gay poem. Then, after suggesting that such an idea is not far off wishful-thinking on his own part, Merrill points his readers to what the greater part of the poem may be about: the "young imagination" sustaining "itself alone". However, I suspect there is some idealizing going into this version of the imagination, which has stagnated and got Robinson into a terrible pickle before Friday comes along "to put an end to the monologue". "Just when I thought I

---

38. *Remembering Elizabeth Bishop*, 265: "in spite of the awful people here, I am feeling more myself than I have in 4 or 5 years, I think, and it is very pleasant. I have finished a long poem and have four more going".

39. *Remembering Elizabeth Bishop*, 333.

40. Kalstone, *Becoming a Poet*, 255.

41. *Ibid.*, 257. The exchange of letters between Bishop and Merrill is cited and discussed in Harrison, 191–92.

couldn't stand it / another minute longer, Friday came": this is how the poem's
tenth verse begins. What has come before is the history of a solitary, self-
reliant creativity, and, as I have suggested, it is hard not to feel that the story
ends in failure.

Here is the section of the poem devoted to Friday, who also appears in the
closing pair of lines:

> Just when I thought I couldn't stand it
> any minute longer, Friday came.
> (Accounts of that have everything all wrong.)
> Friday was nice.
> Friday was nice, and we were friends.
> If only he had been a woman!
> I wanted to propagate my kind,
> and so did he, I think, poor boy.
> He'd pet the baby goats sometimes,
> and race with them, or carry one around.
> – Pretty to watch; he had a pretty body.
>
> And then one day they came and took us off.

Bishop's line "If only he had been a woman!" has a foreshadowing in Valéry's
notes:

> Tentation de Robinson.
> Le pied marqué au sable lui fait croire à une femme.
> Il imagine un Autre. Serait-ce un homme ou une femme?
> Robinson divisé – poème.[42]

This thought about Friday's gender does not seem to cross the mind of Defoe's
Robinson:

> It happen'd one Day about Noon going towards my Boat, I was
> exceedingly surpiz'd with the Print of a Man's naked Foot on the Shore,
> which was very plain to be seen in the Sand: I stood like one Thunder-
> struck, or as if I had seen an Apparition ... .[43]

The original Robinson is too concerned about his physical safety to find it in
his mind to wonder if it might be a large-footed woman. Both Valéry's and
Bishop's figures inhabit physically safe places in which it is their mental security
that most concerns their creators.

---

42. Paul Valéry, *Oeuvres*, 1960, 415.

43. Daniel Defoe, *Robinson Crusoe,* ed. M. Shinagel, 1994, 112.

Perhaps there is an allusion here to John Donne's "We kill ourselves to propagate our kind".[44] What this prompts is the thought that Bishop's passage about Friday is also alive with half-suppressed reflections on the non-reproductive nature of gay sexuality. After all, if there is an echo of Donne here, it starts thought about an ambivalence towards heterosexual coupling embedded in the curious phrasing with which Bishop's Crusoe expresses the desire to have children. There might even be an ambiguity in the phrase "my kind" (as in the Isherwood title *Christopher and his Kind*), which would underline the compulsory contradiction in homosexuality, for however active you are in the promotion of gay culture, it nonetheless happens that, for the most part, you need heterosexuals to propagate gays. Numerous critics have taken "Crusoe in England" to be an implicitly lesbian poem, yet it is perhaps worth bearing in mind that Bishop was hardly the poet to produce an anthem, however discreetly or indirectly. Her George Washington handicap would oblige her to look more squarely at the case than such a piece of counter–cultural propaganda would allow. She had, after all, lived during the previous twenty years through two important lesbian relationships both of which had ended painfully, and "Crusoe in England" seems to have been finally completed in a lull after her "secretary" had returned to North America from Ouro Prêto for psychiatric treatment.

Six

In her acute reading of "Crusoe in England", Joanne Feit Diehl addresses by means of Melanie Klein's writings and object-relations theory the issue of Bishop's art as reparation. She contrasts the poem with Bishop's memoir "In the Village": "If 'In the Village' sketches a psychically successful journey from mourning to reparation, 'Crusoe in England' delineates a similar trajectory with a more somber outcome". She goes on to outline what this "somber outcome" is caused by:

> Friday's loss proves irreparable because in this poem of unreconciled mourning, no other object comes to take his place. The haunting singularity that marks Crusoe's island speaks to Friday's reality as well, for he can neither be forgotten nor replaced. Reparation here would mean the internalization of Friday into the self and substitution for him in the external world.[45]

---

44. John Donne, "An Anatomy of the World: The First Anniversary", II, 110. Travisano notes: "Images of frustrated or meaningless propagation have cycled through the poem, and they reach their culmination here", (182).

45. Diehl, 104.

This seems to confuse the narration in the poem with the poem as a psychic narrative about the poet herself. As I have suggested elsewhere, the poetry of reparation, so as not to be merely wishful, is obliged to include an account of actual damage as irreparable. What is required for reparation is not the replacement of the object lost, or the undoing of the damage done, but an emblematic action which makes a reparative gesture even as it narrates the damage. This work is achieved, if it is achieved, by the made poem in its figuration as an art object. In this light, there is no need for a happy ending to a work to perform a reparation.[46]

In the conclusion to her book, though, Feit Diehl offers a way of viewing "Crusoe in England" as a reparative action:

> Thus, a text such as "Crusoe in England" can be understood as the delineation of an insufficient holding environment and the narrator's attempts to create his own idiom of care against a background of wondrous depletion. Indeed, the compensatory nature of object-relations aesthetics gestures towards a fundamental theory of art: namely, that creativity springs from the desire to make reparation to the limited mother, to return to the holding environment reconceived by the daughter-poet, an environment that through its reformulation attempts to make up the deficit of the original, infantile relation.

While this outlines in psychoanalytic terms what a reparative poetic text might be doing, it remains uncommitted about whether "Crusoe in England" is such a text, for, as she had earlier concluded: "If, as in Bishop's case, the relationship (with the mother) is marked by disruption and abandonment, is it any wonder that all the inventiveness in Crusoe's possession cannot redress his subsequent loss?"[47] No, I suppose not; but more difficult questions might be: can all the poetic inventiveness in Bishop's possession redress, or offer an emblematic reparation for her subsequent loss? Is "Crusoe in England" an attempt to do this? Feit Diehl's account seems to conclude that the poem is an attempted reparation, one that fails at the narrative level. My version of reparative poetry would *expect* it to fail at the narrative level, but allow for its achieving something in its diction, tone, and form – if read as working in contrapuntal relation to the narrative of loss.

Lota's psychiatrist in Rio had been trained by Melanie Klein, and in a letter to Robert Lowell of 30 March 1959, she refers to the object relations theorist in the context of literary rivalry: "I am delighted to hear that Elizabeth [Lowell's then wife] has been writing so much – although envious, too, I suppose. (See

---

46. See Robinson, *In the Circumstances*, 1–23.

47. Diehl, 108, 105.

a grim little book by Melanie Klein, *Envy and Gratitude* – superb in its horrid way.)"[48] Bishop's response to the theory appears both divided and uncommitted. Moreover, there is another possibility beyond Joanne Feit Diehl's, which is that "Crusoe in England" is a refusal of reparation, an account of someone who, however in need of repair, prefers for the sake of loyalty to loss, the harder way of doing without it. Thus, for "Crusoe in England", the exploration of solitude and imagination is not a separate issue from isolation and sexual orientation; the isolation is also an instance of a sensibility suffused with its experiences, sexual or otherwise.

One last reason why the poem seems to turn its back on consolations of whatever kind is that in this poem's view, the art of poetry is not to be idealized as an unequivocal good, standing off from the accidents and incoherences of experiences in and of the world, able to bring to bear upon narrations of suffering its healing balms of technique. For Bishop, the benefits of poetry were only to be had in relation to itself:

> People seem to think that doing something like writing a poem makes one happier in life. It doesn't solve anything. Perhaps it does at least give one the satisfaction of having done a thing well or having put in a good day's work.[49]

Poetry, and the life of writing, the solitude and devotion which it requires, are inextricably interwoven with the suffering and the damage. "I wanted to study medicine", Bishop recalled in 1976, "But when I'd gotten out of college I'd already published several things and – and I think Miss Moore discouraged me".[50] In her practice of poetry, to recall Adam Phillips's terms, it is not that "the cure can seem a mirror-image of the disease", but rather that the seeming-cure is an aspect of the apparent sickness. For those of us who, like John Keats, have put faith in the healing powers of poetry, this is the hardest lesson to be experienced when reading "Crusoe in England".

---

48. *One Art: Selected Letters*, 371.

49. *Conversations with Elizabeth Bishop*, 41.

50. *Ibid.*, 57.

METAPHYSICAL SURREALISM IN BISHOP

CHERYL WALKER

It is perhaps obvious that surrealism was bound up with certain metaphysical notions typical of Modernism such as immanent transcendence and super-subjectivity, notions that intersect with religious concerns especially in mysticism. Yet surrealism is often discussed apart from religion, and, since I plan in this essay to consider Elizabeth Bishop's religious preoccupations as they connect to the strategies of surrealism, it may be well to begin by establishing what Neal Oxenhandler calls "the sublime point" in surrealist poetics.[1] In an essay on "the situation of the self" in Cocteau, Breton, and Ponge, Oxenhandler explores Breton's "dynamic, hallucinating movement past a series of disparate landscapes which have a mysterious revelatory power …" (61). He names as "the sublime point" the moment when a deep connection is made between disparate forces threatening the self with meaninglessness and loss:

> The voyage is both concrete and internal. Not only does it reveal strange landscapes, it also reveals the hidden inner landscape of the self, that "sublime point" where all contraries are resolved in a fusion best conveyed through the metaphor, a device more necessary than any other to the surrealist ontology. For it is the metaphor that conveys best the sense of mental process; and the surrealist poem is the mind in act at its most intense, most visionary peak – striving for the "sublime point". (61)

It has recently been suggested by Barbara Page that Elizabeth Bishop's practice was not metaphoric but metonymic. That is, connections in her work are furnished by the continuing process of association rather than by the controlling and subjugating ontology of fixed metaphorical relations. However, metaphor as it functions in Oxenhandler's discussion of surrealism is not the stabilizing totality it sometimes appears to be, because the most consistent aspect of Breton's poetry, according to Oxenhandler, is "the way in which language

---

1. Neal Oxenhandler, "Cocteau, Breton, and Ponge: The Situation of the Self", in *About French Poetry from Dada to "Tel Quel"*, ed. Mary Ann Caws, Detroit, 1974. Further references to this essay are given as page numbers in the text.

reproduces the psyche in a state of free play" (60). For him, the use of analogy, juxtaposition, and metaphor allows the inner self to be revealed "as a constant surging up of words and images in ever new constellations" (62).

In Oxenhandler's discussion of the inner self, and "the various forces that are dynamically at play within the person" (67) one might miss the larger, extra-personal dimensions of Breton's ambitions which aimed at nothing short of resolving the great problems of human existence and achieving the ultimate liberation of humanity. In the section of the first manifesto entitled "Secrets of the Magic Art of Surrealism", Breton speaks of the images that emerge in the mind at play:

> The mind is gradually convinced of the supreme reality of these images. At first only submitting to them, it soon observes that they flatter its reason, thereby increasing its knowledge. It becomes aware of unlimited expanses in which its desires are manifested, in which the *pro* and *con* are forever being minimized, in which its darkness conceals its presence. It proceeds, borne along by those images which give it pleasure, which hardly leave it time to blow on the fire of its fingers. This is the most beautiful of nights, *the night of lightning* ; compared to it, day is night.[2]

Should one have missed the distinctly religious valence of this language, Breton goes on to quote Novalis to the effect that the human tendency to fall short of pursuing the ideal relations genuinely desired by the mind, and accessible through its spontaneous imagery, might be compared to the fall from Reformation Protestantism into Lutheranism. In the ending to this famous essay, Breton vatically proclaims "Existence lies elsewhere".

Elizabeth Bishop's attraction to surrealism seems at first blush nowhere near as grandiose or as optimistic as Breton's. One might conclude that her use of it comes down to nothing more than an appreciation for the "marvellous" as it is revealed by surprising juxtapositions. In an untitled essay on the year 1968, held in the Bishop archive at Vassar College, she writes about the San Francisco rock and roll scene as bizarre and chaotic "but NOT surrealistic[.] [T]he marriage of an umbrella and a sewing machine – that's poetry – this was just childish".[3] Here Bishop, like Breton, invokes Lautréamont's statement that a certain sensation might be as "beautiful as the chance meeting of an umbrella and a sewing machine on a dissection table".[4] For Bishop this formula does have something important to say about poetry. As Thomas Travisano

---

2. André Breton, "Secrets of the Magic Art of Surrealism", in *Modern Continental Literary Criticism*, ed. O.B. Hardison, Jr. New York, 1962, 308–09.

3. Elizabeth Bishop, *Papers*, Vassar College Library, Poughkeepsie.

4. Michael Benedikt, *The Poetry of Surrealism: An Anthology*, Boston, 1974, xviii.

puts it, surrealism's way of looking, its delight in incongruous juxtapositions, "got in the bone".[5] But just how much of a surrealist was Elizabeth Bishop?

A number of critics – Travisano, Barbara Page, Richard Mullen – have pondered the relations, both positive and negative, between surrealism and Bishop's own poetics. All agree that she too cultivated the interpenetration of the conscious mind with material from the unconscious. In "Off-Beat Claves, Oblique Realities", Barbara Page comments:

> Like the surrealists, Bishop refused to make sharp distinctions between the conscious and the unconscious, and sought glimpses into truths that cannot be seen "full-face", although she did not share their enthusiasm for irrationalism in art. In this regard Bishop might be aligned with another American poet, Robert Frost: both valued the glimpse as a means of reaching beyond systematic observation, yet both balanced skepticism against outbreaks of the marvellous and insisted that poetry should be regulated by formal order.[6]

Richard Mullen begins his essay on "Elizabeth Bishop's Surrealist Inheritance" by saying:

> Some of the enchanted mystery which permeates Elizabeth Bishop's poetry arises from her preoccupation with dreams, sleep, and the borders between sleeping and waking. Her poems contain much of the magic, uncanniness and displacement associated with the works of the surrealists, for she too explores the workings of the unconscious and the interplay between conscious perceptions and dream. Although she draws very little from the surrealists' extreme experiments in technique, she does inherit the liberating bequest of their imaginative breakthroughs, and in an original and unobtrusive manner, she assimilates various surrealist aspirations into her poetic practice.[7]

In addition to building upon these critics' insights, I would like to focus particularly on this idea of "aspirations", the loftiness and hunger that Breton insists upon when, in the section of the first "Surrealist Manifesto" entitled "Against Death", he proclaims: "Whether you like it or not, there is matter here to satisfy several requirements of the mind. All these images seem to

---

5.   Thomas J. Travisano, *Elizabeth Bishop: Her Artistic Development*, Charlottsville, 1988.

6.   Barbara Page, "Off-Beat Claves, Oblique Realities: The Key West Notebooks of Elizabeth Bishop", in *Elizabeth Bishop: The Geography of Gender*, ed. Marilyn May Lombardi, Charlottesville, 1993, 200.

7.   Richard Mullen, "Elizabeth Bishop's Surrealist Inheritance", in *American Literature*, 54 (March 1982), 63.

testify that the mind is ripe for something other than the anodyne pleasures it usually permits itself" (309–10).

It is my belief that Bishop was always interested in something beyond mere delight, even the delight of putting things together in new ways. Symbolism and, to a greater extent, surrealism offered her a vault and a purchase, a leap out of unanswerable pain and the deadly dailyness of life but also the promise of access to, of a grip on, another level of reality we might well describe as the province of religion.

In many of Bishop's early surrealist poems, as Thomas Travisano rightly shows, the failure to achieve this level of "purchase" is rehearsed in poem after poem: "The pattern of search and frustration", Travisano writes, "is typical of Bishop's early dream poems. They are enigmatic because they present a writer grappling with the enigma of self. Their irony is often, in a veiled way, self-directed, because she longs to get outside herself but can't escape".[8]

Strange as it seems, from some perspectives, one might even speak of the theme of frustration that emerges here as related to the death of God. In "Paris, 7 A.M." the poet asks:

> Where is the ammunition, the piled-up balls
> with the star-splintered hearts of ice?
> This sky is no carrier-warrior-pigeon
> escaping endless intersecting circles.
> It is a dead one, or the sky from which a dead one fell.
> The urns have caught his ashes or his feathers.[9]

And then the poet asks "When did the star dissolve … ?" I take this questioning to be paradigmatic of the search and the longing in so many of Bishop's poems, a hunger for the metaphysical that Bonnie Costello also notes where she writes:

> Religious rhetoric of the soul and of divinity haunts Bishop's poems. Even in her most descriptive work, she searches for a supersensible meaning or authority to which she might submit.[10]

Bishop's principal disagreement with the surrealists had to do not with their metaphysics but with the inadequacy of their psychology, their refusal to take seriously the destructive obsessions locked in the psyche. "(As if a river should carry all / The scenes that it had once reflected / shut in its waters, and not

---

8. Travisano, 45.

9. Elizabeth Bishop, *The Complete Poems: 1927–1979*, New York, 1984, 26. All further references to this edition are given in the text.

10. Bonnie Costello, *Elizabeth Bishop: Questions of Mastery*, Cambridge, MA, 1991, 91.

floating/ on momentary surfaces)", she muses in "The Weed". Bishop pondered material that, despite the surrealists' claims, was not so readily accessible: eternity ("the sea / gone off with the sun" as her favorite Rimbaud passage put it), also the past and its legacy.

Few readers have noted how often Bishop takes up, in different guise, the great theological themes – pride, human obtuseness, the fall, and abandonment by God – themes also addressed by two of her favourite poets, George Herbert and Gerard Manley Hopkins. She once declared to Anne Stevenson, in a letter of January 8, 1964, that her sense of loss was not religious.[11] But for all her disclaimers, no modern poet was more thoroughly devoted to the questions, the puzzles, the psychological penetration, the serious aims, and the absurd practices of religion than Bishop. In an interview Richard Wilbur comments that, despite her insistence that she had no "philosophy", she remained attached to religious speculation, "Because of her bringing up, (she) had many Christian associations, cared about many Christian things, and had got (them) into her poems here and there. I think that's what she was left with, the questions, if not the answers, of a person with a religious temperament".[12]

Even "The Weed" might be read as not only surrealistic (as Mullen reads it) but theological. In an interview with Ashley Brown, Bishop mentioned that the poem was "modelled somewhat" on Herbert's "Love Unknown", but another telling connection might be made between it and Francis Thompson's "The Hound of Heaven", a poem Bishop surely knew. In a central passage which might well have lodged in Bishop's unconscious, Thompson writes:

> I slept, methinks, and woke,
> And slowly gazing, find me stripped in sleep.
> In the rash lustihead of my young powers,
> I shook the pillaring hours
> And pulled my life upon me; grimed with smears,
> I stand amid the dust o' the mounded years –
> My mangled youth lies dead beneath the heap.
> My days have crackled and gone up in smoke,
> Have puffed and burst as sun-starts on a stream.
> Yea, faileth now even dream
> The dreamer, and the lute the lutanist.[13]

11. Elizabeth Bishop, *One Art, Letters*, ed. Robert Giroux, New York, 1994.

12. Gary Fountain and Peter brazeau, *Remembering Elizabeth Bishop: An Oral Biography*, Amherst, 1994, 349.

13. Francis Thompson, "The Hound of Heaven", in *Chapters Into Verse*, ed. Robert Atwan and Laurence Wieder, Vol. II, Oxford, 1993.

Then the speaker turns to his divine pursuer to ask, "Ah! is Thy love indeed / A weed, albeit an amaranthine weed, / Suffering no flowers except its own to mount?" Both Herbert's "Love Unknown" and Thompson's "Hound of Heaven" concern the hardening of the heart and the need for penetrating grace. Bishop's weed, unlike Thompson's, provides no ultimate answer but does offer renewal: "I grow," it said, "but to divide your heart again."

Bishop wrote "The Weed" during her Key West period when she was often gripped by a depressed sense that her youth had "gone up in smoke" and that, as a poet, she was a failure. "Yea, faileth now even dream / The dreamer, and the lute the lutanist". It was also a period in which she was reading Kierkegaard. In a Key West Notebook[14], she records a passage from the Danish philosopher: "Poetry is illusion before knowledge: religion illusion after knowledge. Between poetry and religion the worldly wisdom of living plays its comedy. Every individual who does not live either poetically or religiously is a fool".

I think Bishop must have felt similarly that both poetry and religion negotiate between truth and artifice: in life, however, the comic aspect of ordinary experience is closer and more insistent. Even in poetry and religion, Bishop believed, serious matters are best apprehended with a light touch. To Anne Stevenson she wrote: "The good artist assumes a certain amount of sensitivity in his audience and doesn't attempt to flay himself to get sympathy or understanding. (The same way I feel the 'Christians' I know suffer from bad manners – they refuse to assume that other people can be good, too, and so constantly condescend without realizing it." "I don't like *heaviness*", she insisted in the same letter).[15]

For a way around heaviness, surrealism, and especially "the-always-more-successful surrealism of everyday life" appealed to her. She was especially fond of bizarre religious artifacts which she shared with her equally amused, and amusing, friend, Flannery O'Connor, once sending the orthodox Catholic a cross immured, like a ship, in a bottle. In an unpublished letter to Robert Lowell of January 8, 1955, Bishop tells a typical story of investigating the awful but delightful – that is, the marvellous – side of Brazilian Catholicism:

> The other night, Sunday, after the movies I went into a very primitive sort of funeral parlor in Petropolis. The door was open and loud samba music was coming out of the back room. There wasn't anything much in the shop but one large coffin pasted over with purple and gilt paper, and a few white wax babies, almost life size – votive offerings. But I bought a small wood Benedito, the crudest kind of whittling and painting, that is really terrifying – he's holding out the baby, who is stuck on a small nail, exactly like an hor d'oeuvres.

---

14. Elizabeth Bishop, *Key West Notebook* 75, 3a, 41.

15. Letter to Anne Stevenson, January 8, 1964.

Having declared herself an unbeliever, Bishop surrounded herself with religious artifacts, haunted churches, read Augustine, Ignatius Loyola, and St. Theresa for pleasure, and submitted seven Christian hymns instead of English poems for her *Poetry Pilot* selection, insisting that her reasons for admiring them "have almost nothing to do with theology".[16] Yet her flirtation with the trappings of religion was lifelong. At one point she thought she might use the word "Concordance" for the title of *A Cold Spring*, writing to Lowell, in another unpublished letter of August 19, 1951:

> It's now called "Concordance" – I hope you like that. From the title of one poem. ("Over 2,000 Illustrations and a Complete Concordance"). I had my doubts but yesterday morning, just as I was leaving the hotel in Halifax, I picked up the Gideon Bible and thought I'd make one of those test-samplings, you know. My finger came right down on the concordance column, so I felt immensely cheered.

Poetry and religion were always conjoined at some level in her mind and "concordance" alludes to that conjunction. She used surrealist techniques – especially metaphoric displacement, negation, incongruous juxtaposition, and the uniting of loftiness with the mundane – as means to suggest that concordance without insisting upon it. The bifurcated heart in "The Weed" might be an acknowledgment of the failure of belief or the premise of belief as it is in Herbert and Thompson. Bishop denied that she was a believer but she hovered about, never totally disdaining the importance of the religious life. To Robert Lowell she wrote on May 20, 1955: "I ... wish I could go back to being a Baptist! – not that I ever was one – but I believe now that complete agnosticism and straddling the fence on everything is my natural posture – although I wish it weren't".

The two rivers in "The Weed", the divided heart, assertion and denial – though in our secular academic discourse these are usually seen as problems for faith, they are quite close, as Michael Sells has recently shown, to traditions of mysticism, traditions that Bishop maintained a lifelong connection to through her reading. For Sells *apophasis* or un-saying is at the core of mysticism because it insists that "the source of emanation" is no-thing, "not a being or entity at all." Much of Sells' argument in *Mystical Languages of Unsaying* seems quite close to Bishop:

> Thus the hierarchical levels of being that are posited are unsaid from within. At the heart of that unsaying is a radical dialectic of transcendence

---

16. Elizabeth Bishop, "Seven Christian Hymns", *Poetry Pilot*, 1964, 14.

and immanence. That which is utterly "beyond" is revealed or reveals itself as most intimately "within": within the "just act", however humble ... within the basic acts of perception ... within the act of interpreting ... or within the act of love.[17]

These four concerns – the just act, the basic acts of perception, the act of interpreting, and the act of love – could be used to map the four directions of Bishop's poetry.

As part of that mapping, I would like to go back to the two rivers that first appear in "The Weed" where "two rivers glanced off from the sides, / one to the right, one to the left, / two rushing half-clear streams". I am particularly interested in what happens to the poet's vision at the point of their reappearance in "Santarém". It will be remembered that, during Bishop's early surrealist phase, the struggle for what I am calling "a vault and a purchase" was frequently attended by a sense of frustration and failure. This is only rarely the case in Bishop's later Brazilian phase to which "Santarém" belongs.

Bishop visited Santarém in February 1960. She loved the place, with its two rivers – the Amazon and the Tapajôs – coming together: "I'd like to go there for a rest cure or something – no pavements, – just deep orange sand, beautiful houses and absolute silence".[18] Though she began the poem within a year, she did not finish it until 1978 and Brett Millier comments that it "escapes its author's commitment to accuracy and takes on the air – of myth" (308). The whole poem has precisely that air of miracle, of the marvellous, that belongs to metaphysical surrealism, suggesting that Bishop did not abandon her surrealist training in her later years as some have suggested. One might focus, for example, on the blue zebus, the blue eyes left by the slavers, followed by the "blue pharmacy", bizarre and wonderful like the wasp's nest she finally obtains as a gift in response to her appreciation for it. "Of course I may be remembering it all wrong", she begins, in a gesture of apophasis. With the rivers "grandly, silently flowing, flowing east", the golden light "under a sky of gorgeous, under-lit clouds", it appears as one of her strange revelatory landscapes. "I liked the place; I liked the idea of the place", she comments. The place and the ideas to which it gives rise offer that vault and purchase so important to surrealism and to Bishop's conception of art.

To put it simply, "Santarém" is a visionary poem, as visionary in its way as moments in Vaughan and Herbert:

> Two rivers. Hadn't two rivers sprung
> From the Garden of Eden? No, that was four

---

17. Michael A. Sells, *Mystical Languages of Unsaying*, Chicago, 1994, 7.

18. Brett C. Millier, *Elizabeth Bishop:Life and the Memory of It*, Berkeley, 1993, 308.

and they'd diverged. Here only two
and coming together. Even if one were tempted
to literary interpretations
such as: life/death, right/wrong, male/female
– such notions would have resolved, dissolved, straight off
in that watery, dazzling dialectic. (185)

The whole poem is built on two-ness rendered as difference, opposition, and convergence, unification. It is not unlike what Michael Sells describes as the water-sun-fire (here river-light-embers) language of mystical paradox and parallax. Pairs and pairings – the two rivers, teams of zebus, hooves and feet, blues and yellows, miscegenation, a cow about to be married:

A river schooner with raked masts
and violet-colored sails tacked in so close
her bowsprit seemed to touch the church. (186)

But there are also pairs of things that diverge "in that watery, dazzling dialectic": the "modest promenade" in front of the Cathedral and the belvedere "about to fall into the river", the one tower cracked by lightning (during a "night of lightning" like Breton's?), but the priest out of town ("It was a miracle"). Of course, the gravest illustration of parallax, where two views of the object see it quite differently from different perspectives, occurs at the end when Mr. Swan considers the wasp's nest and asks, "What's that ugly thing?"

Is this a surrealistic poem, a religious poem, a poem about poetry and the imagination? I think the answer is yes on all three counts. It tells a story Bishop was always telling – surprise and delight in the material universe, fusion in the midst of confusion, a found object: arrival, longing for refuge "I wanted to stay awhile", and then departure, what Brett Millier describes as a return to "the difficult journey" (310). Bringing diverse materials together and then the moment of vision and transfiguration, these are what link poetry, surrealism, and religion in the world of Elizabeth Bishop. Like "Grandmother's Glass Eye" in her 1930s draft essay, her poems look "Heavenward, or off at an angle" while at the same time, their "real eye look[s] at you".[19]

---

19. Barbara Page, "Elizabeth Bishop and Postmodernism", in *The Wallace Stevens Journal*, 19, (Fall 1995), 166–79.

JOHN ASHBERY AND LANGUAGE POETRY

PETER NICHOLLS

The connection between John Ashbery and the Language poets is important for several reasons. In the first place, the way in which we read Ashbery perhaps more than any other contemporary American poet situates us, defines our position in relation to an artistic practice which, it seems to me, is ever more divided against itself. To put this another way, consider the following proposition from a well-known essay by Joseph Epstein published in the magazine *Commentary* in 1988. Epstein begins with a daunting question: "Who killed Poetry?" he asks. His answer is as follows:

> Institutional, linguistic, historical factors have also doubtless exerted their influence in pushing poetry into the dark corner it now inhabits. Yet nearly every explanation of the situation of poetry in our time ... seems to let the poets themselves off the hook.[1]

Poets, it seems, don't write what people want to read, and even though more and more work is being produced, with creative writing programmes ever in the ascendant, poetry in America has been driven into a "dark corner". It is possible, though, to read this situation very differently, as does Language poet Ron Silliman in his afterword to a recently published anthology of contemporary poetry: "[W]e in North America", claims Silliman, "are living in a poetic renaissance unparalleled in our history".[2] Poetry, it seems, is either dead or exuberantly alive, and this quite staggering difference in view typifies a widening rift in American literary culture, a rift of disagreement which turns

---

1. Joseph Epstein, "Who Killed Poetry?", in *Commentary*, 86.2 (August 1988), 17.

2. Ron Silliman, "The Practice of Art", in Dennis Barone and Peter Ganick, eds *The Art of Practice: Forty-Five Contemporary Poets*, Elmwood, 1994, 377. This volume is intended as a kind of supplement to two earlier path-breaking anthologies, Ron Silliman's *In the American Tree*, Orono, 1986, and Douglas Messerli's "Language" Poetries: *An Anthology*, New York, 1987. In his afterword to *The Art of Practice*, Silliman projects yet another wave of contemporary writing, giving a long list of younger poets deserving of consideration.

less on whether a particular poem is any good or not, but on whether it actually deserves to be called a poem at all.

A brief quotation from Language poet Charles Bernstein puts a finger on the problem. This is from his poem-essay called "Artifice of Absorption"; Bernstein is considering Helen Vendler's introduction to *The Harvard Book of Contemporary American Poetry*:

> ... perhaps the most irritating thing about Vendler's manner of argument is that it is always referring to what "all" poems do, making it impossible for her to even consider that some poems may come into being just because they don't do what some other poems have done. Vendler says she hopes readers will be provoked by some of the anthologized poems to say – "Heavens, I recognize the place, I know it!" I would hope readers might be provoked to say of *some* poems, "Hell, I don't recognize the place or the time of the 'I' in this sentence. I don't know it."[3]

The flashpoint of disagreement is an exemplary one: for Vendler, a great poem restores the world to us as something new yet familiar – "It insists," she says, "on a spooling, a form of repetition, the reinscribing of a groove, the returning upon an orbit already traced."[4] For Bernstein, however, that looping back upon an experience already lived produces only a kind of epistemological deadlock. For him, the linguistic world of the poem is a radically disjunctive one where the subject may easily misrecognize itself and others. In Vendler's view, poets "attempt that accuracy – of perception, of style"; Bernstein comments, "& what does accuracy have to do with it anyway?" This rejection of the residual mimeticism Bernstein finds in Vendler's position indicates a fundamental divergence or, indeed, an unbridgeable difference in aesthetic thinking. For the writing Bernstein represents – a writing which is "language–centered", deploying strategies of "diminished reference" – this writing spurns the allegedly second-order experience of "re-cognition" and accepts nothing but itself by which to measure its own "accuracy". One cannot but be impressed by the distance which separates Vendler and Bernstein; it is unlikely, one might think, that their bookshelves contain many of the same contemporary poets.

It is here that Ashbery's work occupies a pivotal position, for with the partial exception of Wallace Stevens he is the one recent poet to be admired on both sides of the poetry divide. Not that he is admired in exactly the same way, of course, for, as is well-known, it is precisely the part of Ashbery's work that so

---

3. Charles Bernstein, *A Poetics*, Cambridge, MA, 1992, 42.

4. Helen Vendler, "Introduction" to *The Harvard Book Of Contemporary American Poetry*, Cambridge, MA, 1985, 2.

upset Harold Bloom which has exerted a lasting appeal for many of the Language poets. This is the Ashbery of the 1962 volume *The Tennis Court Oath*, notable in Helen Vendler's view for its "wilful flashiness and sentimentality".[5] Of course, it helps if Bloom and Vendler are so negative about these poems – as Geoff Ward puts it in *Statutes of Liberty*, "if Harold Bloom dislikes them so intensely, there must be something in them".[6] As presumably there must, since the poets who have admired them – poets like Bruce Andrews, Barrett Watten and Susan Howe – are something more than the "rabblement of poetasters" Bloom intemperately described as the book's main audience. What is striking is the consensus amongst these writers about the central importance of *The Tennis Court Oath*. Bruce Andrews, for example, writes to Lyn Hejinian in 1978 that "(It is his most important book, even if Ashbery is now too scared or heedless to recognize it) ...",[7] and in a piece called "Misrepresentation (A Text for *The Tennis Court Oath* of John Ashbery)", Andrews declares that the volume "poses for us a radical questioning of established forms, yet at the same time, and so appropriately in its own form, it explores the implications of that questioning – not as an idea, but as an experience and a *reading*".[8] Susan Howe has similarly testified to the volume's importance to her development,[9] and Barrett Watten has written in some detail about the general impact of *The Tennis Court Oath* and its particular relevance to the work of Clark Coolidge.[10] Perhaps not surprisingly, this way of seeing Ashbery's career in terms of an early radicalism later sold short reappears in the work of some of the pro-Language critics. Jerome McGann, for example,

---

5. Helen Vendler, "Understanding Ashbery", in Harold Bloom, ed. *Modern Critical Views: John Ashbery*, New York, 1985, 180. For Bloom's dismissal of *The Tennis Court Oath*, see his "The Charity of Hard Moments", *ibid.*, 52. As noted in John Shoptaw, *On the Outside Looking Out: John Ashbery's Poetry*, Cambridge, MA, 1994, 125, the other influential text for the Language writers has been Ashbery's *Three Poems*.

6. Geoff Ward, *Statutes of Liberty: The New York School of Poets*, London, 1993, 110.

7. Bruce Andrews, letter to Lyn Hejinian, in The Lyn Hejinian Papers, Mandeville Department of Special Collections, University of California at San Diego, Box 1, Folder 6, May 27, 1978.

8. Bruce Andrews, "Misrepresentation (A Text for *The Tennis Court Oath* of John Ashbery)", in Ron Silliman ed. *In The American Tree*, Orono, 1986, 522.

9. Shoptaw, 42.

10. Barrett Watten, *Total Syntax*, Carbondale and Edwardsville, 1985, 90–91. See also George Hartley, *Textual Poitics and the Language Poets*, Boomington and Indianapolis, 1989, 23.

sees Ashbery's work after 1972 as a falling away from innovation and a growing cultivation of what he calls "suburban and personal interests".[11]

In what follows I shall be less concerned with this representation of Ashbery's later career than with the significance of *The Tennis Court Oath* as an apparently pivotal text. For with the benefit of some critical hindsight it is easy to see how various features of this volume might provide a forceful example for poets like Bruce Andrews. While, as John Shoptaw observes, the poems are not uniformly disruptive,[12] the work is marked by a mordantly humorous management of genre, voice and context. The most striking poems from this point of view are those which set the pronominal self adrift in a kaleidoscopic whirl of tones and idioms. (The technique, of course, would become a recurring feature of Ashbery's work, though the aggressive abruptness of the self's mutations in *The Tennis Court Oath* would be eased into the more sinuous mutations of the extended period in many of the later volumes.) Ashbery has often commented on this aspect of his writing – for example: "I find it very easy to move from one person in the sense of a pronoun to another and this again helps to produce a kind of polyphony in my poetry ... ."[13] Pronouns are thus envisaged as merely linguistic items rather than distinct positionalities, and this dissolution of the self in writing would have important reverberations for younger poets. In the interview from which I have quoted, for example, Ashbery goes on to remark "a loosening of syntactical connections that allows experience to happen rather than to make sense".

It is not just a case, then, of fractioning the self into different "voices", but of defining subjectivity as a process which unfolds as the poem, ostensibly without an end in view. Compare this comment by Rae Armantrout, one of the most interesting of the Language poets:

> The pronouns are fairly arbitrary in my poetry. I would imagine this is so for many other writers as well. Like the characters in dreams, pronouns are aspects of oneself. I may choose a pronoun for the tone it creates.

---

11. Jerome McGann, "Contemporary Poetry, Alternate Routes", *Critical Inquiry*, XIII, Spring, 1987, 627. See also Andrew Ross, "The New Sentence and the Commodity Form: Recent American Writing", in Cary Nelson and Lawrence Grossberg, eds *Marxism and the Interpretation of Culture*, London, 1988, 370. For a critique of this view of Ashbery's development, see Vernon Shetley, *After the Death of Poetry: Poet and Audience in Contemporary America*, Durham NC and London, 1983, 144–48.

12. Shoptaw, *On the Outside Looking Out*, 44. "Only a third of the volume's poems aggressively disrupt grammar, syntax, punctuation and physical layout. The rest are written in an 'intermediate' style and some (ten or so) would not be out of pace in *Some Trees*."

13. Interview with Ashbery in 1972 quoted in Margorie Perloff, *Poetic License: Essays on Modernist and Postmodernist Lyric*, Evanston, 1990, 280.

For instance, using *you* can make a poem sound either seductive or confrontational. I provide *little* context for these pronouns partly because I am not necessarily trying to establish them as solid identities, separate from myself. I'm interested in the multiplicity, and also the duplicity, of inner voices ... the ideation is the process of forming ideas – that is more than one. Thinking may be mainly sensing relations. I can connect ideation in this way with my interest in internal voices.[14]

Armantrout's way of linking multiplicity with duplicity has a curious relevance to the work I am considering here. It is as if, for Ashbery, the force of the lyric convention and the range of its "authentic" voices are so powerful that the poet is compelled to take evasive action. In the first place, the poems are radically decontextualised; the more detail we are given, the less securely situated the language seems to be (as Bruce Andrews observes, "a welter of adjectives has not added up to an external world").[15] Yet while there is an obvious fascination with forms of concealment and hiding in the poems – Ashbery constantly conjures with clues which have dropped out of detective stories – the question remains as to what was there to be hidden in the first place. If there is, as he says in the much later *Self-Portrait*, "no point of view / like the 'I' in a novel",[16] we can begin to see how the Language poets might have found hints of their own view, that (in Barrett Watten's words) "inner speech is social", and that "there is a substrate in which 'language' itself speaks, not just is spoken by a speaker".[17] In *The Tennis Court Oath*, Ashbery clearly taps one vein of the tradition running through Dada and Surrealism for which, once more in Watten's words, "language and psyche (are) a kind of vast reservoir for collage".[18] It is the *principle* of collage which is important here, rather than the materials themselves. In what is in one sense almost a parody of Poundian modernism, Ashbery tends to choose trivial, often banal texts on which to work. John Shoptaw's account of the poem "Europe" and its debt to *Beryl of the By-plane*, for example, tells us much about Ashbery's methods of composition but it does not really help us to understand the poem any better. Indeed, the customary use here of ellipsis (the "leaving out business"[19]) and

14. Interview in Manuel Brito, *A Suite of Poetic Voices: Interviews with Contemporary American Poets*, Santa Brigida, 1992, 19–20.

15. Bruce Andrews, "Misrepresentation: (A Text for *The Tennis Court Oath* of John Ashbery)", 525.

16. John Ashbery, *Self-Portrait in a Convex Mirror*, Manchester, 1977, 56.

17. Manuel Brito, "An Interview with Barrett Watten", in Ron Smith, ed. *Aerial 8: Barrett Watten*, Washington, DC, 1995, 27, 29.

18. Barrett Watten, *Total Syntax*, 40.

19. John Ashbery, "The Skaters" in *Rivers and Mountains*, New York, 1977, 144.

the pseudo-declarative sentence not only block immediate understanding but assert its impossibility, even its undesirability.

This is a poetry of "how it feels, not what it means", as Ashbery puts it in the later *Houseboat Days*,[20] a poetry in which "thought" is not something to be articulated but rather something that is encountered in the making of the poem ("I always begin at zero", says Ashbery, "and discover my thought by writing"; compare Lyn Hejinian's related observation, that "where one once sought a vocabulary for ideas, now one seeks ideas for vocabularies"[21]). It is this aspect of *The Tennis Court Oath* which now seems so prescient, so indicative of things to come. For this reordering of priorities denies us the forms of identification we assume from conventional lyric at the same time as it also blocks the sort of hermeneutic impulse encouraged by *The Cantos* or *The Maximus Poems*. Take the first stanza of "Leaving the Atocha Station", a celebrated or, depending on how you look at it, infamous example of Ashbery's new style:

> The arctic honey blabbed over the report causing darkness
> And pulling us our of there experiencing it
> he meanwhile ... And the fried bats they sell there
> dropping from sticks, so that the menace of your prayer folds ...
> Other people ...   flash
> the garden are you boning
> and defunct covering ...   Blind dog expressed royalties ...
> comfort of your perfect tar grams nuclear world bank tulip
> Favourable to   near the night pin
> loading formaldehyde.   the table torn from you
> Suddenly   and we are close
> Mouthing the root   when you think
> generator   homes enjoy leered [22]

Ellipses and typographical spaces produce moments where sense simply fails, and in that failure we are meant to discover both pleasure and a certain eerie foreboding of incompletion. For poems like this (to adapt what Charles Bernstein has said of Clark Coolidge) "refuse ... the syntactic ideality of the complete sentence, in which each part of speech operates in its definable place

20. John Ashbery, "Saying It to Keep It from Happening", in *Houseboat Days*, Harmondsworth, 1978, 29.

21. Ashbery quoted in Shoptaw, *On the Outside Looking Out*, 6. Lyn Hejinian, "If Written is Writing", in Bruce Andrews and Charles Bernstein, eds *The L=A=N=G=U=A=G=E Book*, Carbondale and Edwardsville, 1984, 29.

22. John Ashbery, *The Tennis Court Oath*, Middletown, 1982, 33.

so that a grammatic paradigm is superimposed on the actual unfolding of the semantic strings".[23] If there is something a little too cute about some of Ashbery's periphrastic moves here – "tar grams" for "cigarettes", for instance – any attempt to transcode the lines confronts us with an unrelenting banality (as in Shoptaw's gloss for the "blind dog" lines: "While reading the newspaper … and smoking … we watched the seeing eye dog dig up a tulip garden for a buried bone"[24]). It is the rapidity of the transitions – often, as for the Language poets, a result of suppressing transitive verbs in favour of passive constructions and unhooked participles – which would make this volume so significant for later experimental writers. As Andrews observes, in *The Tennis Court Oath* "the construction is not a shawl, enveloping & smoothing the shifts, as in later work, but is at the heart of our experiencing these shifts at all – the jagged kaleidoscope of melancholia and expiration".[25]

One way of describing this effect is to say that syntax has somehow become absolute (or "total", to use Barrett Watten's word). To put it another way, the poem has set its face against what Andrews calls "communicative competence" and in doing so has repudiated any notion of linguistic "transparency".[26] It is here perhaps that we can see Ashbery's relation to a particular version of Surrealism. What is at issue is less the poetics of dream imagery than a sense of the anti-referentiality of some Surrealist language. This is Surrealism as, for example, William Carlos Williams had understood it in the thirties: "Surrealism does not lie. It is the single truth. It is an epidemic. It is. It is just words".[27] That view of Surrealism not as a poetics of the inner life but as a practice of *writing* is the one which helps us to understand how "Surrealism" could become a sort of portmanteau word for an alternative non-image based poetics in America running from Gertrude Stein to the Language writers ("It is simple," wrote Williams, "There is no symbolism, no evocation of an image").[28]

There is plenty of straightforwardly Surrealist imagery in Ashbery's poems, of course ("the spoon of your head", and so on,[29] the kind of thing exploited by the more "orthodox" of Breton's American follows such as Kenneth Patchen and Charles Henri Ford). Yet the line of development in which we might situate

---

23. Charles Bernstein, *A Poetics*, 60.

24. Shoptaw, *On the Outside Looking Out*, 44.

25. Bruce Andrews, "Misrepresentation: (A Text for *The Tennis Court Oath* of John Ashbery)", 522–23.

26. *ibid.*, 521

27. *A Novelette* (1932) in William Carlos Williams, *Imaginations*, New York, 1971, 281.

28. *ibid.*, 299.

29. John Ashbery, *The Tennis Court Oath*, 28.

Ashbery is actually closer to what has frequently been called "literary Cubism", a tendency best represented by one of his favourite poets, Pierre Reverdy. It was Reverdy, of course, who gave Breton the original definition of the Surrealist image as "a pure creation of the mind. It cannot be born from a comparison but from a juxtaposition of two more or less distant realities".[30] But where Reverdy differed from Breton was in the latter's refusal of any conscious "juxtaposition": "In my opinion", wrote Breton, "it is erroneous to claim that 'the mind has grasped the relationship' of two realities in the presence of each other. First of all, it has seized nothing consciously".[31] The difference in emphasis is finely caught in Kenneth Rexroth's account of Reverdy's work:

> Poetry such as this attempts not just a new syntax of the word. Its revolution is aimed at the syntax of the mind itself. Its restructuring of experience is purposive, not dreamlike, and hence it possesses an uncanniness fundamentally different in kind from the most haunted utterances of the Surrealist or Symbolist unconscious.[32]

The "restructuring" of which Rexroth speaks is primarily a praxis of writing, not of recollection; and it is here that we can begin to discern a sort of faultline which separates the canonical works of Anglo-American modernism – *The Waste Land, The Cantos, Paterson, A* – from what Rexroth calls "literary cubism". In the great modernist works, says Rexroth:

> … as in Apollinaire's "Zone", the elements, the primary data of the poetic construction, are narrative or at least informative wholes. In verse such as Reverdy's, they are simple, sensory, emotional or primary informative objects capable of little or no further reduction. Eliot works in *The Waste Land* with fragmented and recombined arguments; Pierre Reverdy with dismembered propositions from which subject, operator and object have been wrenched free and re-structured into an invisible or subliminal discourse which owes its cogency to its own strict, complex and secret logic.[33]

---

30. Quoted in André Breton, *Manifesto of Surrealism* (1924), in Richard Seaver and Helen R. Lane, trans. *André Breton: Manifestoes of Surrealism*, Ann Arbor, 1972, 20.

31. Breton, *ibid.*, 36–37.

32. Kenneth Rexroth, "Introduction" to trans. *Pierre Reverdy: Selected Poems*, New York, 1969, vii.

33. *ibid.*, vi–vii.

So in place of the unconscious as an absent scene to be represented we have this "secret logic" which, for Ashbery, entails a constant movement between "meaningfulness" and "randomness", as he puts it.[34] The terms Rexroth uses here – "dismembered", "wrenched" – point up the violence which shadows this act of poetic "reduction", a violence which in *The Tennis Court Oath* attends both the literary echo and the twisted references to "ordinary" speech. What results is a certain linguistic *opacity*, which is rather different from the referential *difficulty* or "the eternal dead weight of symbolism and allegory" which Ashbery finds in Eliot, Pound, Yeats and Joyce.[35] As Bernstein suggests in another context, we are witnessing a "shift of attention from the rhetorical effect (the thing said/depicted) to the rhetoricity",[36] by which he seems to mean that the primary focus of our reading now proves to be the prosodic intersection of different registers and idioms. And with this goes an emphasis on reading as a productive act – the reader not now working to restore a context to the poem on the page, to reconstitute fragmented propositions and bits of knowledge, but engaged rather in what Lyn Hejinian calls a "generative" as opposed to a "directive" reading: "Reader and writer engage in a collaboration from which ideas and meanings are permitted to evolve".[37] This is not just some sort of free play, however, at least not in theory, for the Language poets are intensely interested in the ways in which readers interpret messages whose context they cannot assume.[38] In such cases, a powerful self-consciousness is developed, one paralleling that of the writer. As syntax departs increasingly from the normative structures of everyday exchange, so the breakdown of simple, extrapolable "meaning" yields a proliferation of social frames or contexts, often triggered at the level of the individual word. In Bernstein's words, "Meaning is no where *bound* to the orbit of purpose, intention, or utility",[39] and when it escapes it reveals language as an endlessly rich but common environment.

---

34. Interview with Ashbery (1974) quoted in Helen Vendler, 'Understanding Ashbery', 185: "In the last fiew years I have been attempting to keep meaningfulness up to the pace of randomness ... but I really think that meaningfulness can't get along without randomness and that they somehow have to be brought together".

35. John Ashbery, "Reverdy en Amérique", *Mercure de France*, 344 (January / April 1962), 111, (my translation).

36. Charles Bernstein, *A Poetics*, 79.

37. Lyn Hejinian, "The Rejection of Closure", in Bob Perelman, ed. *Writing/Talks*, Carbondale and Edwardsville, 1985, 272.

38. See for example Manuel Brito, "An Interview with Barrett Watten", 38, on "quoted cultural conundra that, taken as far out of context as possible, work to lay bare the prior assumptions of communication ... as the possibility of poetic speech".

39. Charles Bernstein, *A Poetics*, 13.

It is here that we can begin to approach the limits of Ashbery's interest for the Language poets, for as Christopher Beach observes, Ashbery "does not appear to be deeply committed to a fundamental critique of language itself or of its operations within a social or ideological context".[40] Nonetheess, Ashbery's experiments in *The Tennis Court Oath* surely implied a sort of negative knowledge of social discourse which had a significant impact on early Language poetry. I am thinking particularly of some of the more extreme effects here, effects which create what is a now familiar packing or jamming of the poetic line (as in the passage which so dismayed Bloom in "Leaving the Atocha Station": "for that we turn around / experiencing it is not to go into / the epileptic prank forcing bar. to borrow out onto tide-exposed fells / over her morsel", etc.[41]). Ashbery's lines might be said to produce, in Bernstein's phrase, a deliberate "viscosity of thought" [42] which requires us to consider not only the obtrusive materiality of words, but also the tendency they have to swerve away from the paths of normal communication. Take, for example, Ashbery's use of what Shoptaw calls "crypt words", by which he means "both a puzzle, something encoded, and a burial plot, something hidden, forgotten, or simply covered over":[43] For instance, "it all came / gushing down on me", where the crypt word is "crashing", or "emotions / The crushed paper heaps", where "crushed hopes" gives the encrypted echo; or, in "Leaving the Atocha Station", "establishing the vultural over / rural area cough pollution", where the crypt word is presumably "cultural" ("culture vulture"?). Shoptaw's idea of a cryptonymic reading (drawn from the psychoanalytic theory of Nicolas Abraham and Maria Torok) is suggestive, though not pursued in sufficient detail to make it fully convincing. Indeed, one might wonder whether the very idea of a readability, at which cryptonomy aims, is misplaced in relation to *The Tennis Court Oath*, for when the apparently effaced word is restored, what we acknowledge is not exactly a repression – whose would it be? – but rather the jarring proximity of "poetic" to everyday language.

Ashbery, of course, would continue to be fascinated by the intricacies of everyday language, by its cliches and platitudes, yet this fascination would increasingly produce a play of tones and voices caught up within the paradoxically monological order of a reflective language. I generalise too much, perhaps, yet one can see how the measured movements of a poem like "Self-

---

40. Christopher Beach, *ABC of Influence: Ezra Pound and the Remaking of American Poetic Tradition*, Berkeley, Los Angeles, 1992, 240.

41. See Bloom's account ("The Charity of Hard Moments", 52) of his "outrage and disbelief" when confronted by this poem.

42. Charles Bernstein, *Content's Dread: Essays 1975–1984*, Los Angeles, 1986, 67.

43. Shoptaw, *On the Outside Looking Out*, 7.

Portrait in a Convex Mirror" might disappoint admirers of *The Tennis Court Oath*. For their part, the Language writers have variously – very variously, as Douglas Messerli's recent anthology demonstrates[44] – pursued forms of linguistic opacity in the conviction that this is the way to avoid the commonplace imaginary of expressive conventions and to confront instead the determining forces of language. It is important to grasp the political locatedness of this endeavour, for Language writing had its origins in the Vietnam period, as Lyn Hejinian has observed. When questioned in interview about the collectivity of writers associated with Language, she explained that "We discovered each other in the intense aftermath of the Vietnam war era, having had intense experience of institutions and disguised rationality. And by some coincidence, we all individually had begun to consider language itself as an institution of sorts, determining reasons, and we had individually begun to explore the implications of that".[45] What that exploration has often entailed are extreme forms of self-reflexivity in language use, forms which exceed lyric self-interrogation. Barrett Watten, for example, writes of one of Steve Benson's performances that:

> the performer acts out a continually reflexive encounter with his language, trying to hear what it is saying and respond verbally at all points. The total self-involvement can only undermine its own authority; the other is rendered intact, but it is simultaneously the speaking subject that is the other. Benson's work casts the shadows of lyrical self-consciousness in Ashbery and O'Hara into the light of public discourse.[46]

For many of the Language writers, that move toward "public discourse" has been the crucial one, and while many of their most powerful devices may have been learned from Ashbery and O'Hara, their push toward extreme forms of opacity has been intended to open an ethical dimension of writing more expanded than anything attempted in the lyric mode, however ironized. I want to conclude with some problematic, though characteristic, propositions from Charles Bernstein. To support his view that "Language is the commonness in being", Bernstein proposes that:

---

44. See Douglas Messerli, ed. *From the Other Side of the Century: A New American Poetry 1960–1990*, Los Angeles, 1994.

45. Lyn Hejinian, interview with Tyrus Miller, *Paper Air*, 4, 2 (1989), 34. Cf. Hejinian, interview in Brito, ed. *A Suite of Poetic Voices*, 84: "A major component of my poetics, or let's say of my poetic impulse, is a result of that war and the meaning of its never being named".

46. Barrett Watten, *Total Syntax*, 113–14.

The move from purely descriptive, outward directive, writing toward writing centered on its wordness, its physicality, its haecceity (thisness) is, in its impulse, an investigation of human self-sameness, of the place of our connection: in the world, in the word, in ourselves. [47]

Note how Bernstein takes linguistic opacity not simply as a means by which to enact or embody certain forms of mental process. For him, to grasp the "wordness" of writing, as he puts it, is also to understand language as "the place of our connection". If poetic language is "political", then, it is apparently because it can make a certain practice of reading the basis of an ethical relation which has been exiled from the conventional category of the aesthetic – this is, though, an "ethics" in almost the Levinasian sense, a recognition of the claims of others rather than a body of moral rules and values. We can now begin to see how far poets like Bernstein have travelled from the disruptive moment of *The Tennis Court Oath* at the same time as making its necessity absolute. For any kind of "clarity" or "transparency" is now taken to signal a lapse into conventional formalism. This is what Bernstein has to say about George Oppen, a poet whose major work, we remember, was appearing around the time of *The Tennis Court Oath* and who, more persistently than Ashbery, tried to construct a "social" poetics. Bernstein suggests that while Oppen manages to understand language as "the place of our connection", for him the temptation often still remains to speak *about* that connection. Bernstein notes acutely that Oppen's:

> often claimed commitment to clarity, however qualified annuls a number of possibilities inherent in his technique ... That is, he tends, at times, to fall back onto "clarity" as a self-justifying means of achieving resolution through scenic motifs, statement, or parable in poems that might, given his compositional techniques, outstrip such controlling impulses. [48]

Bernstein's observation invites us – rightly, I think – to read Oppen's work as a sort of hinge between modernism and Language poetry. In each case, he implies, a certain opacity in the writing directs attention away from self-expression toward language as the medium of social connection. Ashbery's work has moved in a different direction, though the experimental vein of *The Tennis Court Oath* seems to have gestured toward this horizon. We might think that Ashbery's refusal of linguistic opacity was wise; or we might think that it

---

47. Charles Bernstein, *Content's Dream*, 32. See also *ibid.*, 20, "... political writing becomes disoriented when it views itself as description and not discourse; as not being *in* the world but *about* the world".

48. Charles Bernstein, "Hinge/Picture", *Ironwood*, 26 (Fall 1985), 241.

led him to then produce affecting but ultimately comfortable work. Either way, the development of the devices of *The Tennis Court Oath* in Language poetry leave us to confront one of the major paradoxes of contemporary American writing: namely that its pursuit of a "commonness" in language has become wedded to forms of often intractable linguistic opacity. Does that, finally, relegate poetry to Epstein's "dark corner", or does it testify to Silliman's unparalleled "poetic renaissance"? The question is not one to be too hastily resolved, though Ashbery's work seems – tantalisingly and magisterially – to countenance both possibilities.

BEFORE AND AFTER LANGUAGE:
THE NEW AMERICAN POETRY

GEOFF WARD

One

This is an essay about voice, syntax and panic. After looking at a poem published by Charles Bernstein in the 1990s, I will ask questions about the relationship between that text and the poetic procedures and discoveries of an earlier generation, the one anthologized by Donald Allen in 1960 as *The New American Poetry*. The main focus of what follows is however John Ashbery's work in the Nineties. And so if this essay is about how we might situate Language-writing after the "new" American poets of 1960, (and vice versa), it also asks how we should view the continuing prolificity of a poet from the earlier generation, John Ashbery, in the light of both. Here however is the complete text of "Time and the Line" by Charles Bernstein, a prime instigator as well as practitioner of avant-garde writing since the first issue of *L=A=N=G=U=A=G=E*, co-edited with Bruce Andrews, appeared in February 1978:

> George Burns likes to insist that he always
> takes the straight lines; the cigar in his mouth
> is a way of leaving space between the
> lines for a laugh. He weaves lines together
> by means of a picaresque narrative;
> not so Hennie Youngman, whose lines are strict-
> ly paratactic. My father pushed a
> line of ladies' dresses – not down the street
> in a pushcar but upstairs in a fact'ry
> office. My mother has been more concerned
> with her hemline. Chairman Mao put forward
> Maoist lines, but that's been abandoned (most-
> ly) for the East-West line of malarkey
> so popular in these parts. The prestige
> of the iambic line has recently
> suffered decline, since it's no longer so
> clear who "I" am, much less who *you* are. When
> making aline, better be double sure
> what you're lining in & what you're lining

out & which side of the line you're on; the
world is made up so (Adam didn't so much
name as delineate). Every poem's got
a prosodic lining, some of which will
unzip for summer wear. The lines of an
imaginary are inscribed on the
social flesh by the knifepoint of history.
Nowadays, you can often spot a work
of poetry by whether it's in lines
or no; if it's in prose, there's a good chance
it's a poem. While there is no lesson in
the line more useful than that of the pick-
et line, the line that has caused the most ad-
versity is the bloodline. In Russia
everyone is worried about long lines;
back in the USA, it's strictly soup-
lines. "Take a chisel to write," but for an
actor a line's got to be cued. Or, as
they say in math, it takes two lines to make
an angle but only one lime to make
a Margarita.[1]

The extent to which this 1991 poem typifies either Bernstein's practice or the work of the Language group as a whole is open to debate. Its inclusion in the Norton *Postmodern American Poetry* anthology (1994) suggests that it appeared emblematic to at least one editor–reader. And "Of Time and Line" does exhibit a high-velocity absurdist wit, prevalent with local and personal variants across a whole spectrum of recent poetry, from Carla Harryman or Bob Perelman in the USA, to Lisa Robertson and Steven McCaffery in their different wings of Canadian writing, to Tom Raworth or Rod Mengham in the United Kingdom. Although the whole armoury of poetic Modernism (from defamiliarization, parataxis, and non-sequitur to surrealist image-making, dadaist provocation and dysfunctional lyricism) remains on permanent loan to the current generation, it is significant that the devices most frequently deployed in the significant poetry of the 1990s are those that lead most readily to *humour* . A number of possible causes propose themselves, chief among which is the leverage of poetry onto political and social reality at the macro-level. It is tenuous. Poets know this. The very incongruity of invoking Chairman Mao, East-West conflict, the bloodline and soup-lines in the throwaway one-liners of a lyric restates simultaneously both the utopian ambition and the actual impotence of any poetics, setting them in a vertiginous oscillation, an *unheimlich* agitation that is increasingly poetry's home.

---

1. Charles Bernstein, "Of Time and the Line" in, *Postmodern American Poetry: A Norton Anthology,* ed. Paul Hoover, New York and London, 1994, 570–71.

The poem in the Nineties is both a model of unalienated work, (to draw on a formulation of Ron Silliman's) and something that doesn't work at all because it is a purely verbal model, (to draw on the socially obvious). By contrast many of the New American Poets of the 1960 anthology were imbued with political energy and the hope for radical change. Interviewed by David Ossman in 1961, around the time of publication of his first collection, Edward Dorn was quick to turn the conversation away from the technical preoccupation with "the line" that had featured so prominently in his training under Charles Olson at Black Mountain College. Questions of measure could only snare both poet and reader in "a false problem":

> One of the things being more recognized now and listened to, I hope, is that poets are saying things important for every human being, and not being just poets so much. I guess I sound dogmatic, but I think we have to face, finally, that there has to be some hope for something actionable to come out of all of this.[2]

In the context of that interview and those times, "all of this" means the conjoining of what Dorn terms "a political poetry" and the attitude of protest brought to boiling point by the Civil Rights movement. What is "actionable" in this context entails not so much the settlement of grievance by recourse to law (to defer to the OED's meaning for "actionable") as an identification of the law itself as part of the grievance. At this stage Dorn was clearly able to share the giddy but combative optimism of what Allen Ginsberg term "the new consciousness" when interviewed for the same radio series. Of course the case is often made that the new consciousness retreated quite rapidly into stoned oblivion, the hope for something actionable bought off by the modest libertarian gains of the later 1960s. To Dorn, whose work both flowered and withered in the overly long sequence *Gunslinger* (1967–75) there would remain only the ashes of self-parody; "I guess I sound dogmatic" is the only phrase from the 1961 interview with any bearing on his recent work. Meanwhile, Ginsberg rose in cultural prominence as his work declined in power; the revolutionary aspirations of Diane DiPrima or LeRoi Jones / Amiri Baraka were never realised; Olson's fabulous aim of a Jericho-in-reverse, "to build out of sound the walls of the city" dwindled to a one-man Republic of gloom on Watchhouse Point. However, the tracing of a direct line from political disillusion in the late 1960s to absorption by irony in the 1990s offers the reader a questionable allegorization, disguised as a real map; (though it is an allegorization that institution-based critics who want to domesticate poetry will find cartographically irresistible in the future). By contrast with Dorn one could look to Robert Duncan and read real political success, however belated or

---

2. *The Sullen Art*, ed. David Ossman, New York, 1963, 85.

partial, in his writing on behalf of gay rights or against the war in Vietnam. And even where political outcomes have arguably been so partial as to be negligible, as in the "green" politics of Gary Snyder's poetry, (and no matter what one thinks of the actual texts) the relationship between writing and political efficacy has not been ironized out of existence in such a case, nor is it lacking in the hope for something actionable. Finally, and most obviously, the manifest political failure of the 1960s to deliver, except in those areas of consuption that would blur into the new world order, is testimony to the triumph of the latter rather than any weakness in 1960s writing.

If the argument has appeared to move away from a consideration of Charles Bernstein's "Of Time and the Line", that is so that the poem may now be re-read from a different coign of vantage. For, just as a narrative of prelapsarian romanticism heading for the 1970s rocks will not serve unequivocally as epitaph to the generation of 1960, so the Bernstein poem, so evidently characteristic of current tendencies, may yield a more complex and conciliatory attitude to that earlier generation than seems apparent at first. It *is* the case that feminism is the only current platform on which a poet could be handed the microphone with even a modicum of hope for legislation, unacknowledged or otherwise; in general, Auden's insistence that "Poetry makes nothing happen" has never been more true than in 1999. Across the enclaves in which the significant new poetry happens today it is fair to say that no political expressiveness occurs without immediate irony. However, it is equally true to say that there is no expression of irony in the new poetry without politics. Irony is (in a poetry that works) not a self-defensive posture into which the voice of the poem can retreat, pre-empting attack, but rather a division or duplicity of tonal approach, which reminds that we are capable of thinking in contradiction, and hence in alternatives, most certainly including the political. This ironic duplicity is at work in the vast textual mirage of Tom Raworth's *Eternal Sections*, in which a simulacrum of macrocosmic thought replaces the simulacrum of personal speech that characterised his early work, but is equally at work in the spoken finale to a reading by Lisa Robertson from parts of *Debbie*, an ongoing epic: "Good evening, Modernism". And it is at work in Charles Bernstein's poem, "Of Time and the Line".

While this poem deploys a witty discontinuity analogous to techniques used by other writers cited here, it also manifests a certain continuity of voice reminiscent of an earlier generation, but relatively unusual in Bernstein's work as a whole. The amnesia of verbal surfing show in "Whose Language", also reprinted in the Norton anthology, is more characteristic: "Who's on first? The dust descends as / the skylight caves in. The door / closes on a dream of default and / denunciation (go get those piazzas) ...". Of course "Of Time and the Line" challenges the kind of emphasis Olson laid on the line by virtue of its surreal facetiousness – you can never be sure where the next line is coming from – but goes on to challenge facetiousness via political memory, of Mao, the fall of the Wall, the "knifepoint of history". The abrupt darkness of Bernstein's jokes is their best feature. But if the poem challenges the Cold War line, the parental way with a poem or a hemline, by so doing it invokes – and actually laments, perhaps ultimately loves – the lost certainty of the parental. The old comedians George Burns and Hennie Youngman are weirdly but not mockingly treated; the same is true for Mother, and for Chairman Mao. Just as the title of the poem appears to satirise but also perpetuates the title of a novel by Thomas Wolfe, so the name "Frank O'Hara" is stitched into the poem's lining. The joke "if it's in prose, there's a good chance / it's a poem" virtually repeats a self-reflexive aside from and on O'Hara's poem of 1956, "Why I Am Not a Painter": "It is even in / prose, I am a real poet". Since Bernstein is far too knowing not to know that we will know this, it has to be asked to what extent the surface whackiness of his pseudo-narrative is at bottom nostalgic or even an *hommage* . (More subtly, it may consciously or otherwise be an apparent *hommage* which deploys semi-nostalgic, semi-surreal rhetoric in order to open up historical questions. If this is so, then the poem has joined a constellation of writings – including the work of Steve Benson, pre-eminently – capable of using O'Hara's work productively, rather than falling into the customary postures of either hypnotiscd fealty to its affectionate lyricism, or a patronising misreading of its manner for its matter.) That Bernstein's poem has a sharp or maybe wounded sense of its contemporaneity is signalled by its most anxious lines: "it's no longer so / clear who 'I' am, much less who *you* are". These lines imply that there was a time, time of the iambic or perhaps as recent as Mao's time, when it was gratifyingly clear who you and I were. Was that the time of Frank O'Hara in the Fifties? Frank O'Hara is the greatest poet of the twentieth century in the special sense that he alone makes the twentieth century seem great. His poems of the 1950s say that no-one was ever so happy in their time and place as Frank O'Hara. Yet they also say the opposite, speak of vipers, self-loathing and necessary cruelty in "In Memory of My Feelings", tell white lies, "the tendrils of fog trailing softly round their throats" in "How to Get There", a truly great poem that never helped anyone get anywhere, murderous though mild in comparison with the cleansing anger of "For the Chinese New Year & for Bill Berkson", poems all, as the painter and fallen-out-with friend Grace Hartigan observed, about "how to be open but not violated, *how not to panic* ". Perhaps American poetry of that earlier generation, often so ebullient and declarative in its stress on performativity and the individual voice, yields its finest moments on the verge of panic. One thinks of Jack Spicer, and of the psycho-babel of *Behind the State Capitol or Cincinnati Pike*, John Wierners' masterpiece of 1975, and of the nervous rhythms of Stephen Jonas's transmutations. These were all poets of the School of Boston, perhaps less a city than the hub of a certain anxiety. Taught by Robert Duncan, these poets were more able than most to see the darkness that lay beyond the control of Duncan's metaphysical rhapsody, and that had perhaps originated it. I read deconstructively, an operation made even more perverse than usual by the relative readiness of texts in this period to rebuff any such approach pre-emptively via their own extreme self-consciousness. What then of the most self-conscious of all, John Ashbery, anthologized by Donald Allen in 1960 as one of a school, considerably less represented than Frank O'Hara, but currently the most esteemed American poet since Wallace Stevens? What follows is an examination of Ashbery's work in the 1990s that must perforce put some of the themes set up so far on hold. Ashbery's is, however, a poetry that never panics, a refusal that gives panic an important, perhaps dominant, role in his work.

Two

Recently I examined a Ph. D. thesis for the University of London by a candidate writing on John Ashbery. The candidate noted in his Preface with an absolutely heroic evenness of tone that Ashbery had published more new poetry in the four years it took to write the thesis than Philip Larkin had published during his entire lifetime. It is true (and some would say, fortunate) that Larkin was relatively costive when it came to output. Nevertheless the prolificity of John Ashbery, now over seventy years old, is remarkable, almost Victorian. Equally nineteenth-century are the quotations from Walter Pater, Thomas Lovell Beddoes *et al* with which the verse is increasingly peppered, most of all towards the end of the 200 page poem *Flow Chart* (1991) with its double sestina on the death of the poet's mother, as far as I know the first use of the form since Swinburne's "The Complaint of Lisa" in 1872, and related quite consciously to that poem by its replication of Swinburne's rebus-words. Like the Ph.D candidate, I have risked losing my paddle in Ashbery's spate. Like one of Ashbery's own speakers about to commit himself when a squall hit, I was just getting ready to review the 100 page *And the Stars were Shining* (1994) when the even longer *Can You Hear, Bird* (1995) – which might have been more appropriately titled, *Can You Keep Up, Reader* – appeared. He must wonder if people now read, or merely dip into, or now feel that they have already read, each successive book. Perhaps this is the reason why the poem called "Like a Sentence" appears in *And the Stars were Shining*, only to turn up again word-for-word in *Can You Hear, Bird*. How many people noticed? Does it really matter? Is Ashbery's canonization now so achieved a phenomenon that were he to publish chunks of the telephone directory as his next book (which he virtually did anyway in parts of *The Tennis Court Oath*) it would not alter one line in a profile that is now set in stone, albeit *Symboliste* – marmoreal rather than craggy-Mount Rushmore in design. It could of course be argued, to return to the repeated poem "Like a Sentence", that to print the same poem in two different collections is not truly to print the same poem. If that sounds overly ingenious, the kind of filigrane from which academics' conference papers are spun, it is also a kind of no-man-steps-into-the-same-river-twice questioning of the passing moment to which the poetry frequently turns: "No two employees know it" as one of the voices in *Flow Chart* intones. So what this paper chiefly intends to ask about the prolific but endlessly valedictory Ashbery of the Nineties is, is it more of the same, a – to draw a phrase from *Can You Hear, Bird* a "being all alike", in at least two senses the *fin de siecle* , or do the self-differences detectable in books and poems from this phase signal more than signification's inveterate *différance*. Alongside the texts mentioned, plus *Hotel Lautréamont* (1992), I shall be referring to a book by the Canadian poet and theorist, Christopher Dewdney, *The Secular Grail*, (1993).[3]

Especially by comparison with his fellow-members of the New York School – Kenneth Koch, James Schuyler, Frank O'Hara – John Ashbery appears to have been born middle-aged. Russet tones and a certain Strether-like or Prufrockian ruefulness and reluctance have shadowed his writing from a surprisingly early point. An observer not a participant (with of course a concomitant exploitation, a la early Eliot, a la late James of all the observer's privileged access to melancholy overview), not so much a Bohemian flâneur as simply one who hangs back, riddled with and riddling through self-doubt, Ashbery's dominant tone is of patient doubting, striated by moments of near-derailment, near-resolution: "A look of glass stops you, and you walk on, shaken: was I the perceived?", "As One Put Drunk Into The Packet-Boat" (1975): "O I have to keep fighting back to find you, and then when you're still there, what is it I know?", and "Did I order that?" (1991). Frank O'Hara's accidental death at the age of forty has stamped for all time a kind of Keatsian, *carpe diem*-style glamour on his work, his poetry was in any case nothing if not vivacious. Of course O'Hara was used to darkness, too, but the overall upbeat and conversational ebullience of his poetry is and wants to be (to descend happily into liberal humanist sentimentality for a moment) life-enchancing. He even ends his lines, often, on an upward lilt, a balletic lift, as the dancers he moved among could do, but in, actually, a reversal of the tendency of the sentence in English to end on a falling cadence. Likewise though less interestingly, Kenneth Koch's poetry is nothing if not lively in its cartoon colours. James Schuyler's poetry, though more tremulous -*hurt* into linebreaks of the kind theorised by Creeley and the Donald Allen generation, rather than showing a vanguardist commitment – is not condemned always to stand outside of the expression of happiness, sociability, achieved communication. By contrast Ashbery has always been the first to rain on his own parade, thereby of course protracting its soggy but indomitable progress towards internment

---

3. Christopher Dewdney, *The Secular Grail,* Toronto, 1993. Subsequent references to this edition are given in the text.

in the canon; the "canon" being a cubicle in which a dead poet appears to continue to meditate; rather like the corpse of Jeremy Bentham, embalmed and on show in the University of London, but without Bentham's happy-go-lucky expression.

Anyway, death was always there in Ashbery's parade, and not just at the end of it, but spiking the drinks, whispering on the breeze, insinuated. "As you find you had never left off laughing at death, / The background, dark vine at the edge of the porch" ("Forties Flick" from *Self-Portrait in a Convex Mirror* [1975]). "One died, and the soul was wrenched out of the other ..." ("Street Musicians" from *Houseboat Days* (1978). While writing the poems that were collected as *A Wave* (1984), Ashbery nearly died, like Byron at the hands of his doctors, and though that crisis is alluded to only once, in the opening lines of the title poem, "To pass through pain and not know it, / A car door slamming in the night. / To emerge on an invisible terrain". *A Wave* is filled as never before with autumnal rumination and memento mori admonitions. "Therefore why weep we, mourners, around / A common block of space?", ("One of the Most Extraordinary Things in Life"); "It all wears out. I keep telling myself this, but / I never believe me, though others do", ("Down by the Station, Early in the Morning"); " ... we may live / With some curiosity and hope / like pools / that soon become part of the tide", ("A Fly"). In sum, Ashbery has always written with a sharp sense of mortality, and in his seventh decade, it is hardly surprising if the poems begin to converge on certain themes. There is however an important linguistic shift between the poetry of the Nineties and the work of earlier decades. However melancholy the cadence in the examples I have quoted, the poems illustrate that melancholy with brilliant images. In the case of a poem such as "Forties Flick", the deathliness exists in a balance, is a ground against which the vivid figures can be played. The poem of the image has dominated this century (at least) and overtly, in poetries as otherwise inimical as Surrealism, Yeats and Imagism in the Modernist period, to the crossword puzzlers so unfortunately popular in the United Kingdom today, Craig Raine or Paul Muldoon. One reason for the popularity of "Self-Portrait in a Convex Mirror" over other works by Ashbery stems from the fact that it is ingeniously but also quite literally a poem of the image. Ashbery's poetry in the Nineties is primarily one of syntax, rather than images.

It is not unprecedented for syntax to elaborate itself, even to the point of virtual take-over of an older writer's productions. The dictation of the later James, the revised versions of *The Prelude* or *Confessions of an English Opium Eater*, are among the obvious canonical examples. Perhaps as the brilliance of life fades, the urge to hold on to it, to map it, to seize it and fill all its space, the comfort that ongoing syntax provides against silence, is what is at work here. Minimalism in Samuel Beckett was always offset against a stoicism of syntactical accretion, the Unnamable's "in the silence you don't know, you

must go on, I can't go on, I'll go on". Or is syntax, in itself, revisionary? I have
not sat down to compare Richard Ford's recent *Independence Day* to the novel
of which it forms the sequel, *The Sports Writer*, but I am sure that a return to a
certain voice, the character Frank Bascombe, has caused the syntax structuring
that voice to lengthen. No doubt the operations of syntax as one uses it and as
one encounters it through reading are dissimilar. I shall read a short section
from *Flow Chart*, and set it against some remarks from Christopher Dewdney's
A Secular Grail:

> I think it was at that moment he
> knowingly and in my own interests took back from me
> the slow-flowing idea of flight, now
> too firmly channelled, its omnipresent reminders etched
> too deeply into my forehead, its crass grievances and greetings
> a class apart from the wonders every man feels,
> whether alone in bed, or with a lover, or beached
> with the shells on some atoll (and if solitude
> swallow us up betimes, it is only later that
> the idea of its permanence sifts into view, yea
> later and perhaps only occasionally, and only much later
> stands from dawn to dusk, just as the plaintive sound
> of the harp of the waves is always there as a backdrop
> to conversation and conversion, even when
> most forgotten) and cannot make sense of them, but he knows
> the familiar, unmistakable thing, and that gives him courage
> as day expires and evening marshals its hosts, in preparation
> for the long night to come.[4]

Language is always movement forward, streamlined into the
anticipation of an ultimate meaning. Meaning is where we are
going, it is our intention. Like a plant growing towards light, a
sentence grows towards its final meaning, it is teleotropic. This
ultimate meaning is the orientation of a sentence at any given
point in time. It is a magnetic field in which syntax is the compass
needle pointing to the true north of intention.

Both speech and writing are anticipatory motions, propelled by
the expectation of sense. The burden of teleotropism, of intention,
creates a performance anxiety deep at the root of our apparent
linguistic facility. The continual flight of the point of
concentration, tracking within the superstructure of intention as
a nomadic moment of attention, makes for a restless, anxious
lack of stasis. Like music, discursive language creates self-relation
structures whose meaning depends on particular successions of
elements. This is both the impatience and the sensuality of the
text. (150)

---

4. John Ashbery, *Flow Chart*, Manchester, 1991, 4.

Setting any two unrelated gobbets together is a cheap trick, not that that is going to stop me. Apparent convergences and discussible differences will always emerge, expressed via syntax and generating more. *Flow Chart* offers tour after tour de force, syntactically, not it would seem in a spirit of showiness but with a chilly hunkering down into the only stratum that can be relied on, only to discover that even those sands are shifting. This late work by Ashbery, the most willing of epics since Mallarmé's *Igitur* to risk all on the reach of its syntactical tendrils, comes the closest of all Ashbery's poems to encrypting Barbara Johnson's suspicion that knowledge is an effect of syntax. This would find a partial corroboration from Christopher Dewdney, who traces what he terms in the excerpt quoted "the performance anxiety deep at the root of our apparent linguistic facility" back to the child's acquisition of language.

> As infants we are fitted with a cognitive prosthesis, in much the same way that wild horses are forced to wear bits, braces and saddles. Not surprisingly then, the central component of language acquisition trauma is performance anxiety, an anxiety we never fully put behind us. (141)

The anxiety of language acquisition is so fundamental as to put into question received ideas of what constitutes the artificial and the natural. Dewdney argues that the brain is physically remodelled by language, a process for which it was already hard-wired, so that "Language can be regarded as a living software that has genetically earmarked a section of our brains for its own accommodation" (140). Dewdney's theory of language is one that has evolved in mutation of William Burroughs' famous dictum, "Language is a Virus". To both, Language is organic, was there before you were, and lives on through its use of individual consciousnesses. The divergence between their thinking shows in Burroughs' thoroughgoing and Gothic pessimism, set against Dewdney's more fascinated sense of our being at home in the world, despite the home's being a house forever haunted by that moment of childhood anxiety.

Apparently more optimistic than either Burroughs or Ashbery is Dewdney's apprehension of syntax as teleotropic. Language is always movement forward, streamlined into the anticipation of an ultimate meaning. Meaning is where we are going ... and yet there is the concession that syntax characterizes the travel more than it makes real the arrival. Elsewhere in *The Secular Grail* he argues that syntax is the stylistic equivalent of individuality, the thread of alignment along which meaning condenses, rather than the pathway to final meaning. Just so, the long sentence I quoted from *Flow Chart* contains condensed meanings en route, with Ashbery content to subdue the brilliant imagery of his younger phases to the point virtually of cliché – "the plaintive sound of the harp of the waves" – but refuses or is unable to use syntax, however correct and athletic, to summarise. Everything in the first two thirds of the sentence builds like a wave only to crash on loss of significance when the unnamed he "cannot make sense of them". All that can be trusted is that "he knows / the familiar, unmistakable thing, and that gives him courage", but as the thing is not named it is not graspable, is not there, is at last only the syntax that conjured its possibility only to refuse it, and the sentence concludes with a characteristically Ashberyan foreboding over "the long night to come". And this of course is death, at which point the line is appropriately broken.

Such fabulous elongation of syntax to form a labyrinth whose heart turns out to be all thread and no minotaur might seem to offer the questing reader little in the way of ultimate purpose. It is more the case that *Flow Chart* offers pleasures en route, to a centre that is not reached, because that is not what poetic syntax can do. This will only be frustrating if the reader wants a poem to be soluble, like a crossword puzzle with an answer, in which case Craig Raine or Paul Muldoon will be happy to oblige, though Mallarmé or Wordsworth would not have been. Or Rilke, who is everywhere in *Flow Chart*, particularly in the first section, which makes heavy use of many of his key-words, even down to or up to, "the god".

There are a few wonderful poems in *Hotel Lautréamont*, the vast collection of lyrics that Ashbery assembled at the same time as *Flow Chart*, but overall it disappoints. The collection was nearly entitled *A Driftwood Altar* and nearly entitled *Still Life, with Stranger*, terrific titles, (though driftwood altar is a tad Robinson Jeffers, coming from a poet who would have agreed with ex-mayor of New York Ed Koch that anything west of the Hudson is just camping out). But it is curious that the collection should have seemed so various to its author that it could equally well have been given names that point in such different directions. I do not know who writes the blurbs for Ashbery's books, though he or she or they clearly write in a state of baffled terror. The blurb on *Flow Chart*, with its hopeful make-believe about "an unnamed significant other" is the funniest. Ashbery's decision to call his next book *Hotel Lautréamont* causes almost audible sighs of relief, as it enabled the blurber to write about a definite, real other, Isidore Ducasse, not that the latter has anything to do with the book, aside from the general relevance of dark Romanticism and nineteenth century Symbolism, an interest confirmed by the next collection *And the Stars Were Shining*. Though never so profound or as moving as *Flow Chart*, this 1994 collection is certainly a rebuttal to the alleged sameness of Ashbery's work in the Nineties. Like *Hotel Lautréamont*, it disappoints, but this time that is the point. One waits for the joke, but it isn't there. In a poem of the early 80s, "The Songs We Know Best", Ashbery has the couplet, "Too often when you thought you'd be showered with confetti / What they flung at you was a plate of hot spaghetti", an appealing MacGonogallism. In "A Hundred Albums" from the 90s collection, "we'd" just stopped by for a mug of hot wine "but it is soup that is being dashed in your face". No joke. Elsewhere there is a malevolence quite unanticipated in Ashbery's work, as in "The Ridiculous Translator's Hopes": "... vulnerable / as a bride left waiting at the church, inching backward / to the cliff's edge as the photographer gets ready to smile". Words recur across poems, giving them a curious resonance and urgency, but they are odd words used oddly: like "stinger" – "Hold my stinger as a stranger and I will be presently". You know that middle-aged men are in real trouble when they start quoting Dr. Johnson, as Ashbery does in this collection, but one returns to the use of "stranger" as a verb, a use listed in Johnson's Dictionary but one that withered over the Romantic period, to speak of Ashbery's strangering the reader. One poem which I shall give in its entirety is entitled "Coventry", a place of course to which one is sent, malevolently, by those who know but now wish to stranger you:

> *There was one who was put out of his house*
> *and another that played by a pond*
> of a lateness growing,
>
> one that scalded his hand.
>
> And now, he said, please deny there was ever a house.
> But there was one and you were my mirror in it.
> These lines almost convey the comfort of it,
> how all things fitted together in their way.
> But it was funny and we left it –
> her address, her red dress.
>
> Just stay out in the country a lot.
> You have no house. The trees stand tentless,
> the marmoral floors sweating ...
> A delusion too.
>
> Good thing. Good luck.
> You'd have to stay in Coventry.
> But I'm already there, I protested.
> Besides, doesn't any leaf or train want me
> for what I'll have stopped doing when I'm there,
> truly there? Yet who am I to keep anything,
> any person waiting? So we diverged
> as we approached the city.
>
> My way was along straight boulevards
> that became avenues, with barrels of trash burning
> at each corner. The sky was dark but the blue light in it
> kept my courage up, until the watch spring
> broke. Someone had wound it too tight, you see.

Then I could only giggle at the odd bricks,
corners of tenements, buildings to be leased.
I fainted, honey.

And I never saw you again
except once walking fast
across the Victorian station
lit by holiday flares
yet strangely dumb and rumorless
like all the sleep and games that jammed us here.[5]

The poem is ominous as a dream is ominous. Its syntax is truncated, agitated. Where *Flow Chart* banked everything on advancing, "Coventry" breaks down, feints, with an e and with a. "I fainted, honey". Fainting is a very late-Romantic, very dark-Romantic thing to do, and also a very female, very powerless display of activity within the Victorian repertoire. Think of all the languid, fainting, sleeping, drifting Ophelias of the pre-Raphaelite painters, of Frederick Leighton, "The Punishment of Luxury", Alma Tadema. Christopher Dewdney's book includes a short biography of Sigmund Freud structured by the handful of occasions in Freud's life on which he is known to have fainted. What do Dewdney's gleeful cartoons have in common with Ashbery's poem? Well, obviously, nothing. Except that everything here: the hysteria of fainting, the science cum black art cum Symbolist oneirism of the talking cure, Dewdney's organicism and his cultural eclecticism, Ashbery's echoes of faded Victoriana in "Coventry", perhaps the whole issue, now, of poetry, and our curious faith in it, a form of spilt religion, however vestigial, are all Romantic, darkly Romantic. Perhaps Romanticism is the only single concept which can include syntax, and not the other way about. Ashbery is gay, it is well-known, but he has never wanted to be read as a "gay poet". It is probable however that the poems, for example "Local Time" in *And the Stars Were Shining*, have become more open on this issue, albeit still in brief references. Would it be too neat to suggest that syntax is associated with a male tradition of authorship, of control, of the fight against the silence which is evidently death, but perhaps also the fight not to disclose the sexual psyche: "I fainted, honey" conjoins intimacy with loss of consciousness, obliteration of syntax in that very Victorian display, a swoon. Yet as the poet Charles Bernstein remarked in another context, poetry may be a swoon that brings you to your senses.

---

5. John Ashbery, *And the Stars Were Shining*, Manchester, 1994, 74–75.

NOTES ON CONTRIBUTORS

Dennis Brown is Professor of Modern Literature at the University of Hertfordshire, specialising in twentieth-century poetry. His publications include *The Modernist Self* (1989), *Intertextual Dynamics: Joyce, Lewis, Pound and Eliot* (1990), *The Poetry of Postmodernity* (1994), and *John Betjeman* (1999). He is currently working on the relationship between poetics and (British School) psychotherapy.

Benjamin Colbert is Senior Lecturer in English at the University of Wolverhampton. He is the co-editor of a forthcoming collection of essays *Romantic Postmodernism / Postmodern Romanticism*, has edited and introduced *The Travels of Marco Polo* (1996), and is a regular contributor to the *Keats-Shelley Journal*. His current research interests include the Shelley circle, travel literature and Romantic period poetry.

Helen M. Dennis is Deputy Chair of the Department of English and Comparative Literary Studies at the University of Warwick. Her publications include *A New Approach to the Poetry of Ezra Pound: through the Medieval Provencal Aspect* (1996), and 'Ezra Pound and Gender' in *The Cambridge Companion to Ezra Pound* (1999). She has edited and contributed to *Willa Cather and European Cultural Influences* (1996), and is the editor of a forthcoming collection *Ezra Pound and Poetic Influence*.

Joanne Feit Diehl is Professor of English at the University of California, Davis. She is the author of many books and articles on American poetry and fiction, including *Dickinson and the Romantic Imagination* (1981), *Women Poets and the American Sublime* (1990), and *Elizabeth Bishop and Marianne Moore: The Psychodynamics of Creativity* (1993).

Mark Ford's first collection of poetry, *Landlocked*, was published by Chatto & Windus in 1992. His study of the French writer Raymond Roussel (*Raymond Roussel and the Republic of Dreams*) is scheduled for publication by Faber & Faber in the Spring of 2000. He is currently working on an edition of the poems of Hart Crane. He teaches in the Department of English at University College, London.

Lionel Kelly is Senior Lecturer in English at the University of Reading where he was Director of American Studies from 1989–95. His research interests are in American poetry and the short story. His recent publications include essays on Emily Dickinson, Ezra Pound, Raymond Carver, and Tennessee Williams, and an edition of Henry James's *The Portrait of a Lady* (1999). He is currently editing a collection of essays on 'North American Short Stories and Short Fictions' for *The Yearbook of English Studies* (2000).

Edward Larrissy is Professor of English Literature at the University of Leeds. He is the author of *William Blake* (1985), *Reading Twentieth-Century Poetry*: *The Language of Gender and Objects* (1990), and *Yeats the Poet: The Measures of Difference* (1994). He has edited *The Oxford Authors Yeats* (1997), and *Romanticism and Postmodernism* (1999).

Krystyna Mazur graduated from the University of Warsaw and did her doctoral studies at the University of Cornell with a thesis on John Ashbery and contemporary American poetry. She now teaches at the American Studies Centre in Warsaw and combines her special interests in American poetry with the Centre's cultural studies programme.

Peter Nicholls is Professor of English and American Literature at the University of Sussex. He is the author of *Ezra Pound: Politics, Economics and Writing* (1985), *Modernisms: A Literary Guide* (1995), and of numerous articles and essays on twentieth-century literature and theory. He is currently writing a book about contemporary American poetry.

John Pilling is Professor of English and European Literature at the University of Reading and Joint Director of the University's Beckett International Foundation. He is the author of *Beckett Before Godot* (Cambridge University Press, 1997) and of other books and articles on Beckett. He is a regular contributor to *PN Review*, which has published two of his earlier essays on John Ashbery.

Peter Robinson is visiting Professor of English Literature at Tohoku University, Sendai, Japan. He has published four books of poetry, *Overdrawn Account* (1980), *This Other Life* (1988), *Entertaining Fates* (1992), and *Lost and Found* (1997). He has edited the poems of Adrian Stokes, a collection of essays on Geoffrey Hill, and an anthology, *Liverpool Accents: Seven Poets and a City* (1996). His translations of contemporary Italian poetry include *Selected Poems* *of Vittorio Sereni* (1990). A collection of his critical essays, *In the Circumstances: about Poems and Poets*, was published by OUP in 1992, and with John Kerrigan, he has edited *The Thing about Roy Fisher: Critical Studies* (1999).

Thomas Travisano is Professor of English at Hartwick College, was co-founder and first President of the Elizabeth Bishop Society, and is the author of *Elizabeth Bishop: Her Artistic Development* (1988), and co-editor of *Gendered Modernisms: American Women Poets and their Readers* (1996). His most recent book is *Midcentury Quartet: Bishop, Lowell, Jarrell, Berryman and the Making of a Postmodern Aesthetic* (1999).

Cheryl Walker is Richard Armour Professor of Modern Languages at Scripps College, California. Her publications include *The Nightingale's Burden: Women Poets and American Culture Before 1900* (1983), *Masks Outrageous and Austere: Culture, Psyche, and Personae in Modern Women Poets* (1991), and *Indian Nation: Native American Literature and Nineteenth-Century Nationalisms*, (1998). She is currently working on a book on Elizabeth Bishop and religion.

Geoff Ward is Professor of English at the University of Dundee. His publications include *Statutes of Liberty: The New York School of Poets* 1993, (rev. ed. 2000) and *Language Poetry and the American Avant-garde* (1993). He has lectured widely in Europe, North America and Japan, and is currently holder of a Fellowship from the Leverhulme Trust, writing a critical biography of John Ashbery.

INDEX